# ATLAS OF LAOS

Contributors:

**Lao People's Democratic Republic**
Co-author: Bounthavy Sisouphanthong (National Statistical Centre).
Coordinator: Vixay Xaovana (National Statistical Centre).
Cartography: Souphab Kuouangvichith (National University of Laos).
Statistical data: Phongxay Phimpachanh (National Statistical Centre).
Administrative maps: Khamkhong Detchanthachack (National Geographic Department).
Scientific Committee and Lao translation: Sisaliao Svengsuksa, Khamphao Phonekeo and Phou Rasphone.

**France**
Co-author: Christian Taillard (LASEMA-CNRS).
Data analysis and modelling: Michel Vigouroux (Université Paul Valéry-Montpellier III, Libergéo) and Franck Auriac (University of Avignon, Libergéo).
Statistical cartography: Patrick Brossier (Université Paul Valéry-Montpellier III, Libergéo).
Cartography: Guérino Sillère (CNRS, Libergéo) and Géodimensions.
Editing, design and layout: Roger Brunet (Libergéo) and Régine Vanduick (Libergéo).
English translation: Madeleine Grieve.

This atlas is the result of scientific cooperation financed by the French National Centre for Scientific Research (CNRS) and the French Ministry of Foreign Affairs. The English edition is sponsored by the Swedish International Development Agency through the Laotian-Swedish statistical cooperation project.

The Nordic Institute of Asian Studies (NIAS) is funded by the governments of Denmark, Finland, Iceland, Norway and Sweden via the Nordic Council of Ministers, and works to encourage and support Asian studies in the Nordic Countries. In so doing, NIAS has published well in excess of one hundred books in the last three decades.

# Atlas of Laos

## The Spatial Structures of Economic and Social Development of the Lao People's Democratic Republic

**Bounthavy Sisouphanthong**

National Statistical Centre, State Planning Committee of Lao PDR

and

**Christian Taillard**

LASEMA-CNRS, GDR Libergéo-CNRS, France

**NIAS**

SILKWORM BOOKS

First published in 2000 by NIAS Publishing
Nordic Institute of Asian Studies
Leifsgade 33, DK–2300 Copenhagen S, Denmark
tel: (+45) 3254 8844 • fax: (+45) 3296 2530
E-mail: books@nias.ku.dk • Website: http://nias.ku.dk/Books/
*and*
published in 2000 for sale in Asia only by
Silkworm Books
104/5 Chiang Mai-Hot Road, M.7, T. Suthep, Muang, Chiang Mai 50100, Thailand
E-Mail: Silkworm@loxinfo.co.th • Web site: http://www.silkwormbooks.com

Originally published in France in 2000 as
Atlas de la République démocratique populaire lao
by CNRS-Libergéo and La Documentation française

Publication of the English edition was assisted by a grant from
the National Statistical Centre, Vientiane, in association with the
Swedish International Development Agency (Sida).

© CNRS-GDR Libergéo and La Documentation française 2000

**British Library Cataloguing in Publication Data**
Bounthavy, Sisouphanthong
    Atlas of Laos : spatial structures of the economic and social
    development of the Lao people's democratic republic
    1. Laos - Maps 2. Laos - Economic conditions - 20th century -
    Maps 3. Laos - Social conditions - 20th century - Maps
    4. Laos - Statistics
    I.Title      II.Taillard, Christian
    912.5'94

ISBN 87-87062-87-9 (NIAS)
ISBN 974-7551-41-1 (Silkworm)

Typesetting by CNRS-Libergéo
Printed and bound in Thailand

# Foreword

The *Atlas of Laos* is one of the most important projects undertaken under the agreement on scientific and technical cooperation between Lao PDR and France. The atlas maps data gathered by the State Planning Committee's National Statistical Centre, notably the population and housing census conducted in 1995 as part of a statistical cooperation project between Lao PDR and Sweden.

The Laotian government authorised the use of statistical data gathered by the various ministries so that small-scale cartography could be produced, on the level of the 133 districts that constitute the administrative divisions of the country.

This socio-economic atlas has two aims. First, through the use of sectoral data, it seeks to assist the Laotian and international scientific community in their analysis of the territorial structures of economic and social development in Laos. Secondly, it is an instrument that enables Laotian planners to base national development strategy on scientific analysis and promote balanced utilisation of the country's natural and human resources.

The atlas redefines the three regions that structure the national territory. The North is centred on the Luang-phrabang–Oudomxay–Luangnamtha axis, which gives access to Kunming, the capital of Yunnan province in China. The Centre converges on the Vientiane–Xamneua axis, which places the Laotian capital on the international axis linking Bangkok to Hanoi. The South is structured around the meridian axis along the Mekong Valley and around the transverse axes that connect the river to the South China Sea and includes the new economic development zone around the Bolovens Plateau.

With the aid of computerised statistical cartography, which makes it possible to update the maps as soon as new data are available, this atlas studies the integration of these three regions into the national territory. It also analyses the new position occupied by Lao PDR in the reorganisation of continental South-East Asia and in a rapidly changing world.

Lastly, the atlas stresses the importance of the policy of openness pursued by the Laotian government in the era of globalisation. Lao PDR's integration into ASEAN, its support for the economic development of the northern quadrangle of the Indochinese Peninsula and for projects in the Greater Mekong Subregion all bear witness to this commitment to openness. The appeal to other countries and to international organisations to participate in these programmes should continue to ensure stability, democracy and peace in the region and in the world.

**Bouathong Vonglokham**
Chairman, State Planning Committee

# CONTENTS

**7**

# Introduction

The *Atlas of Laos: The Spatial Structures of Economic and Social Development in the Lao People's Democratic Republic* is the first atlas of its kind produced in Laos. It was preceded only by the *Atlas of Lao PDR*, a booklet published by the National Geographic Department in 1995. Although that publication had the merit of demonstrating the value of this type of exercise, it was only 25 pages long and was limited by the data available (around a dozen socio-economic maps).

## A computerised atlas, the product of Franco-Laotian scientific cooperation

The results of the 1995 census of population and housing, conducted by a joint team from Laos and Sweden, provided much-needed quality data. This was the first reliable census conducted in Laos. No general censuses were carried out during the colonial period and only urban censuses were possible during the years of insecurity that followed. The population census carried out in 1985, ten years after the country's reunification, provided the first nationwide evaluation, although it had a number of shortcomings. The use of computer processing and small-scale geo-referencing (at the level of village, district and province) in the 1995 census made statistical mapping possible. With this new information available, the Laotian National Statistical Centre, in cooperation with the Research Centre for South-East Asia and the Austronesian World (LASEMA) at the National Centre for Scientific Research (CNRS) and the geographical research network RECLUS (now Libergéo) in France, decided to produce an atlas of Laos, along the lines of the *Atlas of Vietnam* published in 1993, and the *Atlas of Thailand*, due to be published at the end of 2000. The objectives of the exercise were: to process the territorialised statistical data to make it easier for the State Planning Committee to integrate a spatial dimension into its development strategies; to reduce territorial inequalities; to give regional scope to planning; and to promote the regional integration of the countries of the Indochinese Peninsula by highlighting their complementarities.

This type of atlas contributes to the reflection initiated by the Asian Development Bank (ADB) on development in the Greater Mekong Subregion, which includes China's Yunnan province. The capacity to update the maps rapidly, through computerised cartography, will improve monitoring and evaluation of territorial development policies. The three editions of the atlas—in Lao, French and English—will facilitate cooperation between technical ministries; between central, provincial and district administrations; and between Laotian economic agents and their foreign partners. The atlas will also be a valuable tool for Laotian secondary and university students and teachers.

The National Statistical Centre appointed a team to carry out this joint scientific project. In addition to the centre's director and deputy director, the group comprised: the deputy director of the National Geographic Department, who provided the administrative maps at district level; the dean of the faculty of social science at the National University, who was responsible for the cartography; the scientific editor of the university geography manual, a PhD from the University of Bordeaux, who was in charge of the translation into Lao; and two other Laotian geographers responsible for revising the translation. The cooperation agreement for the project was signed in December 1996. The years 1997 and 1998 were spent training the Laotian participants, collecting and processing the data and constructing the maps during research visits by the Laotian partners to France and by the French partners to Laos. The atlas was edited during 1999, and in early 2000 the scientific results were presented to users and a training course in automatic cartography software was organised for staff from the statistical sections of the technical ministries.

## Statistical, spatial and temporal references of the atlas

There are too few provinces in Laos (17 plus one special administrative zone, compared with 61 provinces in Vietnam and 76 in Thailand) and the ecological and human environments they cover are too heterogeneous (Mekong flood plains, plateaux and mountains; and 2-4 ethnolinguistic families) for this to be a relevant scale. The atlas is therefore based on the 133 districts that existed in 1995. This choice allows for interpretation at two levels: national, where territorial development policy is defined; and local, where the development areas are managed. It also provides a base for constructing diachronic maps in the future, even if the number of provinces increases.

The atlas is based largely on the approximately 30 variables extracted from the census of population and housing as at 1 March 1995. It also comprises socio-economic data from technical ministries that have district-level databases, such as the Ministry of Education; and thematic data, from the Ministry of Agriculture (on irrigation), the State Planning Committee, the Committee for Investment and Foreign Economic Cooperation, the National Tourism Authority and the National Bank of Laos. The provincial statistics bureaux that collect data at district level were also involved, because the information that reaches national level is usually only aggregate data for each province. This made it possible to compile data on health and a consistent body of information on crop systems and livestock, which provides a valuable interim picture of Laotian agriculture at this level, while awaiting the results of the 1999 agricultural census, to be published in 2000. The atlas also includes data collected by the provinces on banks and industrial and trading enterprises in the four urban districts of Vientiane municipality and the districts of the provincial capitals.

The data gathered were subjected to critical analysis, both internal and external, during the statistical and cartographic processing stages. They are necessarily of variable quality. Some—such as those contained in the 1995 census and in the specialised, small-scale thematic surveys—are of high quality; others—such as the provincial-level data from the technical ministries—leave room for improvement. The statistical units of these ministries have made considerable advances, particularly through computerisation, with the support of the National Statistical Centre. Through its extensive use of statistics, the atlas has contributed to improving the processing of existing data and demonstrated the value of expanding data collection at district level.

The statistics gathered paint a reliable picture of the situation prevailing in 1995 (census data) and in 1996 (socio-economic data). This first national atlas thus aims to reveal the spatial structures of Laos at a given point in time, rather than to show a process of change. It is a reference that can serve as a basis for diachronic analyses in the future, especially as it has been produced at a key moment in the country's evolution. The years 1995 and 1996 provide a picture of national integration 20 years after the founding of Lao PDR and just before the Asian crisis of summer 1997, which poses a new challenge to national development.

## Technical and methodological bases for statistical mapping

This atlas was produced with the aid of several computer techniques. Some of the reference maps—such as the relief, forest cover and mineral resources maps—are taken from sources that used remote sensing or a geographical information system. Others were constructed for the atlas using computer-assisted cartography. These include the maps of the axes and nodes that structure the national space, the climate maps, and the maps of the electricity, transport and communications networks. Most of the maps were produced using automatic cartography to process territorialised statistics gathered at district level, or where this was not possible, at provincial level. Because of the strong spatial differentiation in Laos, Jenks method was the most commonly used technique for the discretisation of data because it is well suited to representing extremes.

There are several types of computerised maps in the atlas. The most common are analytical maps showing the territorial distribution of a single variable, represented by shading for relative values and by circles for absolute values (Roger Brunet, *La Carte mode d'emploi*, 1987). Structure maps were also constructed to measure simple but significant groups of data combining two or three variables, represented on rectangular or triangular diagrams. For each type, a table included in the key of these maps indicates the ranges of the variables considered. To make the maps easier to read, the values corresponding to the dominant variable(s) are in bold type. This type of map allows, for example, the representation of agricultural systems before the more specific maps for each type of crop.

Synthetic maps, combining a large number of the variables mapped in the atlas, were also produced for the chapter conclusions under the direction of Franck Auriac. These reflect the territorial structures and dynamics characterising each sector of the country's economic and social life. Multivariate analytical techniques (principal component analysis and cluster analysis) are used to highlight similarities and dissimilarities, connections and contrasts between the variables (S) that describe the spatial units (P), and between the spatial units themselves. In the figure opposite, the set of data in the table (1) is subjected to a classification/partition procedure, whereby the spatial units are reduced step by step into a smaller number of classes based on their degree of similarity. These classes can then be mapped.

The classification by cluster analysis, shown here on a rectangular diagram (2), is represented in the map legends by a linkage tree (3). In the example opposite, province 5 is most similar and therefore closest to province 1, and together they are linked to province 2. These three provinces are then linked to provinces 3 and 6, which form another cluster, while province 4 is so differentiated from all the others that it is only linked to them at the very end of the process of clustering. The classification is therefore expressed as a typology of four classes (3), shown on the map by four shaded areas (4) that represent the territorial structures belonging to the group formed by these six provinces. To make it easier to

interpret the linkage tree and the map, a table in the legend (5) indicates the degree of positive or negative contribution of the most significant variables used to define the classes. The commentary makes additional remarks about these variables.

The atlas is divided into ten chapters. The first nine focus successively on: the national territory; settlement patterns; population dynamics; educational level and activity; agriculture; mining and industry; transport and communications; trade and tourism; and education, health and culture. Wherever the data allow, two synthetic maps are constructed for each chapter: one for the population as a whole and the other for the urban population. The final chapter, which deals with the spatial organisation of Lao PDR, compares these maps related to the spatial structures of each sector of activity.

First, the territorial structures and urban hierarchy are presented in terms of intra-regional and inter-regional connections. These national structures are then set in the context of the Indochinese Peninsula, from a long-term perspective (the caravan trails from the pre-colonial period and their disappearance between the colonial period and 1975) and from a short-term perspective (their re-emergence with the network of main transportation axes studied by the ADB). These spatial analyses on the scales of Lao PDR and of the Indochinese Peninsula are shown in a model, which—although not intended as a plan for territorial development—highlights the territorial constraints that any strategy of regional planning should take into account.

## Mapping the data

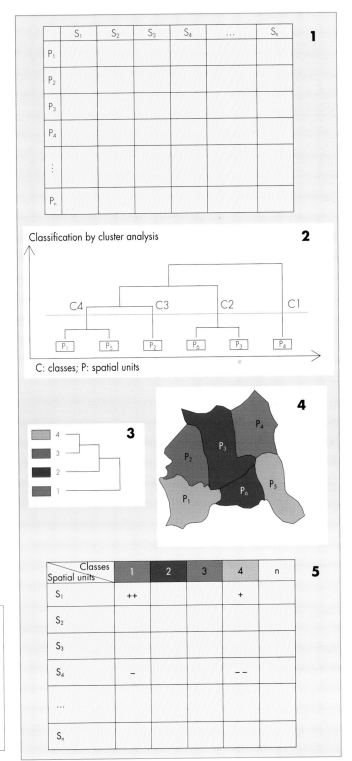

**1**

|     | $S_1$ | $S_2$ | $S_3$ | $S_4$ | ... | $S_n$ |
|-----|-------|-------|-------|-------|-----|-------|
| $P_1$ |     |       |       |       |     |       |
| $P_2$ |     |       |       |       |     |       |
| $P_3$ |     |       |       |       |     |       |
| $P_4$ |     |       |       |       |     |       |
| ⋮   |       |       |       |       |     |       |
| $P_n$ |     |       |       |       |     |       |

**2**

Classification by cluster analysis

C4     C3     C2     C1

$P_1$   $P_5$   $P_2$   $P_6$   $P_3$   $P_4$

C: classes; P: spatial units

**3**

4
3
2
1

**4**

$P_4$
$P_3$
$P_2$
$P_6$
$P_5$
$P_1$

**5**

| Classes / Spatial units | 1 | 2 | 3 | 4 | n |
|-------------------------|---|---|---|---|---|
| $S_1$ | ++ |   |   | + |   |
| $S_2$ |    |   |   |   |   |
| $S_3$ |    |   |   |   |   |
| $S_4$ | –  |   |   | – – |   |
| ...   |    |   |   |   |   |
| $S_n$ |    |   |   |   |   |

### Interpreting the table in the legend

Class 1: extremely positive contribution of the variable $S_1$ and negative contribution of the variable $S_4$

Class 2: positive contribution of the variable $S_1$ and extremely negative contribution of the variable $S_4$

Class 3: no variable with a significantly positive or negative contribution

# Chapter 1. Territory

The Lao People's Democratic Republic (Lao PDR) is the least populous country in the Indochinese Peninsula. The 1995 census recorded a population of 4,575,000, which is just under half that of Cambodia (9.8 million), and between 10-6% of that of Myanmar (46.5 million), Thailand (59.4 million) and Vietnam (75.5 million). Its total area of 236,800 km$^2$ makes it the second-smallest country, between Cambodia (181,000 km$^2$) and Vietnam (330,400 km$^2$), and a long way behind Thailand (513,100 km$^2$) and Myanmar (676,600 km$^2$). Like Myanmar and Thailand, Laos is located in a river basin. However, unlike the basin in those countries, the Mekong Basin is shared by six countries, with Laos occupying 26%, China and Myanmar 22% together, Thailand 23%, Cambodia 20% and Vietnam 9%.

## A multi-ethnic state with a territory off-centre from the Mekong

The dominant ethnic group accounts for a much smaller proportion of the population in Laos than in the neighbouring countries. In the 1995 census, the Lao made up only 52% of the population. With the other related ethnic groups, the Tai-Kadai ethnolinguistic family constitutes two-thirds of the population, which is slightly less than the 69% generally attributed to the Burmans in Myanmar. This is far below the domination of the Tai-Kadai family in Thailand (estimated at 83%), the Mon-Khmer in Cambodia (87%) and the Vietnamese/Kinh in Vietnam (87% in the 1989 census). Each of these dominant ethnic groups created its own state after a "march south". The Lao, following the Mekong, settled in the valleys of the river and its tributaries, where they practised wet rice cultivation, pushing the Austro-Asiatic indigenous people towards the slopes, whence they derived their respective names of Lao Loum (Lao of the lowlands) and Lao Theung (Lao of the slopes).

This fragmented river space and pronounced multi-ethnic structure can be explained by the relatively late timing of the Lao's "march south". The capital of the kingdom of Lan Xang was moved from Luangphrabang to Vientiane in 1553, and the southward movement halted there. The Thai shifted their capital from Chieng Mai to Sukothai and reached Ayuthaya, at the head of the Chao Praya delta, in 1350. They took over the declining Khmer empire in 1431 and blocked the Lao's access to the Mekong Delta. Deprived of a delta base for rice cultivation and of access to international maritime trade essential for building a nation of size, the Lao were unable to rival their neighbours (Christian Taillard, 1989).

The unequal balance of power with the kingdom of Siam manifested itself in the 19th century with the loss of the territories on the right bank of the Mekong, which today make up north-eastern Thailand and which include the broadest plains of the middle river basin. And twice in half a century—in 1778 and 1828—the Lao peoples of the left bank were deported to the Siamese bank. As a result, the Lao in Lan Na, the former kingdom of northern Thailand, and in Isan in the north-east, estimated at respectively 30% and 20% of the population of Thailand, are nine times more numerous than the 2.4 million Lao in Lao PDR. The arrival of new waves of Miao-Yao and Tibeto-Burman immigrants in the 19th century further reduced the proportion of Lao. The latter groups settled on the mountain peaks, whence the term Lao Soung (Lao of the summits) used to designate them.

The nation's history explains why Laos is currently the most mountainous and most ethnically diverse country in the peninsula and why its territory is off centre in relation to the Mekong. The width from east to west attains 500 km in the north of Lao PDR, but is only 150 km at Thakhek in the Centre, accentuating the effects of meridian elongation (1,835 km by road and 1,865 km along the Mekong) and hampering territorial integration.

## The configuration of a buffer state and territorial management

The importance of Laos in continental South-East Asia stems mainly from its political function as an intermediate space in the heart of the peninsula. This position has preserved it over the centuries, despite a frequently unfavourable balance of power with its neighbours, first to the north and south, then to the west and east. Until the 14th century, the Lao principalities separated the successive kingdoms in Yunnan from those centred on the Mekong Delta. Subsequently, the founding of Lan Xang established an intermediate space between the Burmese and Siamese kingdoms on one side, and the Viet on the other. The political split between Communist and free-market systems in the peninsula cut through the middle of Laotian territory during the war years, at the time of the meridian partition between the zone controlled by the royal government in Vientiane and the zone controlled by the Pathet Lao in Xamneua. This fault line established itself on the Mekong, from the time of the country's reunification in 1975 until Vietnam, Laos, Myanmar and Cambodia joined Thailand as members of ASEAN.

This difficult process of nation-building left Lao PDR with two legacies. First, the country had to repair the damage done by the war, which had displaced a quarter of the 1973 population (730,000 people) within national borders and caused 12% of the 1986 population (414,000 people) to leave the country. Between 1975 and 1979, the return of 550,000 people to their provinces of origin was organised, despite transport difficulties (C. Taillard, 1989). Mine clearance in the territories bordering the roads of the former controlled zone of Xamneua will need to continue for many years to make all the farming areas accessible again.

Because of its meridian structure, Lao PDR soon discarded the centralised model of territorial management adopted in 1975, as the Siamese and the French had been obliged to do in the past. Indeed, from as early as the 16th century, Fa Ngum, after having reunited the Lao principalities, organised Lan Xang into three entities, with the royal territory in Luangphrabang extended south by two successive territories in the Mekong Valley. On their own scale, these three territories reproduced the concentric spatial model marked by diminishing integration from the core to the periphery, characteristic of Thai political systems. Lao PDR has also sought to achieve the delicate balance that existed between these three territories in the past, and which today governs relations between the central government and the provinces, and between the provincial administrations and the districts.

Since 1975, the territorial organisation of Lao PDR has been redrawn, with the number of provinces increased from 13 to 18. Vientiane province, where 20% of the country's population was located, was divided into three. Luangnamtha and Saravane provinces were split into two because of difficulties travelling between the Mekong Valley and the mountainous hinterland. The special zone of Xaysomboun, located between Xiengkhuang and Vientiane, was also created. Together with Bokeo province in the northern economic development quadrangle—between Laos, Myanmar, Thailand and China's Yunnan province—studied by the Asian Development Bank (ADB), and Sekong province east of the Bolovens Plateau, Xaysomboun is a strategic region for development.

Four types of provincial territories can be distinguished in the current administrative organisation. The provinces in the Centre, the narrowest part of the country, combine a range of natural landscapes and ethnic structures from the Mekong to the Annamese Cordillera. These provinces are highly heterogeneous and open to both Thailand and Vietnam. The provinces of the second type are bordered by the Mekong and Thailand. These become increasingly homogeneous as they move from Bokeo to Vientiane municipality. There is also Champassack province, which includes both banks of the Mekong and borders Thailand and Cambodia. The provinces of the third type are located along the land borders and are open to either two countries—Luangnamtha (Myanmar and China) and Phongsaly (China and Vietnam)—or one—Huaphanh (Vietnam). Sekong and Attapeu provinces are isolated, despite the old network of the Ho Chi Minh Trail. The provinces of the fourth type are in an intermediate position between the river and mountainous border provinces of the North. They are ecologically more homogeneous, with the Nam Beng basin in Oudomxay, a river junction in Luangphrabang (Nam Ou, Xuang and Khan), and a plateau in Xiengkhuang.

## Territorial organisation

This territorial organisation highlights the meridian structure of the buffer state formed by Lao PDR, which favours relations to the west with Thailand and to the east with Vietnam, all the way along the respective 1,835 km (1,500 km of which are constituted by the Mekong) and 2,060 km of common borders. There are also transverse sections along this stretch, in the form of three unofficial regions: the North, comprising the seven provinces located north-west of a line that goes from Huaphanh to Xayabury; the Centre, which includes the seven provinces lying between this line and Savannakhet; and the South, which covers the four southern provinces. This division reproduces the three founding territories of Lan Xang, which became separate kingdoms in the 18th century: Luangphrabang, Vientiane and Champassack (M. Stuart-Fox 1997, p. 17). These regions are now highly unequal, with the Centre containing half the population, the North a third and the South a fifth. The province of Savannakhet is sometimes attached to the South to reduce this imbalance. This atlas hopes to contribute to the design of new regional divisions, better suited to the needs of economic and social development.

| Code | Provinces, Districts | Code | Provinces, Districts | Code | Provinces, Districts | Code | Provinces, Districts |
|---|---|---|---|---|---|---|---|
| **100** | **Vientiane municipality** | **600** | **Luangphrabang** | **1000** | **Vientiane province** | 1313 | Atsaphone |
| 101 | Chanthabuly | 601 | Luangphrabang | 1001 | Phonhong | **1400** | **Saravane** |
| 102 | Sikhottabong | 602 | Xieng Ngeun | 1002 | Thoulakhom | 1401 | Saravane |
| 103 | Xaysetha | 603 | Nan | 1003 | Keo oudom | 1402 | Ta Oi |
| 104 | Sisattanak | 604 | Pak Ou | 1004 | Kasy | 1403 | Toomlarn |
| 105 | Naxaithong | 605 | Nambak | 1005 | Vangvieng | 1404 | Lakhonepheng |
| 106 | Xaythany | 606 | Ngoi | 1006 | Feuang | 1405 | Vapy |
| 107 | Hadxaifong | 607 | Pak xeng | 1007 | Xanakham | 1406 | Khongxedon |
| 108 | Sangthong | 608 | Phonxay | **1100** | **Borikhamxay** | 1407 | Lao Ngarm |
| 109 | Maypakngum | 609 | Chomphet | 1101 | Pakxanh | 1408 | Samuoi |
| **200** | **Phongsaly** | 610 | Viengkham | 1102 | Thaphabath | **1500** | **Sekong** |
| 201 | Phongsaly | 611 | Phoukhoune | 1103 | Pakkading | 1501 | Lamarm |
| 202 | May | **700** | **Huaphanh** | 1104 | Bolikanh | 1502 | Kaleum |
| 203 | Khua | 701 | Xamneua | 1105 | Khamkeuth | 1503 | Dakcheung |
| 204 | Samphanh | 702 | Xiengkhor | 1106 | Viengthong | 1504 | Thateng |
| 205 | Booneua | 703 | Viengthong | **1200** | **Khammouane** | **1600** | **Champassack** |
| 206 | Nhot Ou | 704 | Viengxay | 1201 | Thakhek | 1601 | Pakse |
| 207 | Boontai | 705 | Huameuang | 1202 | Mahaxay | 1602 | Sanasomboon |
| **300** | **Luangnamtha** | 706 | Xamtay | 1203 | Nongbok | 1603 | Bachiangchaleunsook |
| 301 | Namtha | **800** | **Xayabury** | 1204 | Hinboon | 1604 | Paksong |
| 302 | Sing | 801 | Xayabury | 1205 | Nhommalath | 1605 | Pathoomphone |
| 303 | Long | 802 | Khorb | 1206 | Bualapha | 1606 | Phonthong |
| 304 | Viengphoukha | 803 | Hongsa | 1207 | Nakai | 1607 | Champassack |
| 305 | Nalae | 804 | Ngeun | 1208 | Xebangfay | 1608 | Sukhuma |
| **400** | **Oudomxay** | 805 | Xienghone | 1209 | Xaybuathong | 1609 | Moonlapamok |
| 401 | Xay | 806 | Phiang | **1300** | **Savannakhet** | 1610 | Khong |
| 402 | La | 807 | Paklai | 1301 | Khanthabuly | **1700** | **Attapeu** |
| 403 | Namor | 808 | Kenethao | 1302 | Outhoomphone | 1701 | Xaysetha |
| 404 | Nga | 809 | Botene | 1303 | Atsaphangthong | 1702 | Samakkhixay |
| 405 | Beng | **900** | **Xiengkhuang** | 1304 | Phine | 1703 | Sanamxay |
| 406 | Houn | 901 | Pek | 1305 | Sepone | 1704 | Sanxay |
| 407 | Pakbeng | 902 | Kham | 1306 | Nong | 1705 | Phouvong |
| **500** | **Bokeo** | 903 | Nonghed | 1307 | Thapangthong | **1800** | **Xaysomboun (z.sp.)** |
| 501 | Huoixai | 904 | Khoune | 1308 | Songkhone | 1801 | Xaysomboun |
| 502 | Tonpheung | 905 | Morkmay | 1309 | Champhone | 1802 | Thathom |
| 503 | Meung | 906 | Phookood | 1310 | Xonbuly | 1803 | Hom |
| 504 | Pha Oudom | 907 | Phaxay | 1311 | Xaybuly | 1804 | Longsan |
| 505 | Paktha | | | 1312 | Vilabuly | 1805 | Phun |

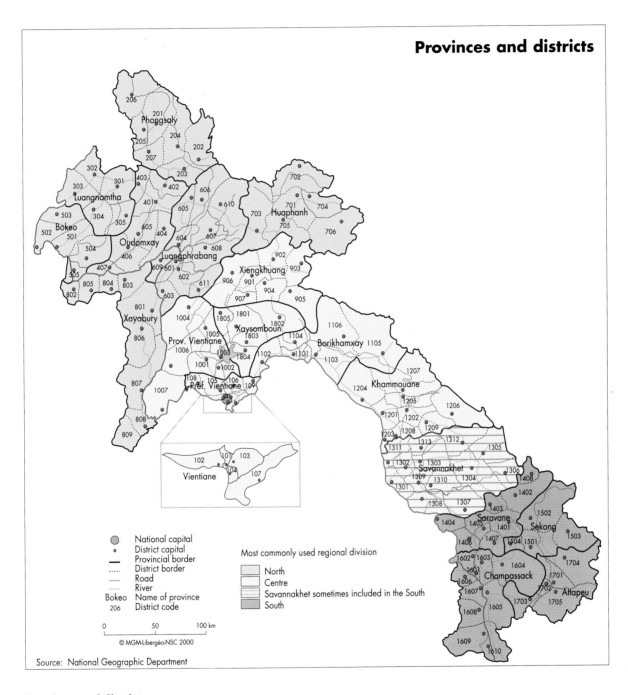

## Provinces and districts

The spelling of the names of the provinces and districts varies considerably in official documents and even in those produced by the National Geographic Department. We have therefore adopted the spellings used in the 1995 census—the main reference for this atlas—which are used in the statistical yearbooks. The codes in the table refer to the map.

# Relief and settlement

Northern Laos, the most mountainous region, echoes the pattern of the Yunnan fan some 500 km further south. The tributaries of the Mekong follow a NE–SW direction, recalling that of the upper Irrawadi River, while the Nam Ma follows a NW–SE direction, like the eastern basin of the Red River. Only the Xiengkhuang Plateau, with the Plain of Jars at its centre, disrupts this fan pattern. Like an umbrella radiating in all directions, it binds northern Laos to the Annamese Cordillera. The cordillera separates the Mekong Valley from the coastal plains of Central Vietnam and provides the junction with the Bolovens Plateau, an extension of the Vietnamese plateaux.

The Mekong Valley is undergoing abrupt changes of direction in relation to its general meridian orientation, between Huoixai and Luangphrabang in the North, and between Xanakham and Pakxanh in the region of Vientiane. Beginning as a narrow corridor in the north, the valley then broadens into a series of plains between Vientiane and Thakhek, although these are less expansive than those on the Thai bank. The Laotian plains broaden out in the region of Savannakhet, before being hemmed in again in by the southern plateaux. The differences in relief between the plains along the Mekong disrupt navigation. Transport is notably restricted by the rapids of Khemmarat, south of Savannakhet, and blocked altogether by the Khone Falls at the Cambodian border.

The population density map shows the discontinuity of settlement on the three main plains along the river: Vientiane, Savannakhet and Champassack. Settlement by the Lao ethnic group exceeds 50% almost continuously from Xayabury to the south. It surpasses 87% from Paklai to Vientiane, and from the districts bordering Saravane province to the Cambodian border. The proportion of Lao is just over 18% in the highlands between Xamneua and Vientiane and in Khammouane province in the Centre, creating a break between the Austro-Asiatics of the North and South.

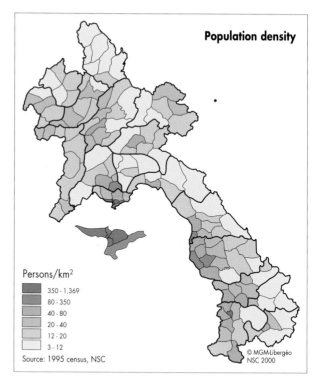

**Population density**

Persons/km²

- 350 - 1,369
- 80 - 350
- 40 - 80
- 20 - 40
- 12 - 20
- 3 - 12

Source: 1995 census, NSC

© MGM-Libergéo
NSC 2000

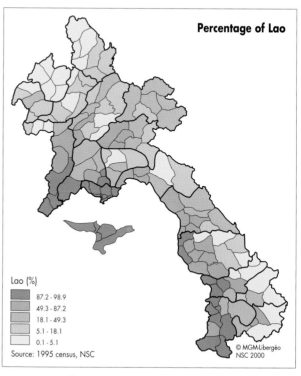

**Percentage of Lao**

Lao (%)

- 87.2 - 98.9
- 49.3 - 87.2
- 18.1 - 49.3
- 5.1 - 18.1
- 0.1 - 5.1

Source: 1995 census, NSC

© MGM-Libergéo
NSC 2000

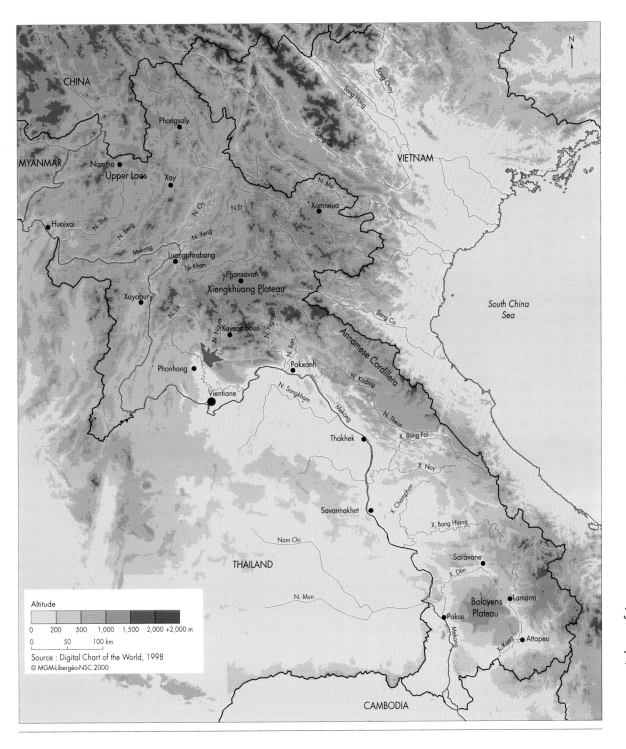

**Altitude**

| 0 | 200 | 500 | 1,000 | 1,500 | 2,000 | +2,000 m |

| 0 | 50 | 100 km |

Source : Digital Chart of the World, 1998
© MGM-Libergéo-NSC 2000

*Atlas of Laos*

# Road network and accessibility

Laos is a mountainous country where elevations of below 200 m account for only 16% of the total area. More than 20 years after reunification, territorial and economic integration is seriously hampered by the difficulty of travelling within the country. Travel is particularly arduous during the wet season because of poorly constructed and poorly maintained roads.

Road 13, between Namtha on the Chinese border and Kinak on the Cambodian border, is the only meridian axis usable all year round, even though the section south of Savannakhet has not yet been paved. It links the capital Vientiane (population: 233,000) to Luangphrabang in the North (population: 31,800), and to Thakhek (population: 25,800), Savannakhet (population: 62,200) and Pakse (population: 47,600) in the South. It also services Namtha (population: 14,400) and Muong Xay (population: 15,000) in the North. It is connected to the Thai network by a bridge in Vientiane; another bridge is under construction in Pakse. The second main road, Road 1, runs east of Road 13 and parallel to it, across the Xiengkhuang Plateau, through the interior of the provinces of the Centre, the Sekong Valley and Attapeu. It handles interprovincial traffic. During the war years, this road linked the southern provinces on the border with Vietnam to Xamneua in the zone controlled by the Neo Lao Haksat. Located west of the Ho Chi Minh Trail, it also suffered from bombing.

During the same period, the main transverse road in the North, linking Muong Sing to Xamneua, had a similar strategic role connecting the border provinces of the North. The Chinese-built road that follows the Nam Beng Valley joined up with the Mekong at Pakbeng, but was not extended to Thailand. There is no direct road link between the Xiengkhuang Plateau and Vientiane. In the Centre, Roads 8 and 9 link up with central Vietnam, via the mountain passes of Keo Neua and Lao Bao (the lowest in the cordillera, elevation 420 m). A third bridge planned at Savannakhet, with Japanese financing, as part of the East–West Corridor highway project studied by the ADB, will give prominence to Road 9.

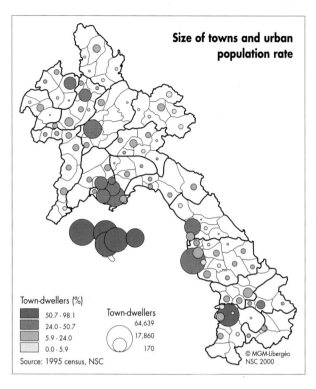

**Size of towns and urban population rate**

Town-dwellers (%)
- 50.7 - 98.1
- 24.0 - 50.7
- 5.9 - 24.0
- 0.0 - 5.9

Town-dwellers
- 64,639
- 17,860
- 170

Source: 1995 census, NSC

© MGM-Libergéo
NSC 2000

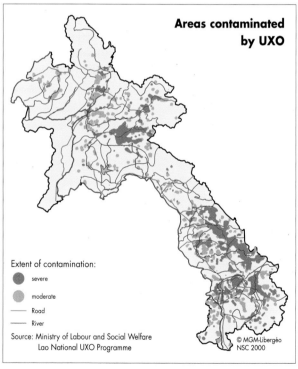

**Areas contaminated by UXO**

Extent of contamination:
- severe
- moderate
- Road
- River

Source: Ministry of Labour and Social Welfare
Lao National UXO Programme

© MGM-Libergéo
NSC 2000

# Road network: axes and nodes

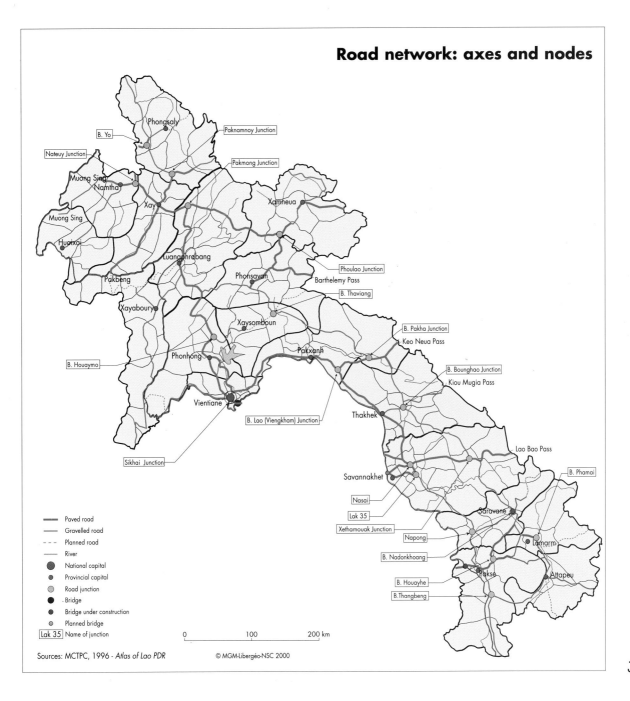

B. Yo

Nateuy Junction

Paknamnoy Junction

Pakmong Junction

Phongsaly

Muong Sing
Namtha

Muong Sing

Huaixai

Xay

Xamneua

Pakbeng

Luangphrabang

Phonsavan

Phoulao Junction

Barthelemy Pass

B. Thaviang

Xayaboury

Xaysomboun

B. Pakha Junction

Keo Neua Pass

Pakxanh

B. Houaymo

Phonhong

B. Bounghao Junction

Kiou Mugia Pass

Vientiane

B. Lao (Viengkham) Junction

Thakhek

Lao Bao Pass

Sikhai Junction

Savannakhet

B. Phamai

Nasai

Lak 35

Xethamouak Junction

Saravane

Napong

Lamarm

B. Nadonkhoang

B. Houayhe

Pakse

Attapeu

B.Thangbeng

**Legend**

— Paved road
— Gravelled road
- - - Planned road
— River
● National capital
● Provincial capital
● Road junction
● Bridge
● Bridge under construction
● Planned bridge
Lak 35 Name of junction

0    100    200 km

Sources: MCTPC, 1996 - *Atlas of Lao PDR*    © MGM-Libergéo-NSC 2000

# Forest environment

A massive 85% of Laos is forested, with 47% classed as forests in the 1989 inventory and 38% as unstocked and bamboo forests as a result of slash-and-burn techniques or relative aridity. Rainfall of less than 1,800 mm around the Xiengkhuang Plateau has reduced the forested area in the province to less than 48%, and to as low as 33% in Huaphanh and even 27% in Oudomxay and 22% in Luangphrabang, where slash-and-burn is most widespread, which appears clearly in the forest cover map of 1992-1993. Forest covers 40% of Savannakhet, despite much lower rainfall (below 1,400 mm), which hampers wet rice cultivation and favours dry dipterocarp forest. There is also a clear correlation between the heaviest rainfall (more than 2,600 mm) and the evergreen and mixed forests in the highlands of Borikhamxay and Khammouane in the Centre and those of Attapeu and Champassack in the South, and the deciduous forests of Luangnamtha and Bokeo in the North-West.

The inventories of 1982 and 1989 provide data on deforestation on a regional scale. This is evaluated at 70,000 ha per year, due to slash-and-burn, but also to logging (timber being the second export item by value in 1997) and to collection of firewood (which is used as a cooking fuel by 93% of households). At this pace, forests probably only covered 42% of the total area of Laos in 1999, compared with 70% in 1940, i.e. a fall of 28 percentage points in 60 years. The table below supports the evidence in the forest cover map of 1992-1993, which shows that the biggest reductions have occurred in the North and the Centre.

| Cover % | North | Centre | South[2] | Total 1989 |
|---|---|---|---|---|
| Forest [1] | 36 | 52 | 59 | 47 |
| Unstocked and bamboo forest | 56 | 28 | 21 | 38 |
| Savannah and scrub | 3 | 8 | 9 | 6 |
| Crops | 1 | 4 | 7 | 4 |
| Other | 4 | 8 | 4 | 5 |
| Total | 100 | 100 | 100 | 100 |
| **Deforestation 1982-1989** | | | | |
| Forested area (ha 000s) | 203 | 188 | 78 | 469 |
| Deforestation (%) | 43 | 40 | 17 | 100 |
| 1. Continuous canopy >20% ; 2. Including Savannakhet province. | | | | |

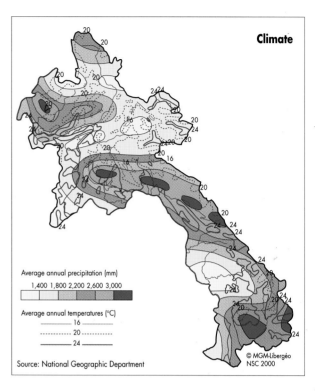

**Climate**

Average annual precipitation (mm)

1,400 1,800 2,200 2,600 3,000

Average annual temperatures (°C)

——— 16 ———
----------- 20 -----------
——— 24 ———

Source: National Geographic Department

© MGM-Libergéo
NSC 2000

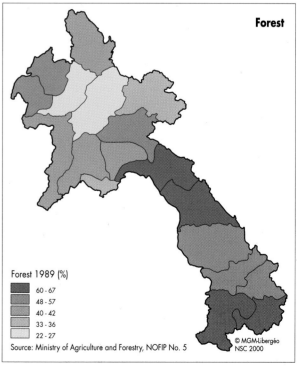

**Forest**

Forest 1989 (%)

- 60 - 67
- 48 - 57
- 40 - 42
- 33 - 36
- 22 - 27

Source: Ministry of Agriculture and Forestry, NOFIP No. 5

© MGM-Libergéo
NSC 2000

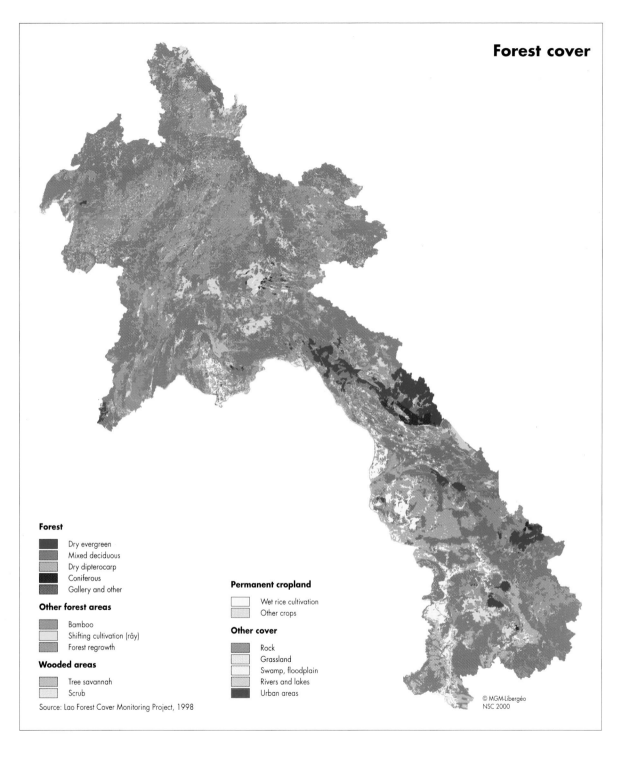

# Forest cover

**Forest**
- Dry evergreen
- Mixed deciduous
- Dry dipterocarp
- Coniferous
- Gallery and other

**Other forest areas**
- Bamboo
- Shifting cultivation (rây)
- Forest regrowth

**Wooded areas**
- Tree savannah
- Scrub

**Permanent cropland**
- Wet rice cultivation
- Other crops

**Other cover**
- Rock
- Grassland
- Swamp, floodplain
- Rivers and lakes
- Urban areas

Source: Lao Forest Cover Monitoring Project, 1998

© MGM-Libergéo
NSC 2000

# Land use and human environment

The land use map is like a negative of the forest cover map. Crop areas in the mountains and east of Savannakhet Plain account for less than 3% of the total, with two exceptions. The proportion of crop areas is higher on the Bolovens Plateau, which, unlike the Xiengkhuang Plateau, was not as heavily bombed, and along the southern roads of Oudomxay and Luangphrabang provinces. This map also highlights the three nuclei of settlement shown in the population density map (page 16), between Vientiane and Pakse. Crop areas account for less than 10% in the districts bordering the Mekong in Savannakhet, between 10% and 12% in the districts in Saravane and Pakse provinces. Crop areas rise to between 13% and 19% in Vientiane city and along the northward road to Thoulakhom, peaking at 28% in the two riparian districts on the road to the bridge over the Mekong.

The natural reproduction rates reflect the spatial structures of the land use map in the four southern provinces, but they contrast with land use in the Centre and the North. The fastest growth is found in Huaphanh and Xiengkhuang (2-3.5%), the most heavily populated regions to be bombed, and in the neighbouring provinces (1.7-2%), which have experienced a post-war baby boom.

The jewels of Lao cultural heritage are strung out along the Mekong Valley, from the city of Luangphrabang, the original capital of Lan Xang, included on UNESCO's World Heritage List; via Vientiane, which replaced it in the 16th century; to the Khmer temple of Wat Phou, the ancient capital of the kingdom of Champassack; and the Khone Falls. The prehistoric site of the Plain of Jars (even if the pagodas of the Phouane principality were destroyed during the war), the Buddhist sites of the Sekong Valley and the Xamneua caves that sheltered the Pathet Lao administration during the bombings are among the country's most famous other sites. Hotel capacity is concentrated along the Mekong and Road 13, with Muong Xay (a new city) and Namtha governing access to China.

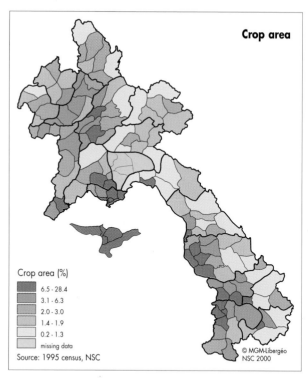

**Crop area**

Crop area (%)
- 6.5 - 28.4
- 3.1 - 6.3
- 2.0 - 3.0
- 1.4 - 1.9
- 0.2 - 1.3
- missing data

Source: 1995 census, NSC

© MGM-Libergéo
NSC 2000

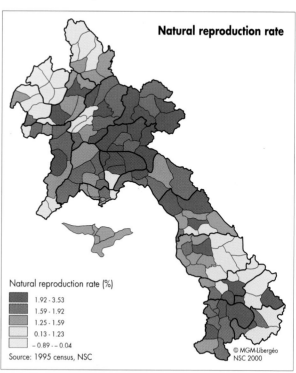

**Natural reproduction rate**

Natural reproduction rate (%)
- 1.92 - 3.53
- 1.59 - 1.92
- 1.25 - 1.59
- 0.13 - 1.23
- – 0.89 - – 0.04

Source: 1995 census, NSC

© MGM-Libergéo
NSC 2000

# Natural, historic and religious heritage

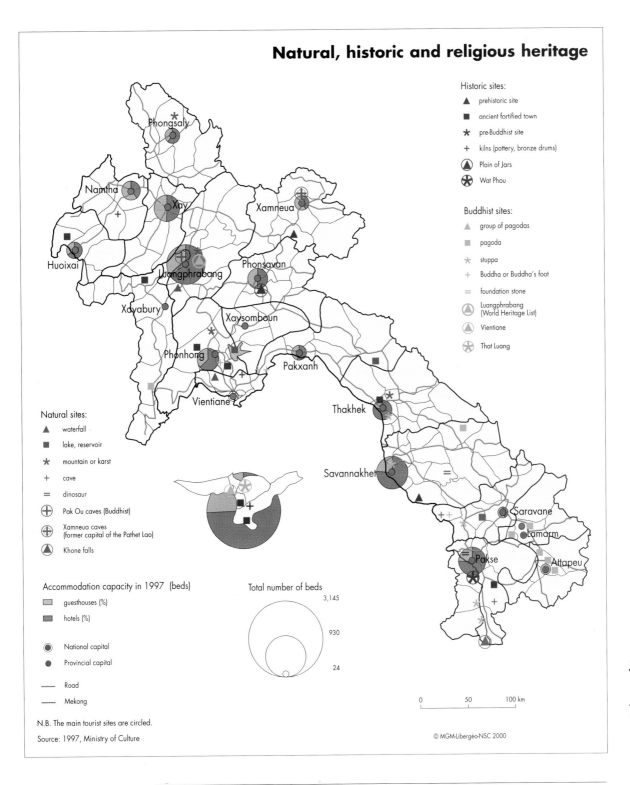

**Historic sites:**
- ▲ prehistoric site
- ■ ancient fortified town
- ✶ pre-Buddhist site
- + kilns (pottery, bronze drums)
- Ⓐ Plain of Jars
- ✳ Wat Phou

**Buddhist sites:**
- ▲ group of pagodas
- ■ pagoda
- ✶ stuppa
- + Buddha or Buddha's foot
- = foundation stone
- Ⓐ Luangphrabang (World Heritage List)
- Ⓐ Vientiane
- ✳ That Luang

**Natural sites:**
- ▲ waterfall
- ■ lake, reservoir
- ✶ mountain or karst
- + cave
- = dinosaur
- ⊕ Pak Ou caves (Buddhist)
- ⊕ Xamneua caves (former capital of the Pathet Lao)
- Ⓐ Khone falls

**Accommodation capacity in 1997 (beds)**
- ▦ guesthouses (%)
- ▦ hotels (%)
- ◉ National capital
- ● Provincial capital
- —— Road
- —— Mekong

**Total number of beds**
- 3,145
- 930
- 24

N.B. The main tourist sites are circled.

Source: 1997, Ministry of Culture

© MGM-Libergéo-NSC 2000

0        50        100 km

Map labels: Phongsaly, Namtha, Xay, Xamneua, Huoixai, Luangphrabang, Phonsavan, Xayabury, Xaysomboun, Phonhong, Pakxanh, Vientiane, Thakhek, Savannakhet, Saravane, Lamarm, Pakse, Attapeu

## Manpower by sector and distribution of wealth

Since agriculture is high throughout the country, the map of manpower by economic sector excludes this dominant variable. The first three types show values far higher than the national average. In Vientiane city, the main activities, in decreasing order of importance are: construction, timber, business services, electricity/radio/television, transport and trade. The second type—the district linking Vientiane to the bridge over the Mekong—is dominated by timber and fisheries. The northern peri-urban districts of the capital show a similar pattern to the four cities bordering the Mekong and the district bordering the Nam Ngum reservoir. This third type is distinguished from the first by the lesser importance of timber and fisheries, which come after trade. The two districts north and south of the Nam Ngum reservoir form a fourth—intermediate—type, where business services and electricity generation remain above the national average, while the other sectors, particularly construction, are below it. The last two types are the most rural. The fifth comprises the regions where the Tai-Kadai dominate in the Mekong Valley, from Xayabury to Cambodia, and the provinces of Huaphanh and Xiengkhuang in the North-East. The sixth consists of the mountains of the interior populated by ethnic minorities. The deviation from the average of this last area is more strongly negative because of its isolation.

There are no available figures on the breakdown of Laotian gross domestic product by province. An insight can be gained, however, from the 1997-1998 Lao expenditure and consumption survey, despite its shortcomings. Per capita income is 4.5 times higher in Vientiane municipality (781,000 kip = $437) than in Oudomxay (175,000 kip = $98), and 2.3 times higher than the national average (336,900 kip = $189). Xayabury and Champassack appear relatively well-off, with over 500,000 kip ($280), as do, to a lesser extent, Vientiane and Borikhamxay provinces, which surround the capital (over 375,000 kip = $210).

Four types of province can be distinguished according to income structure. Income from trade and wage employment is ahead of agriculture only in Vientiane municipality and in Champassack. In the second type, rental income and transfers from abroad equal or exceed trade and wage employment. This is the pattern in the provinces of Khammouane and Savannakhet and in Sekong, where numerous development projects have been implemented. The third type, which comprises most of the provinces of the northern half of the country plus Attapeu in the South, combines income from agriculture and income from trade and wage employment. The last type, almost exclusively agricultural, consists of isolated provinces such as Phongsaly and Xaysomboun, and provinces in intermediate locations, such as Oudomxay in the North and Saravane in the South.

Per capita household spending gives an idea of the distribution of wealth. Annual average rural consumption is equivalent to 65% of urban consumption, at 303,000 kip and 466,000 kip ($170 and $260) respectively. The disparity between the extremes is much wider in the countryside (3.4) than in urban areas (2.1). The highs are comparable at 612,000 kip and 671,000 kip ($345 and $376) for Vientiane municipality because of the large peri-urban area, but the lows differ considerably, from 179,000 kip ($100) in highly rural Muong Xay to 312,000 kip ($175) in recently urbanised Xaysomboun.

The structure of spending in both rural and urban areas in the first two types of province is dominated by food. With respective proportions of 76% and 67%, the peripheral provinces of Phongsaly and Luangnamtha in the North, and Sekong and Attapeu (rural areas only) in the South, food accounts for a larger share of spending than the neighbouring provinces and those along the Vietnamese border between Huaphanh and Khammouane in the North, and Savannakhet and Saravane in the South (71% and 51%). Personal services (transport, garments, education, health, etc.) are significant in the other two types of province. In the countryside, these items exceed 26% in the Mekong provinces between Vientiane municipality and Xayabury, and 18% in the neighbouring provinces of Luangphrabang and Xaysomboun, and in three provinces of the South. The proportion of these services is highest in the towns, where they usually range from a quarter to a third of the total, except in the peripheral provinces of the North and South (with the exception of Champassack).

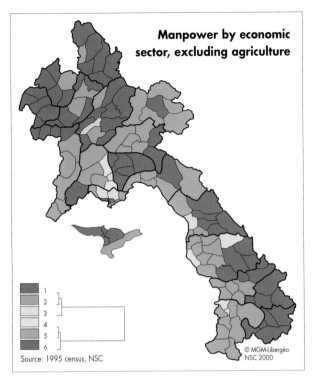

## Manpower by economic sector, excluding agriculture

| | |
|---|---|
| 1 | |
| 2 | |
| 3 | |
| 4 | |
| 5 | |
| 6 | |

Source: 1995 census, NSC

© MGM-Libergéo
NSC 2000

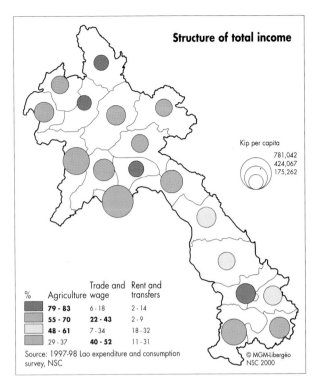

## Structure of total income

Kip per capita
781,042
424,067
175,262

| % | Agriculture | Trade and wage | Rent and transfers |
|---|---|---|---|
| **79 - 83** | 6 - 18 | 2 - 14 | |
| **55 - 70** | **22 - 43** | 2 - 9 | |
| 48 - 61 | 7 - 34 | 18 - 32 | |
| 29 - 37 | **40 - 52** | 11 - 31 | |

Source: 1997-98 Lao expenditure and consumption survey, NSC

© MGM-Libergéo
NSC 2000

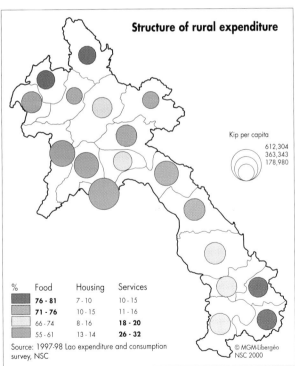

## Structure of rural expenditure

Kip per capita
612,304
363,343
178,980

| % | Food | Housing | Services |
|---|---|---|---|
| **76 - 81** | 7 - 10 | 10 - 15 | |
| **71 - 76** | 10 - 15 | 11 - 16 | |
| 66 - 74 | 8 - 16 | **18 - 20** | |
| 55 - 61 | 13 - 14 | **26 - 32** | |

Source: 1997-98 Lao expenditure and consumption survey, NSC

© MGM-Libergéo
NSC 2000

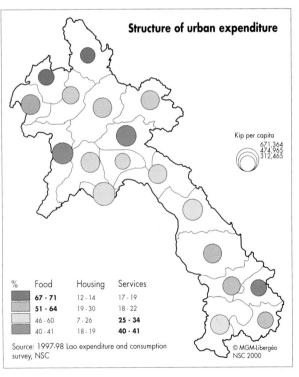

## Structure of urban expenditure

Kip per capita
671,364
474,965
312,465

| % | Food | Housing | Services |
|---|---|---|---|
| **67 - 71** | 12 - 14 | 17 - 19 | |
| **51 - 64** | 19 - 30 | 18 - 22 | |
| 46 - 60 | 7 - 26 | **25 - 34** | |
| 40 - 41 | 18 - 19 | **40 - 41** | |

Source: 1997-98 Lao expenditure and consumption survey, NSC

© MGM-Libergéo
NSC 2000

## Public and foreign investment

Four types of province can be distinguished according to the distribution of public investment in Lao PDR. In the first, roads absorb almost three-quarters of the total, with 2 billion kip, and are ahead of the social sector (education, health, housing). This includes Vientiane municipality, where the roads are being gradually modernised, and Phongsaly, which was isolated for a long time. Industrial investment is only significant in Luangnamtha. In the second type, the social sector comes ahead of roads. This includes the provinces bordering the Mekong from Borikhamxay to Luangphrabang and those centred on its tributaries in the South. The third type is similar to the first, but with a stronger agricultural component. This includes provinces in intermediate positions: Oudomxay and Bokeo in the North, the axis from Huaphanh to Vientiane province in the North-East, and Khammouane and Savannakhet at the junction of the Centre and the South. Xaysomboun stands out because of the absence of the social sector and Champassack because of its dominant agriculture. The relative weakness of agricultural investment in a strongly rural country is striking, especially as foreign investment does not compensate for this deficiency.

In absolute value, Champassack province is the fourth beneficiary of public investment with 2.1 billion kip, behind Phongsaly province and Vientiane municipality, with 2.9 billion kip and 2.7 billion kip respectively. Savannakhet, the largest and most populous province, receives the most funding, with 3.4 billion kip. The two mountainous provinces of the South—albeit sparsely populated—and the two in the North-East, are the least favourably treated, with funding ranging from 1 billion kip to 1.2 billion kip, although they suffered the most war damage. These provinces and more populous Saravane are at a clear disadvantage.

The foreign investment authorised between 1991 and 1997 was even more unequally distributed over the country and was concentrated on the industrial sector and energy. Much investment has been frozen since the Asian crisis. The investments in energy went to the following projects: a lignite-fired power plant in Hongsa, north of Xayabury, financed by Thailand; a hydroelectric dam in Thathom (Xaysomboun), financed by the United States; a part of Nam Theun-Hinboon (210 MW) co-financed by Norway, South Korea and Thailand; studies of Nam Theun 2 (681 MW) co-financed by Japan, Australia and Thailand; dams on the Bolovens Plateau and its southern rim: Xe Kaman (470 MW), co-financed by South Korea, Malaysia and Thailand; and Huay Ho (150 MW), co-financed by South Korea and Thailand. Industrial investment is only significant in the centre of Vientiane.

Investment in services, with the exception of hotels in Luangphrabang, is highly concentrated in three of the four urban districts of Vientiane. In Chanthabouly, the city centre, telecommunications come ahead of banking and trade; telecommunications are practically the only investment sector in the district of Hadxaifong, located upstream from the bridge over the Mekong. Investors mostly come from South-East Asia. In the city centre, the first district, they are joined by others, mainly from East Asia.

Altogether, Thailand is the leading foreign direct investor ($2.7 billion), accounting for 43% of total investment over the period 1991-1997. It is followed by the United States ($1.4 billion, 22%), Australia ($0.53 billion, 8.5%), South Korea ($0.47 billion, 7.5%), Taiwan ($0.43 billion, 7%), Malaysia ($0.33 billion, 5.3%), the European Union ($0.19 billion, 3%) and Japan ($0.14 billion, 2.2%). The Asian countries, now affected by the crisis, accounted for two-thirds of authorised investment.

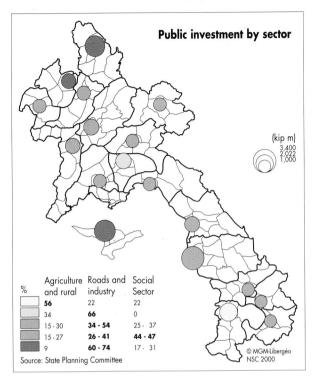

## Public investment by sector

(kip m)
3,400
2,022
1,000

| % | Agriculture and rural | Roads and industry | Social Sector |
|---|---|---|---|
| | **56** | 22 | 22 |
| | 34 | **66** | 0 |
| | 15 - 30 | **34 - 54** | 25 - 37 |
| | 15 - 27 | **26 - 41** | **44 - 47** |
| | 9 | **60 - 74** | 17 - 31 |

Source: State Planning Committee

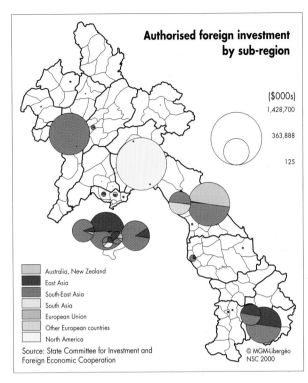

## Authorised foreign investment by sub-region

($000s)
1,428,700

363,888

125

Australia, New Zealand
East Asia
South-East Asia
South Asia
European Union
Other European countries
North America

Source: State Committee for Investment and Foreign Economic Cooperation

© MGM-Libergéo
NSC 2000

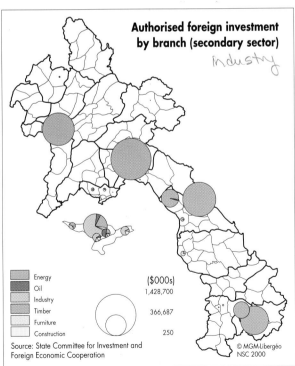

## Authorised foreign investment by branch (secondary sector)

*Industry*

Energy
Oil
Industry
Timber
Furniture
Construction

($000s)
1,428,700

366,687

250

Source: State Committee for Investment and Foreign Economic Cooperation

© MGM-Libergéo
NSC 2000

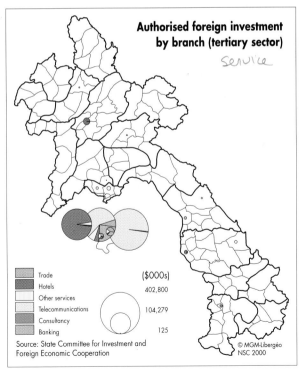

## Authorised foreign investment by branch (tertiary sector)

*Service*

Trade
Hotels
Other services
Telecommunications
Consultancy
Banking

($000s)
402,800

104,279

125

Source: State Committee for Investment and Foreign Economic Cooperation

© MGM-Libergéo
NSC 2000

## Laos in South-East Asia: settlement and demographic indicators

The statistical data used to compare Laos with the rest of South-East Asia are taken from *Key Indicators of Developing Asian and Pacific Countries*, 1996, published by the Asian Development Bank, because they appear to be the most homogeneous. Since the Sultanate of Brunei is not included, the data on Brunei come from the United Nations' *Statistical Yearbook for Asia and the Pacific*

*1995*. The data available, depending on the indicators, range from 1992 to 1995, with this last date being the main reference for this atlas.

Lao PDR is the least populous country in South-East Asia, except for Singapore and Brunei. With 19 persons per km$^2$, Laos is three times less densely populated than Cambodia, Myanmar and Malaysia. Its urban population, although overestimated at 21.7%, remains comparable to that of the rest of the Indochinese Peninsula, excepting Myanmar. Urbanisation is much lower in the continental countries than in the archipelago

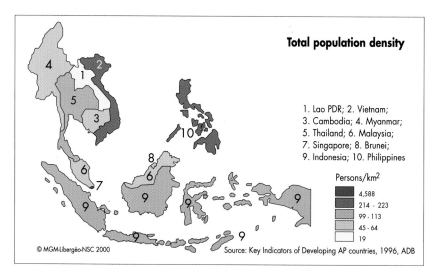

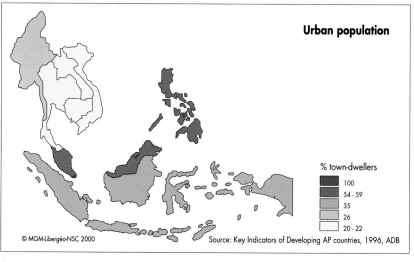

Territory

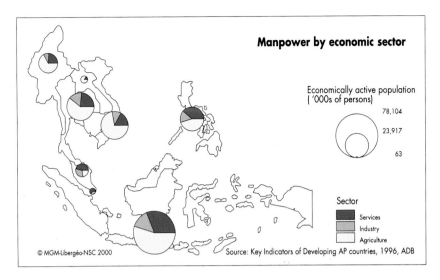

**Manpower by economic sector**

Economically active population
( '000s of persons)

78,104

23,917

63

Sector

Services
Industry
Agriculture

© MGM-Libergéo-NSC 2000

Source: Key Indicators of Developing AP countries, 1996, ADB

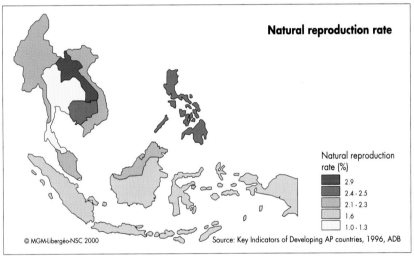

**Natural reproduction rate**

Natural reproduction
rate (%)

2.9
2.4 - 2.5
2.1 - 2.3
1.6
1.0 - 1.3

© MGM-Libergéo-NSC 2000

Source: Key Indicators of Developing AP countries, 1996, ADB

countries of South-East Asia. Laos is also the most ethnically diverse country, with only 53% of Lao, compared with 69% of Burmans, 83% of Thai and 87% of Khmer and Vietnamese in their respective countries.

Laos is also distinguished by the extremely high percentage of its workforce engaged in agriculture (84.7%), an even higher figure than in Vietnam (72.3%) and Myanmar (69.2%). In the other countries with an agricultural base, with the exception of Malaysia, the proportion is between 60% and 45%. It is also the least industrialised South-East Asian country, with the lowest rate of manpower in services.

The rate of population increase—even if it is overestimated here at 2.9% compared with the figure of 2.62% given in the 1995 census—reflects a lag in demographic transition and a post-war baby boom, which are also apparent, to a lesser extent, in Cambodia (2.5%) and Vietnam (2.2%). The Philippines are the only archipelago country in South-East Asia with comparable rates.

## Laos in South-East Asia: crop area and economic indicators

With the exceptions of Singapore and Brunei, the crop area in Laos, where 84% of the land is over 200 m above sea level, is more than four times smaller than in the countries with the smallest crop area in South-East Asia. With average annual per capita income of $320, Laos is richer in income terms than Cambodia ($240) and Vietnam ($190). Laos is nevertheless almost three times poorer than the next richest countries, Indonesia and the Philippines. The income indicator should also be compared with UNDP's Human Development Index (HDI), which ranks Laos alongside Myanmar, and a long way ahead of Cambodia, which is still marked by the legacy of the Khmer Rouge genocide. In the HDI, Laos is ranked after Vietnam, which has far superior health and education systems in the light of its economic performance.

Lao PDR is the biggest recipient of official development assistance per capita in South-East Asia.

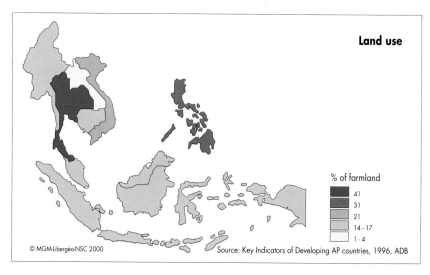

**Land use**

% of farmland
- 41
- 31
- 21
- 14 - 17
- 1 - 4

© MGM-Libergéo-NSC 2000          Source: Key Indicators of Developing AP countries, 1996, ADB

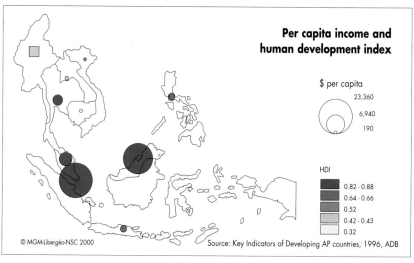

**Per capita income and human development index**

$ per capita
- 23,360
- 6,940
- 190

HDI
- 0.82 - 0.88
- 0.64 - 0.66
- 0.52
- 0.42 - 0.43
- 0.32

© MGM-Libergéo-NSC 2000          Source: Key Indicators of Developing AP countries, 1996, ADB

Territory

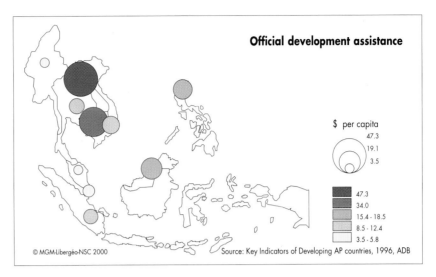

**Official development assistance**

$ per capita
47.3
19.1
3.5

47.3
34.0
15.4 - 18.5
8.5 - 12.4
3.5 - 5.8

© MGM-Libergéo-NSC 2000

Source: Key Indicators of Developing AP countries, 1996, ADB

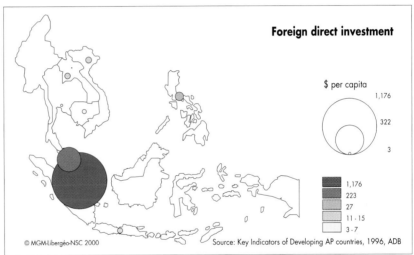

**Foreign direct investment**

$ per capita
1,176
322
3

1,176
223
27
11 - 15
3 - 7

© MGM-Libergéo-NSC 2000

Source: Key Indicators of Developing AP countries, 1996, ADB

With $47.30, it is a long way ahead of Cambodia ($34), the Philippines ($18.50) and Vietnam ($12.40), which come next. Almost 67% of this aid to Laos, estimated at $142 million by the International Monetary Fund (IMF) in 1992, comes from international financial institutions (28% World Bank, 22% ADB, 11% UN agencies and 5.6% IMF) and only 31% comes from bilateral aid (13.6% Japan, 11% Sweden, 5.1% Australia, 1% European Union), a trend that the Asian crisis is likely to accentuate.

The ranking is reversed for direct investment per capita. With the exception of Thailand, which receives an abnormally low amount of direct investment per capita, Lao PDR, with $13, falls into a category that combines the smallest countries by population and the least developed economically, and the largest countries by population, Indonesia and Vietnam, where foreign financing is low in relative figures. Only middle-sized Malaysia is really privileged in this regard ($223), with the exception of Singapore, of course.

*Atlas of Laos*

**31**

# Chapter 2. Settlement

In a country as ethnically diverse as Laos, the distribution of the population by ethnolinguistic families and ethnic groups is a key to understanding the maps. The 1995 census provides this information at district level. The table opposite recognises five ethnolinguistic families according to their scientific classification, which is rare for a country of this size. Of the 47 ethnic groups recorded in the census, this table includes only those that number over 25,000 members, with the exception of the Hor, who, although less numerous, represent the fifth ethnolinguistic family.

The Tai-Kadai family, designated by the term Lao Loum (i.e. Lao of the plains and valleys), make up two-thirds of the country's population. This family includes the Lao—who account for just over half of the total—and only five other ethnic groups. After the Lao, the term Phutai covers a number of smaller groups from this family, such as the White Tai, Black Tai, Red Tai and Tai Phouan, which together account for 10% of the total population and 16% of the Tai-Kadai.

The second ethnolinguistic family, the Austro-Asiatics, 23% of the total population, consists of two branches, distinguished in the table: the dominant Mon-Khmer and the small minority of Viet-Muong in Laos. This family comprises 30 ethnic groups, i.e. 64% of those listed in the census: some of these groups have only a few thousand members, while the dominant group—the Khmu—comprises half a million people. This family is designated by the term Lao Theung (Lao of the slopes), because these groups were driven off the plains with the arrival of the Lao.

The next two families, the Miao-Yao (called Hmong-Yao in Laos) and the Tibeto-Burmans were only able to settle on the mountain peaks when they arrived in the 19th century, which explains why they are both referred to by the same term Lao Soung (Lao of the summits). They represent respectively 7.4% and 2.7% of the population. The Hmong, with 315,000 members, is the fourth largest ethnic group, behind the Lao, the Khmu and the Phutai. The last group, the Hor, belongs to the Sino-Tibetan ethnolinguistic family and numbers fewer than 10,000 persons.

Another key to the distribution of the population is the differentiation between urban and rural populations, a source of numerous errors of interpretation. The population of Vientiane city is often considered as the 524,000 inhabitants of the municipality, which is composed of nine districts. However, only four of these are urbanised and total 266,500 inhabitants, of which only 233,500 are recorded as town-dwellers in the census. There are also three peri-urban districts, where town-dwellers represent between a third and half of the population, and two rural districts. Altogether, the urbanised population of Vientiane municipality totals 331,000.

The census definition of the urbanised population takes into account only the population of the urban villages, characteristic of urbanisation in this part of Asia. To qualify as "urban", a village must meet three of the following five conditions: it must be located within the vicinity of the administrative capital of the province or district; the majority of households must have electricity and piped water; it must have a market; and it must be accessible to motorised vehicles.

This definition is extremely broad, since the last two criteria apply to any village centre located along a road, and "within the vicinity" remains imprecise. The Housing and Urban Planning Department requires other criteria: residential density of more than 30 persons per hectare; a population of more than 2,000; and the availability of other services beyond a local market. According to these requirements, the population of the capital comes down from 233,500 to 166,500. It would be useful to harmonise the definitions to allow more accurate analysis.

| Ethnolinguistic families | Number of ethnic groups | Population | % | Ethnolinguistic families | Number of ethnic groups | Population | % |
|---|---|---|---|---|---|---|---|
| **Tai-Kadai** | **6** | **3,029,154** | **66.2** | Talieng | | 23,091 | 0.5 |
| Lao | | 2,403,891 | 52.5 | Phong | | 21,395 | 0.5 |
| Phutai | | 472,458 | 10.3 | Tri | | 20,906 | 0.5 |
| Leu | | 119,191 | 2.6 | 17 other groups | | 143,459 | 3.1 |
| Nhuane | | 26,239 | 0.6 | **Viet-Muong** | **3** | **4,071** | **0.1** |
| Yang et Xaek | | 7,375 | 0.2 | **Miao-Yao** | **2** | **338,130** | **7.4** |
| **Mon-Khmer** | **27** | **1,037,655** | **22.7** | Hmong | | 315,465 | 6.9 |
| Khmu | | 500,957 | 11.0 | Yao | | 22,665 | 0.5 |
| Katang | | 95,440 | 2.1 | **Tibeto-Burman** | **8** | **122,653** | **2.7** |
| Makong | | 92,321 | 2.0 | Kor | | 66,108 | 1.4 |
| Xouay | | 45,498 | 1.0 | Phounoy | | 35,635 | 0.8 |
| Laven | | 40,519 | 0.9 | 6 other groups | | 20,910 | 0.5 |
| Taoey | | 30,876 | 0.7 | **Hor** | **1** | **8,900** | **0.2** |
| Thin | | 23,193 | 0.5 | **Others, not specified** | **2** | **34,285** | **0.7** |
| | | | | **Total** | **49** | **4,574,848** | **100** |

The structure of housing also sheds light on this issue. The 1995 census contains information on the size and tenure status of housing, construction materials, water and electricity supply, source of energy used for cooking, and type of sanitation. On the basis of construction materials, for example, a distinction can be made between traditional rural dwellings in wood or bamboo, and permanent dwellings—Chinese compartments typical of Asian cities, villas and apartment buildings.

The information from the census, processed at district level and compared with the rural–urban differentiation, makes it possible to analyse urbanisation in Laos for the first time. This analysis, beginning in this chapter, continues, wherever possible, throughout the atlas. It culminates in the conclusion with a typology of the towns and a hierarchy of the urban network, which are essential for designing a balanced strategy of territorial development.

## Ethnolinguistic families: Tai-Kadai and Austro-Asiatics

The Tai-Kadai family accounts for over 84% of the population along a continuous ribbon that runs through the districts bordering the Mekong from Paklai (Xayabury) to the Cambodian border. The Lao prevail over the other ethnic groups in the Tai-Kadai family from Luangphrabang and this belt widens along the river. The Tai-Kadai make up between 64% and 84% of the population around the provincial border separating Khammouane and Savannakhet, and along the axis between Vientiane and Xamneua. Therefore, Huaphanh and Xiengkhuang provinces cannot be considered as a periphery like the other mountainous provinces of the North and South. A number of maps in the atlas confirm this observation. The Phutai are concentrated in the eastern half of the provinces lying between the Mekong and the Vietnamese border in the Centre.

The Mon-Khmer branch of the Austro-Asiatic family is concentrated in two nuclei of settlement. In the North, the Khmu, centred on the provinces of Oudomxay and Luangphrabang, account for between 43% and 73% of the population. They continue into the neighbouring provinces and are extended by the Thin in northern Xayabury. The other ethnic groups in this family account for over three-quarters of the population in the districts along the Vietnamese border in the South. Unlike the homogeneous Khmu, these groups form a mosaic, reflecting multi-ethnic areas. The largest is the Katang (95,000 persons) in Savannakhet province. The Taoey and Xouay are concentrated in Saravane province, the Talieng in Sekong province, and the Laven on the border between Champassack and Attapeu provinces.

The few Viet-Muong ethnic groups are located on the Vietnamese border of Borikhamxay, in between the two Mon-Khmer settlements in the North and South. They represent the extension of the Vietnamese province of Nghê Tinh, where they form a sizeable majority (85% of the population). The Hor, belonging to the Sino-Tibetan family, are concentrated along the Chinese border in Phongsaly province.

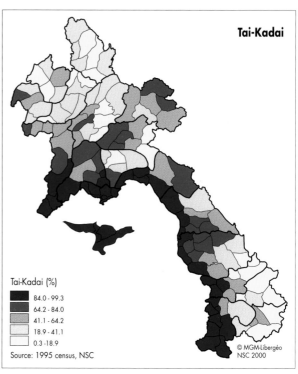

Tai-Kadai

Tai-Kadai (%)

- 84.0 - 99.3
- 64.2 - 84.0
- 41.1 - 64.2
- 18.9 - 41.1
- 0.3 - 18.9

Source: 1995 census, NSC

© MGM-Libergéo
NSC 2000

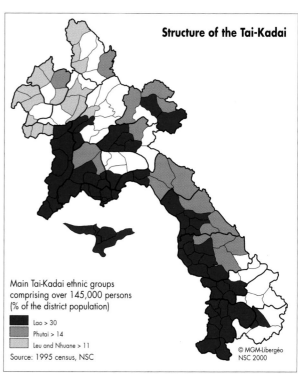

Structure of the Tai-Kadai

Main Tai-Kadai ethnic groups
comprising over 145,000 persons
(% of the district population)

- Lao > 30
- Phutai > 14
- Leu and Nhuane > 11

Source: 1995 census, NSC

© MGM-Libergéo
NSC 2000

*Settlement*

**34**

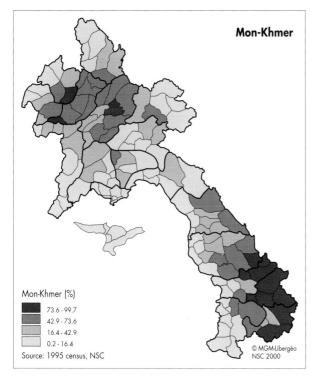

**Mon-Khmer**

Mon-Khmer (%)
- 73.6 - 99.7
- 42.9 - 73.6
- 16.4 - 42.9
- 0.2 - 16.4

Source: 1995 census, NSC

© MGM-Libergéo
NSC 2000

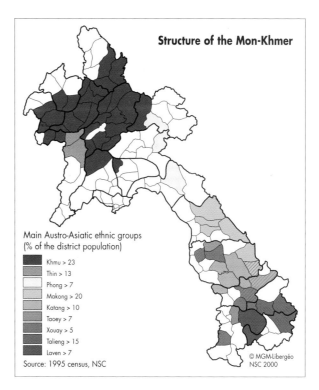

**Structure of the Mon-Khmer**

Main Austro-Asiatic ethnic groups
(% of the district population)
- Khmu > 23
- Thin > 13
- Phong > 7
- Makong > 20
- Katang > 10
- Taoey > 7
- Xouay > 5
- Talieng > 15
- Laven > 7

Source: 1995 census, NSC

© MGM-Libergéo
NSC 2000

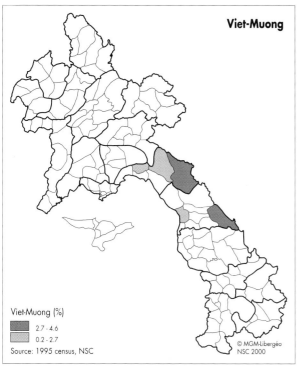

**Viet-Muong**

Viet-Muong (%)
- 2.7 - 4.6
- 0.2 - 2.7

Source: 1995 census, NSC

© MGM-Libergéo
NSC 2000

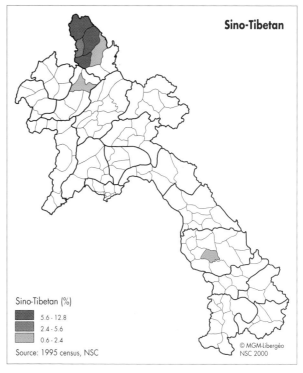

**Sino-Tibetan**

Sino-Tibetan (%)
- 5.6 - 12.8
- 2.4 - 5.6
- 0.6 - 2.4

Source: 1995 census, NSC

© MGM-Libergéo
NSC 2000

*Atlas of Laos*

**35**

## Ethnolinguistic families:
## Miao-Yao and Tibeto-Burman;
## religious affiliations

The Miao-Yao family (called Hmong-Yao in Laos) is spread out across the mountains north of Borikhamxay. In the south-eastern part of this area, the heart of the Hmong settlement borders the Tai-Kadai settlement, from the special zone of Xaysomboun to Huaphanh province. The Yao are located closer to the Mekong and further north, especially in northern Xayabury and western Vientiane province, and in the border districts of Bokeo, Luangnamtha and Phongsaly provinces, alongside the Nhuane and Leu. The Yao rarely make up more than 8% of the population, whereas the Hmong attain 80% at the centre of their area. The Tibeto-Burman family is concentrated in the north-western corner of the country, where Yao and Leu are also found.

The map of religious affiliations shows a meridian division of the country. In the west, along the Mekong from Xayabury to the Cambodian border, is the Buddhist area of the Tai-Kadai. In the east along the Vietnamese, Chinese and Myanmar borders, is the area of the highland animists: Austro-Asiatics, Miao-Yao and Tibeto-Burmans. Between the two areas is a narrow intermediate belt where these two components are combined, particularly along the axis between Vientiane and Huaphanh provinces. Alongside the Buddhists, there are Christians in Pakxanh (Borikhamxay) and Bachiangchaleunsook (Champassack), and Hmong animists in Xaysomboun.

The religious structures in urban areas are more distinct. The Lao population, which is Buddhist, forms the vast majority in the district and provincial capitals, particularly in Luangphrabang city and the two districts upstream and downstream from the centre of Vientiane. The two central districts of the capital also include Christians, although the majority of the population is Buddhist. Christians are more numerous in Savannakhet and Pakse, but are outnumbered there by animists, as they are in the capitals of the districts bordering the Mekong from Pakxanh to southern Savannakhet province.

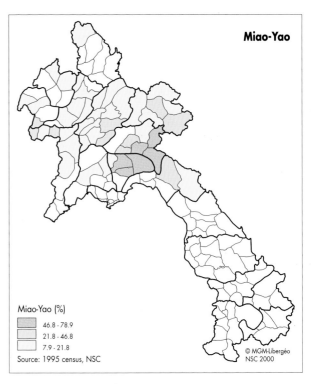

Miao-Yao

Miao-Yao (%)
- 46.8 - 78.9
- 21.8 - 46.8
- 7.9 - 21.8

Source: 1995 census, NSC

© MGM-Libergéo
NSC 2000

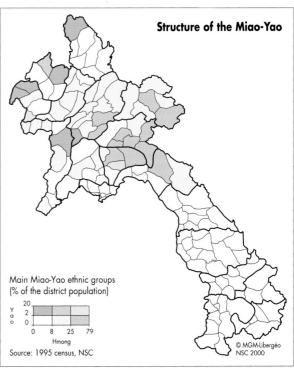

Structure of the Miao-Yao

Main Miao-Yao ethnic groups
(% of the district population)

Source: 1995 census, NSC

© MGM-Libergéo
NSC 2000

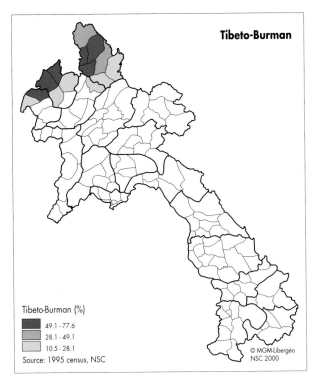

**Tibeto-Burman**

Tibeto-Burman (%)

- 49.1 - 77.6
- 28.1 - 49.1
- 10.5 - 28.1

Source: 1995 census, NSC

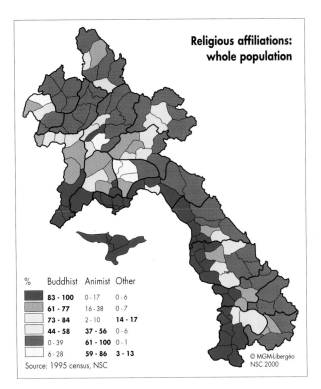

**Religious affiliations:
whole population**

| % | Buddhist | Animist | Other |
|---|---|---|---|
| | **83 - 100** | 0 - 17 | 0 - 6 |
| | **61 - 77** | 16 - 38 | 0 - 7 |
| | **73 - 84** | 2 - 10 | **14 - 17** |
| | **44 - 58** | **37 - 56** | 0 - 6 |
| | 0 - 39 | **61 - 100** | 0 - 1 |
| | 6 - 28 | **59 - 86** | **3 - 13** |

Source: 1995 census, NSC

© MGM-Libergéo
NSC 2000

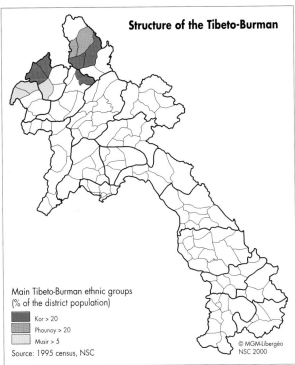

**Structure of the Tibeto-Burman**

Main Tibeto-Burman ethnic groups
(% of the district population)

- Kor > 20
- Phounoy > 20
- Musir > 5

Source: 1995 census, NSC

© MGM-Libergéo
NSC 2000

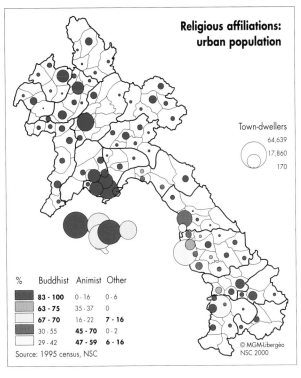

**Religious affiliations:
urban population**

Town-dwellers
- 64,639
- 17,860
- 170

| % | Buddhist | Animist | Other |
|---|---|---|---|
| | **83 - 100** | 0 - 16 | 0 - 6 |
| | **63 - 75** | 35 - 37 | 0 |
| | **67 - 70** | 16 - 22 | **7 - 16** |
| | 30 - 55 | **45 - 70** | 0 - 2 |
| | 29 - 42 | **47 - 59** | 6 - 16 |

Source: 1995 census, NSC

© MGM-Libergéo
NSC 2000

*Atlas of Laos*

## Urban population and tenure status

The two definitions of the urban population—the one used by the census and the one used by the Housing and Urban Planning Department—lead to quite different evaluations of Vientiane city: the first gives a population of 233,400 and the second a population of 166,650. In contrast, the second definition attributes slightly higher populations than the first to the three other large towns in the Mekong Valley. Savannakhet, the second-largest town in Laos, with respective population estimates of 62,200 and 66,800, is 3.5 times less populous than the capital according to the census, and 2.7 times less populous according to the Housing Department. Pakse has a population of between 47,600 and 54,000 and Luangphrabang between 31,800 to 35,700. Savannakhet and Pakse are the same size as one of the four districts of the capital.

The two evaluations differ the most for the other provincial capitals. In the North, according to the Housing and Urban Planning Department, Muong Xay (Oudomxay), a new road junction, is bigger than Namtha (Luangnamtha), the gateway to China (with respective populations of 23,100 and 10,000); however, according to the census, the two towns are of equal size, with populations of 15,000. The same occurs in the North-East, where, according to the Housing Department, Phonsavanh (Xiengkhuang), with a population of 16,800, is much larger than Xamneua (Huaphanh), with a population of 5,900; whereas, according to the census, the two towns are roughly the same size (with respective populations of 5,600 and 5,400). In Thakhek (Khammouane), the population indicated by the Housing Department is also bigger than that shown by the census (34,800 compared with 25,800).

Lao PDR has a low rate of urbanisation, with an urban population of 17% according to the census and 19% according to the Housing Department. The urban population exceeds 50% in the four districts of Vientiane city and in Pakse; it ranges from 28% to 50% mainly in the other towns in the Mekong Valley. Since the vast majority of people own their dwellings, rented and tied accommodation are indicators of urbanisation. In three of the four districts of Vientiane city, each of these indicators accounts for more than 10% of total housing, followed by Savannakhet and Pakse for rented accommodation and by Pakse alone for tied accommodation.

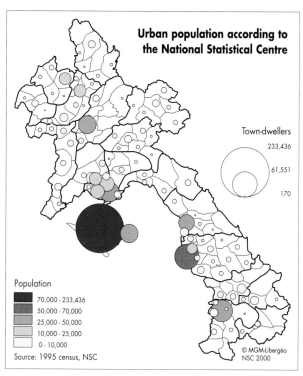

Urban population according to the National Statistical Centre

Town-dwellers
233,436
61,551
170

Population
70,000 - 233,436
50,000 - 70,000
25,000 - 50,000
10,000 - 25,000
0 - 10,000

Source: 1995 census, NSC

© MGM-Libergéo
NSC 2000

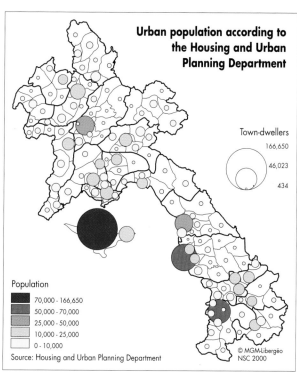

Urban population according to the Housing and Urban Planning Department

Town-dwellers
166,650
46,023
434

Population
70,000 - 166,650
50,000 - 70,000
25,000 - 50,000
10,000 - 25,000
0 - 10,000

Source: Housing and Urban Planning Department

© MGM-Libergéo
NSC 2000

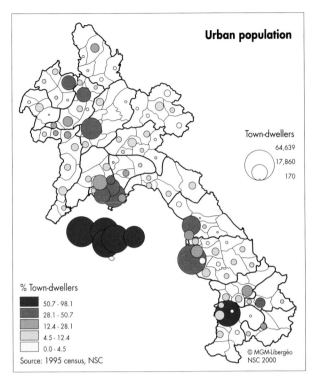

## Urban population

Town-dwellers

64,639
17,860
170

% Town-dwellers
- 50.7 - 98.1
- 28.1 - 50.7
- 12.4 - 28.1
- 4.5 - 12.4
- 0.0 - 4.5

Source: 1995 census, NSC

© MGM-Libergéo
NSC 2000

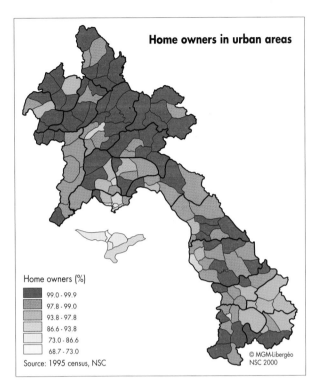

## Home owners in urban areas

Home owners (%)
- 99.0 - 99.9
- 97.8 - 99.0
- 93.8 - 97.8
- 86.6 - 93.8
- 73.0 - 86.6
- 68.7 - 73.0

Source: 1995 census, NSC

© MGM-Libergéo
NSC 2000

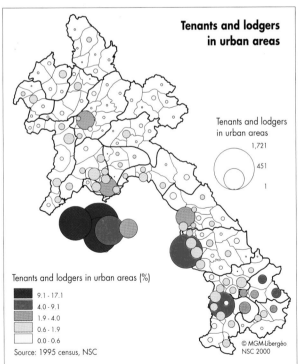

## Tenants and lodgers in urban areas

Tenants and lodgers
in urban areas

1,721
451
1

Tenants and lodgers in urban areas (%)
- 9.1 - 17.1
- 4.0 - 9.1
- 1.9 - 4.0
- 0.6 - 1.9
- 0.0 - 0.6

Source: 1995 census, NSC

© MGM-Libergéo
NSC 2000

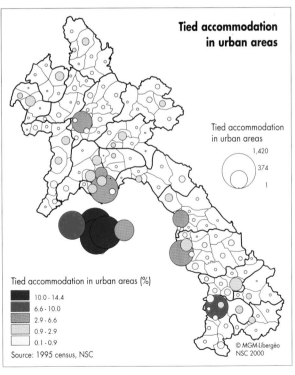

## Tied accommodation in urban areas

Tied accommodation
in urban areas

1,420
374
1

Tied accommodation in urban areas (%)
- 10.0 - 14.4
- 6.6 - 10.0
- 2.9 - 6.6
- 0.9 - 2.9
- 0.1 - 0.9

Source: 1995 census, NSC

© MGM-Libergéo
NSC 2000

# Housing: urban population

The largest living quarters are found in the three biggest towns: Vientiane, Savannakhet and Pakse, and in the peri-urban districts of Vientiane, where villas are common. All the other provincial capitals contain a mixture of large, medium and small dwellings, with the exception of recently urbanised Lamarm (Sekong), where medium-sized and small dwellings predominate. The two other types concern the least urbanised districts.

There are more concrete than wooden dwellings in Vientiane and Luangphrabang, the old royal capital and the most urbanised town in the North. The ratio is reversed for the district capitals on Vientiane Plain and for the three large towns of the Mekong. Wood is also predominant in Saravane and in the riparian districts of the South. There are more semi-permanent dwellings, made of bamboo or salvaged materials, than wooden dwellings in the provincial capitals of the North.

Over 70% of urban dwellings in the Mekong Valley and on Vientiane Plain are connected to the public electricity grid. The dwellings located along the Mekong and upstream from Vientiane and on the axis linking the capital to Xamneua rely on a mixture of public supply and small private generators—petrol generators in the Mekong Valley and hydraulic generators in the North-East. The towns in the three provinces of the North are clearly disadvantaged. As a cooking fuel, wood is predominant throughout the country, except in Savannakhet, where coal is used more. Modern fuels appear only in Vientiane.

Dwellings in the central districts of Vientiane, and in Savannakhet, Pakse and Luangphrabang, are distinguished by piped water and pour-flush latrines. Muong Xay in the North has piped water and Thakhek has pour-flush latrines. The other two districts of Vientiane, and Lamarm and Xamneua, rely on a mixture of piped water, wells and rainwater. Wells are the dominant source of water in the rest of the Mekong Valley and along the Vientiane–Xamneua axis. In the towns of the North, dry latrines predominate. In the other towns in the South and on Vientiane Plain, many dwellings have no sanitation at all.

Settlement

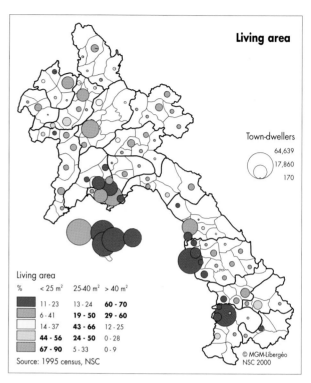

Living area

Town-dwellers
64,639
17,860
170

Living area
| % | < 25 m² | 25-40 m² | > 40 m² |
|---|---------|----------|---------|
|   | 11 - 23 | 13 - 24 | **60 - 70** |
|   | 6 - 41 | **19 - 50** | **29 - 60** |
|   | 14 - 37 | **43 - 66** | 12 - 25 |
|   | **44 - 56** | 24 - 50 | 0 - 28 |
|   | **67 - 90** | 5 - 33 | 0 - 9 |

Source: 1995 census, NSC

© MGM-Libergéo
NSC 2000

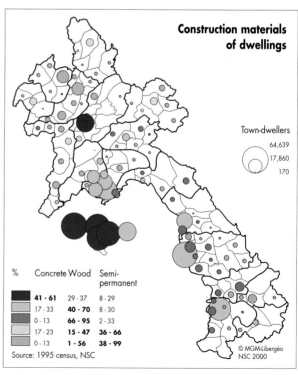

**Construction materials of dwellings**

Town-dwellers
64,639
17,860
170

| % | Concrete | Wood | Semi-permanent |
|---|----------|------|----------------|
|   | **41 - 61** | 29 - 37 | 8 - 29 |
|   | 17 - 33 | **40 - 70** | 8 - 30 |
|   | 0 - 13 | **66 - 95** | 2 - 33 |
|   | 17 - 23 | **15 - 47** | **36 - 66** |
|   | 0 - 13 | 1 - 56 | **38 - 99** |

Source: 1995 census, NSC

© MGM-Libergéo
NSC 2000

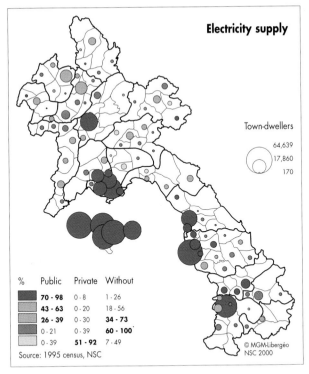

**Electricity supply**

Town-dwellers

64,639
17,860
170

| % | Public | Private | Without |
|---|--------|---------|---------|
| | **70 - 98** | 0 - 8 | 1 - 26 |
| | **43 - 63** | 0 - 20 | 18 - 56 |
| | **26 - 39** | 0 - 30 | 34 - 73 |
| | 0 - 21 | 0 - 39 | **60 - 100** |
| | 0 - 39 | **51 - 92** | 7 - 49 |

Source: 1995 census, NSC

© MGM-Libergéo
NSC 2000

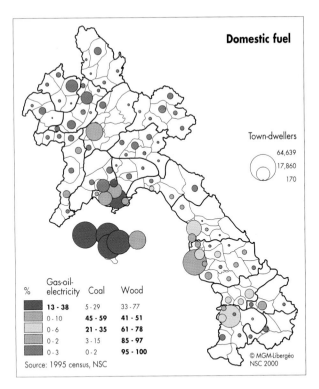

**Domestic fuel**

Town-dwellers

64,639
17,860
170

| % | Gas-oil-electricity | Coal | Wood |
|---|---------------------|------|------|
| | **13 - 38** | 5 - 29 | 33 - 77 |
| | 0 - 10 | **45 - 59** | 41 - 51 |
| | 0 - 6 | **21 - 35** | 61 - 78 |
| | 0 - 2 | 3 - 15 | **85 - 97** |
| | 0 - 3 | 0 - 2 | **95 - 100** |

Source: 1995 census, NSC

© MGM-Libergéo
NSC 2000

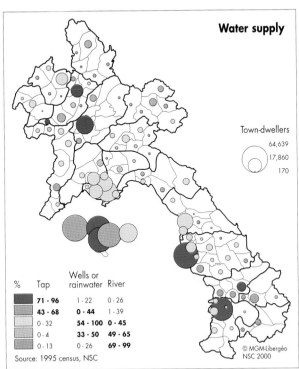

**Water supply**

Town-dwellers

64,639
17,860
170

| % | Tap | Wells or rainwater | River |
|---|-----|--------------------|-------|
| | **71 - 96** | 1 - 22 | 0 - 26 |
| | **43 - 68** | **0 - 44** | 1 - 39 |
| | 0 - 32 | **54 - 100** | **0 - 45** |
| | 0 - 4 | **33 - 50** | 49 - 65 |
| | 0 - 13 | **0 - 26** | 69 - 99 |

Source: 1995 census, NSC

© MGM-Libergéo
NSC 2000

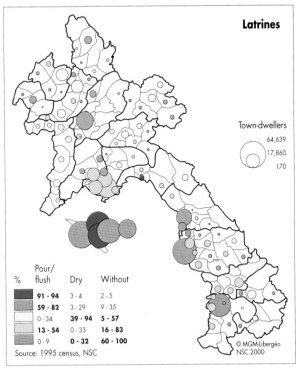

**Latrines**

Town-dwellers

64,639
17,860
170

| % | Pour/flush | Dry | Without |
|---|-----------|-----|---------|
| | **91 - 94** | 3 - 4 | 2 - 5 |
| | **59 - 82** | 3 - 29 | 9 - 35 |
| | 0 - 34 | **39 - 94** | 5 - 57 |
| | **13 - 54** | 0 - 33 | 16 - 83 |
| | 0 - 9 | **0 - 32** | **60 - 100** |

Source: 1995 census, NSC

© MGM-Libergéo
NSC 2000

*Atlas of Laos*

# Housing: whole population

The data for the population as a whole highlight the characteristics of rural housing, on which the analysis focuses here. The size of living quarters is related to the distribution of the two main ethnolinguistic families, the Tai-Kadai and the Mon-Khmer. The belt of Tai-Kadai population, with the largest dwellings, is less continuous in the Mekong Valley. The Mon-Khmer, with its two large settlements in the North and South, live in small and medium-sized dwellings. Between the two, along the Vientiane–Xamneua axis, a mixture of large and medium-sized dwellings is found. The Vientiane Plain and the Mekong Valley show a combination of wooden, concrete and semi-permanent dwellings. Semi-permanent dwellings predominate throughout the North and in the interior of the Centre and the South.

There is wide variation in the distribution of electricity and cooking fuels. A public electricity supply is concentrated on Vientiane Plain, along the bank downstream from the city and between Thakhek and the mouth of the Xe Bang Fai River, where there is pump irrigation. In Huaphanh, there are small hydraulic generators. Wood is by far the most widely used cooking fuel. This is a generally underestimated cause of deforestation.

Wells and rainwater surpass rivers as the main source of water on the plains in the regions of Vientiane and Savannakhet and on the Plain of Jars (Xiengkhuang). This pattern is reversed on the fringe of these regions and in the rest of the Mekong Valley. In the mountainous peripheral provinces of the North and South, people mainly use river water. Dwellings are equipped with either pour-flush or dry latrines from western Vientiane province to Pakxanh, and from the capital to Vangvieng along Road 13. In Xayabury, dry latrines predominate. Everywhere else, i.e. in the vast majority of the country, particularly in the South, over two-thirds of dwellings have no sanitation. An inadequate water supply and a lack of sanitation pose serious public health problems and are indicators of the poverty of the rural population.

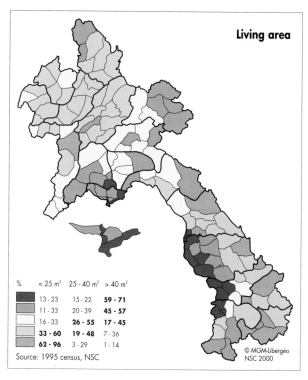

**Living area**

| % | < 25 m² | 25 - 40 m² | > 40 m² |
|---|---|---|---|
| | 13 - 23 | 15 - 22 | **59 - 71** |
| | 11 - 33 | 20 - 39 | **45 - 57** |
| | 16 - 33 | **26 - 55** | 17 - 45 |
| | **33 - 60** | **19 - 48** | 7 - 36 |
| | **62 - 96** | 3 - 29 | 1 - 14 |

Source: 1995 census, NSC

© MGM-Libergéo
NSC 2000

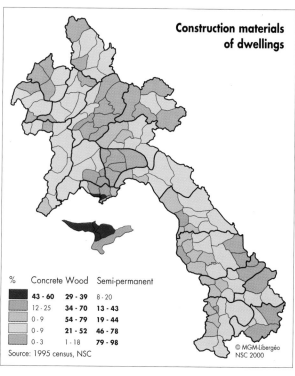

**Construction materials of dwellings**

| % | Concrete | Wood | Semi-permanent |
|---|---|---|---|
| | **43 - 60** | **29 - 39** | 8 - 20 |
| | 12 - 25 | **34 - 70** | **13 - 43** |
| | 0 - 9 | **54 - 79** | 19 - 44 |
| | 0 - 9 | 21 - 52 | **46 - 78** |
| | 0 - 3 | 1 - 18 | **79 - 98** |

Source: 1995 census, NSC

© MGM-Libergéo
NSC 2000

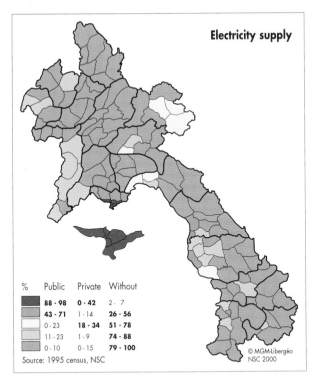

**Electricity supply**

| % | Public | Private | Without |
|---|--------|---------|---------|
| ■ | 88 - 98 | **0 - 42** | 2 - 7 |
| ▨ | 43 - 71 | 1 - 14 | **26 - 56** |
| ☐ | 0 - 23 | 18 - 34 | **51 - 78** |
| ▤ | 11 - 23 | 1 - 9 | **74 - 88** |
| ▥ | 0 - 10 | 0 - 15 | **79 - 100** |

Source: 1995 census, NSC

© MGM-Libergéo
NSC 2000

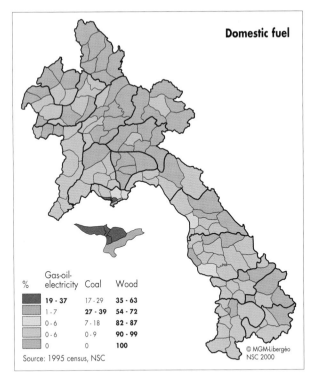

**Domestic fuel**

| % | Gas-oil-electricity | Coal | Wood |
|---|---------------------|------|------|
| ■ | 19 - 37 | 17 - 29 | **35 - 63** |
| ▨ | 1 - 7 | **27 - 39** | **54 - 72** |
| ☐ | 0 - 6 | 7 - 18 | **82 - 87** |
| ▤ | 0 - 6 | 0 - 9 | **90 - 99** |
| ▥ | 0 | 0 | **100** |

Source: 1995 census, NSC

© MGM-Libergéo
NSC 2000

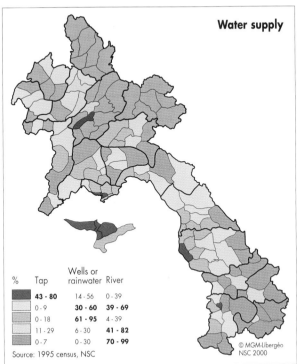

**Water supply**

| % | Tap | Wells or rainwater | River |
|---|-----|--------------------|-------|
| ■ | **43 - 80** | 14 - 56 | 0 - 39 |
| ☐ | 0 - 9 | **30 - 60** | **39 - 69** |
| ▨ | 0 - 18 | **61 - 95** | 4 - 39 |
| ▤ | 11 - 29 | 6 - 30 | **41 - 82** |
| ▥ | 0 - 7 | 0 - 30 | **70 - 99** |

Source: 1995 census, NSC

© MGM-Libergéo
NSC 2000

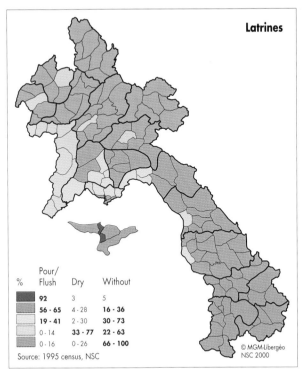

**Latrines**

| % | Pour/Flush | Dry | Without |
|---|------------|-----|---------|
| ■ | **92** | 3 | 5 |
| ▨ | **56 - 65** | 4 - 28 | **16 - 36** |
| ☐ | **19 - 41** | 2 - 30 | **30 - 73** |
| ▤ | 0 - 14 | **33 - 77** | **22 - 63** |
| ▥ | 0 - 16 | 0 - 26 | **66 - 100** |

Source: 1995 census, NSC

© MGM-Libergéo
NSC 2000

*Atlas of Laos*

**43**

# Spatial structures of settlement and housing

The spatial structures of urban housing distinguish Vientiane and Luangphrabang, where all the variables are far higher than the national average, particularly concrete dwellings. The second largest town, Savannakhet, and the district downstream from Vientiane feature next, especially for the use of modern cooking fuels. Then come Pakse, Thakhek and the district capitals on Vientiane Plain, for piped water and electricity supply. The provincial capitals come second-last, followed by the recently urbanised towns of Lamarm and Xaysomboun, which are ranked last for construction materials, water supply and cooking fuel.

The spatial structures of housing for the population as a whole show the same first and second types as urban housing, with the latter extended to include Pakse. The third type encompasses the three other towns of the Mekong Valley and the districts of Vientiane Plain, as the indicators of urbanisation diminish, particularly as the proportion of wood as a cooking fuel increases. The second-last type covers the rest of the Mekong Valley and the Nam Beng Valley, together with parts of Xiengkhuang and Huaphanh, where the population is majority Tai-Kadai. The last type comprises the mountains, where the four other ethno-linguistic families predominate. For these last two types, deficiencies increase for all the variables.

The spatial structures of the ethnolinguistic families are a reference map for this atlas. For each class in the linkage tree, a diagram in the legend gives the positive or negative contribution of all the ethnolinguistic families, measured by the deviation between the average for the class and the national average shown in the first grey-coloured diagram. The Tai-Kadai are the dominant family along the Mekong from Paklai to the Cambodian border. The two nuclei of Austro-Asiatic settlement are found in the mountainous peripheries of the South and North. The extreme North and North-East are inhabited by the Tibeto-Burmans and the Hor. Between the Tai-Kadai of the plains and the highland families is an intermediate area, combining Tai-Kadai and Mon-Khmer. The Miao-Yao are located in between in the north-eastern triangle.

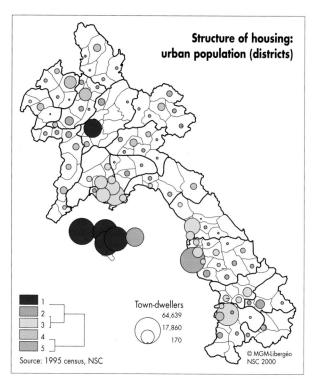

**Structure of housing: urban population (districts)**

1
2
3
4
5

Town-dwellers
64,639
17,860
170

Source: 1995 census, NSC

© MGM-Libergéo
NSC 2000

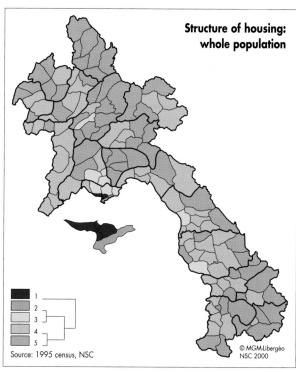

**Structure of housing: whole population**

1
2
3
4
5

Source: 1995 census, NSC

© MGM-Libergéo
NSC 2000

*Settlement*

# Structure of the ethnolinguistic families

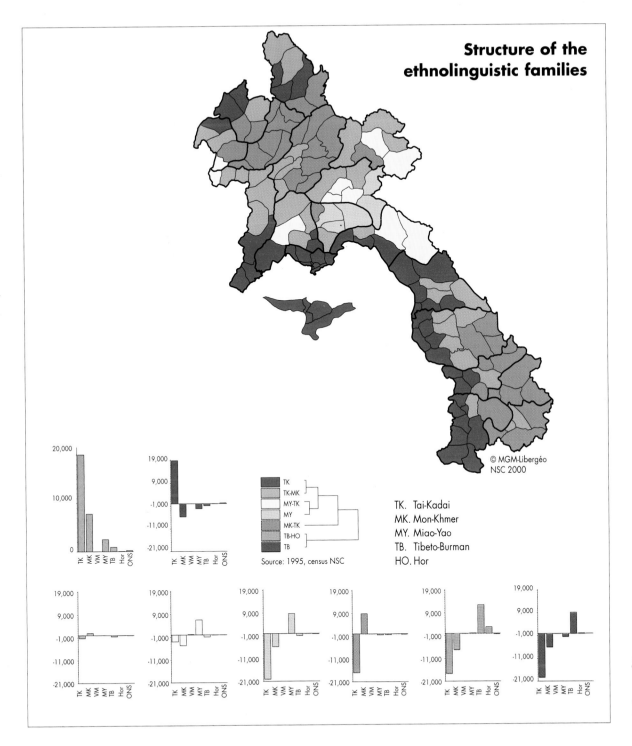

TK. Tai-Kadai
MK. Mon-Khmer
MY. Miao-Yao
TB. Tibeto-Burman
HO. Hor

TK
TK-MK
MY-TK
MY
MK-TK
TB-HO
TB

Source: 1995, census NSC

© MGM-Libergéo
NSC 2000

# Chapter 3. Population dynamics

Alongside the settlement pattern by ethnolinguistic family, population dynamics (natural reproduction rate and population mobility) is another essential dimension of regional, economic and social planning in Lao PDR, in both its rural and urban components.

Because of an under-reporting of births and deaths, the data from the 1995 census cannot be relied on for calculating the natural reproduction rate. Therefore, a survey was conducted at the same time: *Analysis of Fertility, Mortality and Population Growth in Lao PDR,* whose results were published in the census at provincial level only. With a gross birth rate of 4.13% and a gross mortality rate of 1.51%, the natural reproduction rate is 2.62%, which is considerably lower than at the time of the 1985 census. This indicated a gross birth rate of 4.6%, a gross mortality rate of 1.7% and a natural reproduction rate of 2.9%. After the post-war baby boom, the pace of population increase should start to decline and life expectancy at birth should rise from 48 years to 52 years for women and to 50 years for men, chiefly due to a significant drop in infant mortality, from 118 to 104 per 1,000 live births.

The census includes two population projections. The first forecasts a stabilisation of population indicators at the levels recorded in 1995. According to this high hypothesis and with a base population of 4.6 million, the population of Laos would increase to 5.2 million in 2000, 6.8 million in 2010 and 8.7 million in 2020. This forecast has little chance of being fulfilled, because it is contrary to the trend that has emerged over the past ten years. Moreover, the projection made in 1985 that the population would reach 4.8 million in 1995 was already overly optimistic. The second hypothesis forecasts that the demographic transition—until now restricted to the Lao—will spread to the ethnic minorities of the mountains. With a steady decline in the birth rate from

4.1% to 2.5% by 2020, and in the mortality rate from 1.5% to 8%, and in the natural reproduction rate from 2.6% to 1.7%, the population can be expected to reach 5.1 million in 2000, 6.4 million in 2010 and 7.7 million in 2020, i.e. one million less than in the first scenario.

The main conclusion of these forecasts is that population pressure will increase strongly, even if density remains low. The situation may be exacerbated by migration flows, due to rural exodus, to internal migration from the mountains to the lowlands, or to the inaccessibility of certain parts of the territory because of unexploded ordnance (UXO), the legacy of the war years.

Fortunately, population flows are now on an altogether smaller scale than during the war, when 730,000 people, i.e. a quarter of the population, were displaced. From 1985 to 1995, i.e. between the two censuses, 166,200 people changed district, i.e. 3.6% of the 1995 population. This still represents a population the size of the capital's, according to the definition used by the Housing Department. Vientiane city alone accounts for almost half of total population movements, with 80,100, breaking down into 52,400 arrivals and 27,700 departures, i.e. a net inflow of 24,700 persons. With its five other districts, the municipality's share in total population movements increases from 48% to 53%. The four medium-sized towns of the Mekong Valley together account for 25,000 movements, i.e. 15% of the total, or the equivalent of the population of a town like Thakhek, according to the definition used in the census. This breaks down into 9,900 arrivals and 15,100 departures, i.e. a net outflow of 5,200 people.

Movements to and from the largest towns thus account for two-thirds of all population movements, if the whole of Vientiane municipality is included, while movements towards the smallest provincial capitals and rural districts account for just under one third. However, this assessment of migration flows, based on the processing of the census at district level, does not capture the full picture. It does not take into account movements within districts, particularly the resettlement in the lowlands of ethnic minorities from the mountains.

This strategy, accelerated at the beginning of the 1990s, aims to slow one of the three causes of deforestation—slash-and-burn agriculture (the other two being logging and fuelwood collection)—and allow advances in health and education to reach the ethnic minorities, which is difficult and costly because this population is extremely scattered, or even impossible because of their itinerant lifestyle. The survey conducted by ORSTOM for UNESCO-UNDP, under Yves Goudineau, *Resettlement and Social Characteristics of New Villages* (1997), covering 1,000 families from 67 villages in 6 provinces, shows that a third of the population has been resettled over the past 20 years, with proportions of between 50% and 85% for some districts in Xiengkhuang, Attapeu and Luangnamtha. The maps of migration flows in these three provinces and in Sekong indicate that most of these resettlements have taken place within the same district, although they are not quantified. The report also stresses that these movements, in contrast to the pattern in Vietnam, occur from the least populated regions towards the most populated regions, which has caused land pressure in the plains and valleys, although densities are still relatively low.

The reasons most commonly given by villagers for these movements are a shortage of land, particularly for rice cultivation, and the presence of mines, which partly explains the pressure on cropland and the reduction in fallow for shifting cultivation. The survey conducted by Uxo Lao/Handicap International, *Living with Unexploded Ordnance* (1997), provides valuable information on this subject. It covers 2,861 villages, i.e. a quarter of the country. In 42 districts out of 133 and 10 provinces out of 18, at least 35% of the villages live under threat from UXO. In 83% of these villages, the affected area includes the tracks and roads near the village, and in 33% it includes the inhabited areas. In 48% of the villages studied, the affected area extends to the forests, in 25% to slash-and-burn farming areas, and in 35% to ricefields. Thus, the very territory of economic and social reproduction is affected, endangering the lives and future of these population groups, who live mainly in the mountains.

The accidents recorded confirm the contamination of productive land, since 39% occur in developed areas (32% in villages and 7% on access tracks and roads), 36% on farmland (18% in ricefields, 13% on land cleared for shifting cultivation and 5% on grazing land) and 19% in the forest (12% while collecting fuelwood and 7% while hunting). The same pattern shows up in the tasks performed at the time of the accidents: 22% occur during farm work, 17% in the forest or while travelling from one place to another and 12% during domestic tasks in the village. The major cause, handling and playing with explosives, accounts for 35% of accidents, particularly among men and boys, who make up 86% of the injured (59% and 27% respectively). Moreover, one-third of all accidents occur in three provinces—Savannakhet, Xiengkhuang and Saravane—where arable land is the most abundant.

According to *Handicap International*'s report, contamination is so widespread that even if farmers try to avoid the worst affected areas, they can no longer earn their livelihoods by remaining only in the safest areas. The rate of accidents in Laos has fallen from three per day during the first decade after the return of the population, to 0.7 per day in the following decade. Accidents now occur less frequently in ricefields, which were the first areas to be cleared of mines and more frequently in land cleared for shifting cultivation, which is much more extensive because of the duration of fallow. Accidents also occur more often in the new villages of displaced persons, settled in areas that were sparsely populated until the arrival or reconstruction of a road, and therefore still unsafe. Decontamination of the highest-risk productive land remains a priority task for territorial planning. Financing by foreign aid is still insufficient in the light of needs.

## Population growth

The supplementary survey to the census covers 19 spatial units, since, at the beginning of 1995, the four northern districts of the province of Xayabury formed a special zone like Xaysomboun. The birth rate, which is 4.13% for Lao PDR as a whole, is much higher than the national average in the two most populous areas—Savannakhet province and Vientiane municipality—and in two provinces bordering the Mekong—Champassack and Xayabury. The mountainous peripheries in the North-West and South, and, more surprisingly, Vientiane province, have birth rates below 3.9%. More than half the provinces fall between these two extremes.

The overall mortality rate and the infant mortality rate show similar distributions. These rates are higher than the national average (1.51% and 104 per 1,000 live births respectively) in the northern half of the country with a multi-ethnic population, with the surprising exception of Phongsaly and Oudomxay, which have the lowest overall mortality rates in Laos. The Vientiane–Xamneua axis (excluding Huaphanh for infant mortality) is surrounded by the highest rates (over 1.5% and 125 per 1,000 live births respectively). Vientiane municipality and Savannakhet (1.0 to 1.2% for overall mortality and 72 to 80 per 1,000 live births for infant mortality) have among the lowest rates.

The natural reproduction rate, which is 2.6% at national level, breaks down into four territorial groups. Vientiane municipality and the provinces from Savannakhet to Champassack show the highest rates of natural increase, even though these are already the most populous areas. Next, around the average, come the interior provinces in the north and the north-eastern provinces. The rates are below 2.4% in the provinces surrounding Vientiane municipality and in the north-western provinces and the mountainous southern provinces. Sekong and Attapeu provinces show the lowest natural reproduction rate, even though they are the least populous areas. Life expectancy, which is 52 years for women and 50 years for men at national level, exceeds 57 and 54 years respectively in the fastest-growing provinces, and in Phongsaly and Oudomxay, where mortality rates are exceptionally low.

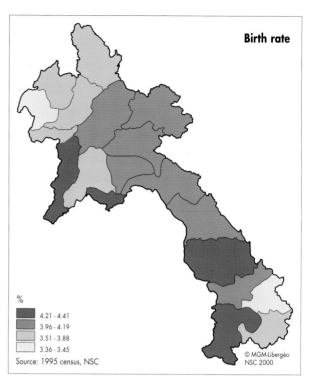

**Birth rate**

%
- 4.21 - 4.41
- 3.96 - 4.19
- 3.51 - 3.88
- 3.36 - 3.45

Source: 1995 census, NSC

© MGM-Libergéo
NSC 2000

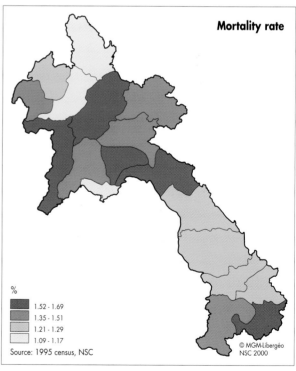

**Mortality rate**

%
- 1.52 - 1.69
- 1.35 - 1.51
- 1.21 - 1.29
- 1.09 - 1.17

Source: 1995 census, NSC

© MGM-Libergéo
NSC 2000

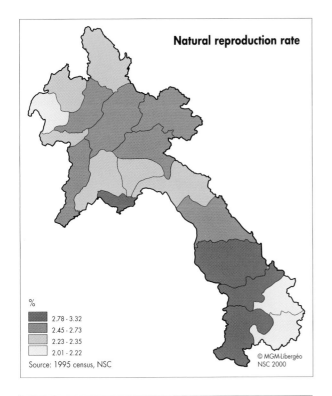

**Natural reproduction rate**

%
- 2.78 - 3.32
- 2.45 - 2.73
- 2.23 - 2.35
- 2.01 - 2.22

Source: 1995 census, NSC

© MGM-Libergéo
NSC 2000

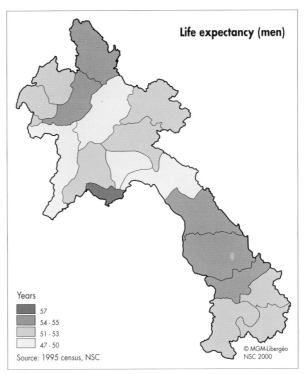

**Life expectancy (men)**

Years
- 57
- 54 - 55
- 51 - 53
- 47 - 50

Source: 1995 census, NSC

© MGM-Libergéo
NSC 2000

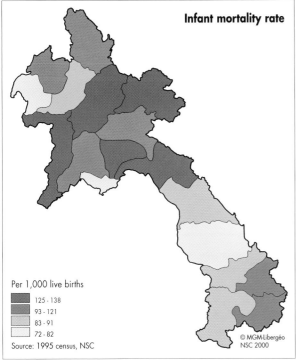

**Infant mortality rate**

Per 1,000 live births
- 125 - 138
- 93 - 121
- 83 - 91
- 72 - 82

Source: 1995 census, NSC

© MGM-Libergéo
NSC 2000

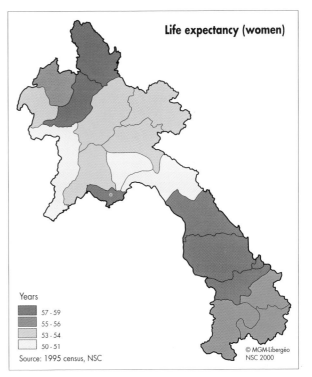

**Life expectancy (women)**

Years
- 57 - 59
- 55 - 56
- 53 - 54
- 50 - 51

Source: 1995 census, NSC

© MGM-Libergéo
NSC 2000

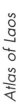

*Atlas of Laos*

## Migration balances in the districts and migration flows in Vientiane municipality (1985-1995)

Migration flows, involving 166,200 people between the last two censuses, occurred mainly in the northern half of the country, with the exception of the Bolovens Plateau and its northern rim. Outflows and a negative balance of migration are visible in a large north-eastern triangle, whose sides are formed by Phongsaly, Vientiane and Huaphanh provinces. Inflows and a positive balance of migration are concentrated in Vientiane municipality and the neighbouring provinces bordering the Mekong and, to a lesser extent, the North-West. This last area shows the emergence of the northern economic development quadrangle between China, Myanmar, Laos and Thailand, even before the meridian highway is rebuilt.

Only 16% of the 52,400 arrivals to the capital come from the four largest towns in the Mekong Valley and 17% from the peri-urban districts of the municipality, shown respectively in green and red on the maps. This means that more than two-thirds of arrivals come directly from the other provincial capitals and rural districts, mainly along the north-eastern axis of Huaphanh–Xiengkhuang, but rarely from the North, with the exception of Luangphrabang. Almost half of the 27,700 departures are towards the peri-urban districts of the municipality and 16% towards the four largest towns in the Mekong Valley, particularly Pakse and Savannakhet. The remaining third are mainly towards the two small urban centres of Vientiane province and towards Phonsavanh, the capital of Xiengkhuang province.

Vientiane shows a positive balance of migration with the provinces situated along three axes: north-east from Xamneua and Xiengkhuang, north from Luangphrabang to Phongsaly, and south along the Mekong as far as Champassack. The balance is negative with the northern rim of the Bolovens Plateau (construction of the dam on the Xe Xet and capital works in the provinces of Sekong and Saravane), Khamkeuth (reconstruction of the road to Vietnam) and Muong Xay (new road node of the North). Differentiation is apparent between the peri-urban districts of the capital: Naxaithong records more departures than arrivals, whereas the reverse occurs in Xaythany and Hadxaifong, which clearly shows the two axes of urbanisation.

*Population dynamics*

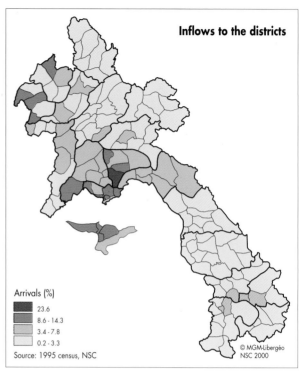

**Inflows to the districts**

Arrivals (%)
- 23.6
- 8.6 - 14.3
- 3.4 - 7.8
- 0.2 - 3.3

Source: 1995 census, NSC

© MGM-Libergéo
NSC 2000

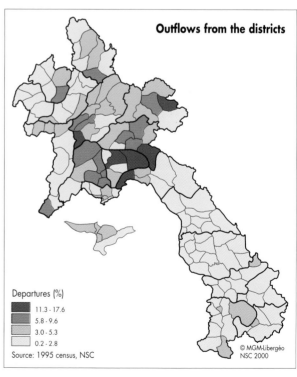

**Outflows from the districts**

Departures (%)
- 11.3 - 17.6
- 5.8 - 9.6
- 3.0 - 5.3
- 0.2 - 2.8

Source: 1995 census, NSC

© MGM-Libergéo
NSC 2000

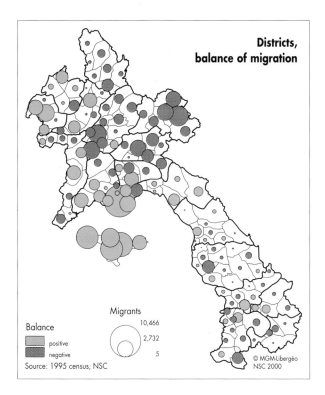

**Districts,
balance of migration**

Balance

Migrants
10,466
2,732
5

positive
negative

Source: 1995 census, NSC

© MGM-Libergéo
NSC 2000

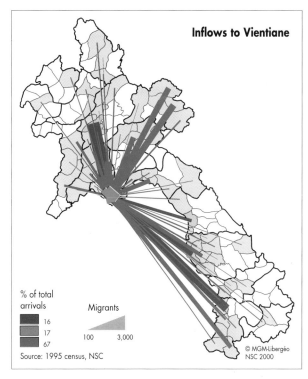

**Inflows to Vientiane**

% of total
arrivals
16
17
67

Migrants
100    3,000

Source: 1995 census, NSC

© MGM-Libergéo
NSC 2000

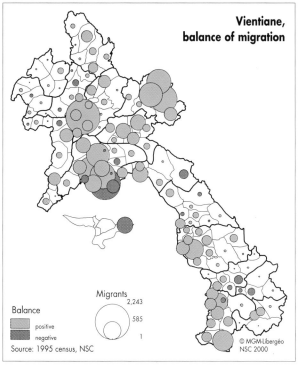

**Vientiane,
balance of migration**

Balance

Migrants
2,243
585
1

positive
negative

Source: 1995 census, NSC

© MGM-Libergéo
NSC 2000

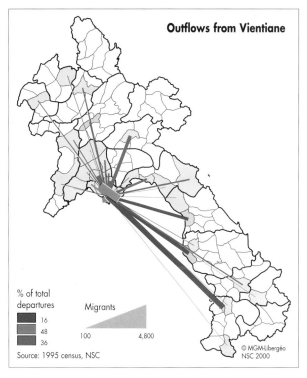

**Outflows from Vientiane**

% of total
departures
16
48
36

Migrants
100    4,800

Source: 1995 census, NSC

© MGM-Libergéo
NSC 2000

*Atlas of Laos*

## Migration flows in Luangphrabang and Thakhek (1985-1995)

The migration balances of the districts on page 51 show that Luangphrabang, the old royal capital, is the only town to have a negative balance of migration of 2,870 over ten years, which represents a reduction of 9% of its population (31,800 in 1995), contrasting with the 10% increase recorded by Vientiane (population 233,400). This decline should be stemmed since the city's inclusion on UNESCO's World Heritage List in 1994, which is generating tourist development (reconstruction of the airport, restoration of traditional houses and colonial buildings). More than three-quarters of the 6,900 arrivals come from the districts of the province, and only 16% from the other provinces of the North and from Huaphanh, which are two indicators of its low power of attraction. Thirty percent of the 9,800 departures are towards Vientiane (even 40% if the entire municipality is included), and 30% towards the districts of Xayabury and the other provincial capitals of the North, with the exception of Phongsaly. The city therefore has more inflows than outflows with its province and those that border it to the east (Huaphanh) and north (Phongsaly). The situation is reversed with the capital and Vientiane province in the south, and the provinces of the economic development quadrangle on the north-western border.

Thakhek, with a population of 25,800 in 1995, located in the narrowest part of Laos, lacks a hinterland. Therefore, 57% of its 3,900 arrivals and 55% of its 1,300 departures occur with the rural districts of Khammouane province, and 23% and 26% respectively with the capital. Since its establishment during the colonial period, the town has profited from tin mining in the Nam Pathene Valley. It has a rate of increase by migration of 5%, comparable to that of Pakse. Interestingly, Thakhek shows contrasting balances of migration with the districts of Vientiane municipality, although these are small.

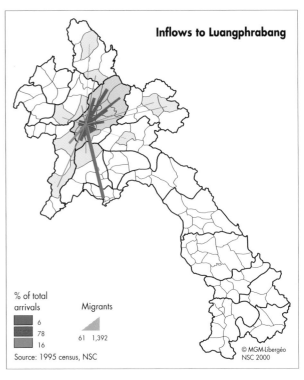

**Inflows to Luangphrabang**

% of total arrivals

6
78
16

Migrants

61   1,392

Source: 1995 census, NSC

© MGM-Libergéo
NSC 2000

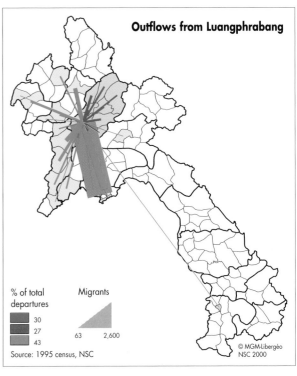

**Outflows from Luangphrabang**

% of total departures

30
27
43

Migrants

63   2,600

Source: 1995 census, NSC

© MGM-Libergéo
NSC 2000

*Population dynamics*

**52**

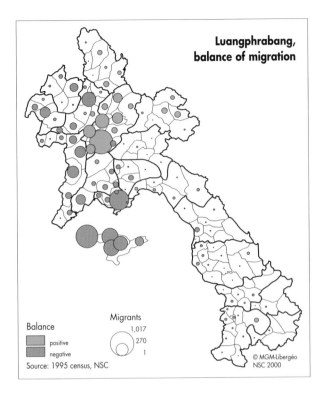

**Luangphrabang,
balance of migration**

Balance
positive
negative

Migrants
1,017
270
1

Source: 1995 census, NSC

© MGM-Libergéo
NSC 2000

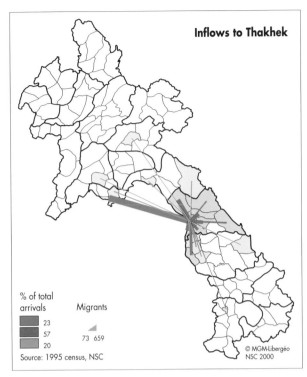

**Inflows to Thakhek**

% of total
arrivals
23
57
20

Migrants
73 659

Source: 1995 census, NSC

© MGM-Libergéo
NSC 2000

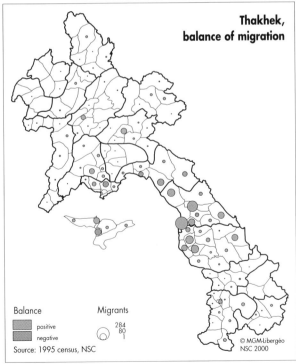

**Thakhek,
balance of migration**

Balance
positive
negative

Migrants
284
80
1

Source: 1995 census, NSC

© MGM-Libergéo
NSC 2000

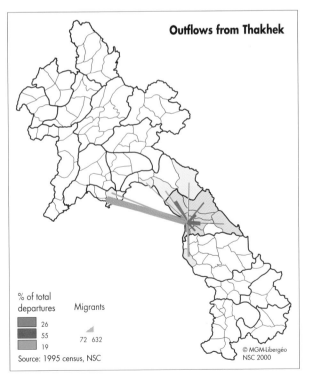

**Outflows from Thakhek**

% of total
departures
26
55
19

Migrants
72 632

Source: 1995 census, NSC

© MGM-Libergéo
NSC 2000

*Atlas of Laos*

## Migration flows in Savannakhet and Pakse (1985-1995)

In Savannakhet, a town with a population of 62,200 in 1995, inflows equalled outflows (7,500). The structure of migration flows is comparable to that of Thakhek because of the same corridor effect; however, the characteristics are more pronounced because the provincial territory is larger. More than two-thirds of the arrivals and departures occur with the districts of the province, and 22% of arrivals and 27% of departures with Vientiane, which receives slightly more people than it loses. Within the province, the town mainly attracts the population of the neighbouring districts, with the exception of Xonbuly to the north, and loses more people to the districts of the eastern part where the Austro-Asiatics dominate and where the administrative control is stronger. Flows with the other provinces are limited to the two capitals of the neighbouring provinces and to Pakse.

Because of its peripheral position, the structure of the migration flows to and from Pakse is similar to that of Luangphrabang, with one slight difference: a positive balance of migration of 2,500, i.e. 5% of the town's population of 47,600 in 1995. Flows with the other districts of the province are unequal: they constitute 72% of arrivals (9,900) and only 44% of departures (7,300). This difference is more marked in Luangphrabang with 78% and 27% respectively. The ratio is reversed for flows with Vientiane, which accounts for 16% of arrivals and 33% of departures (6% and 30% in Luangphrabang). Given the smaller number of provinces in the South, the flows they receive are smaller than in the North. The differentiation of the balances of migration in Pakse is also explained by the settlement pattern. The flows are positive for the districts of Champassack bordering the Mekong and the two central districts of Attapeu, where the Lao population is predominant. They are negative in areas where Austro-Asiatics predominate, such as eastern Savannakhet province.

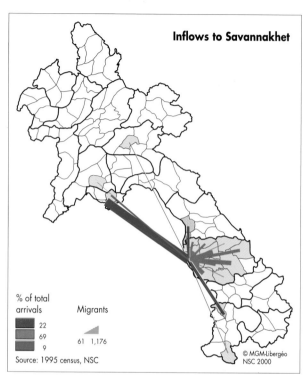

Inflows to Savannakhet

% of total arrivals

Migrants

22
69
9

61  1,176

Source: 1995 census, NSC

© MGM-Libergéo
NSC 2000

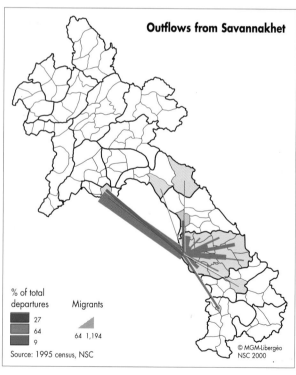

Outflows from Savannakhet

% of total departures

Migrants

27
64
9

64  1,194

Source: 1995 census, NSC

© MGM-Libergéo
NSC 2000

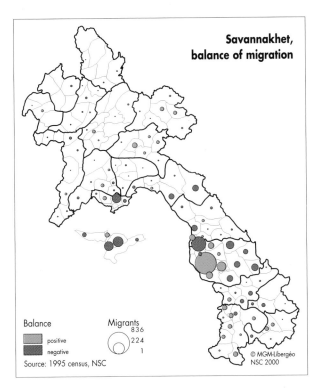

**Savannakhet,
balance of migration**

Balance
- positive
- negative

Migrants
836
224
1

© MGM-Libergéo
NSC 2000

Source: 1995 census, NSC

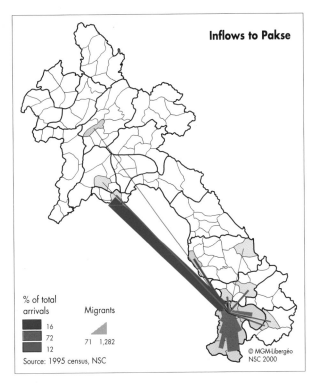

**Inflows to Pakse**

% of total
arrivals
- 16
- 72
- 12

Migrants
71    1,282

© MGM-Libergéo
NSC 2000

Source: 1995 census, NSC

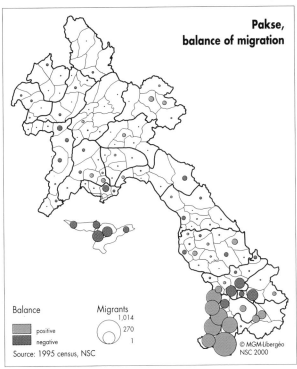

**Pakse,
balance of migration**

Balance
- positive
- negative

Migrants
1,014
270
1

© MGM-Libergéo
NSC 2000

Source: 1995 census, NSC

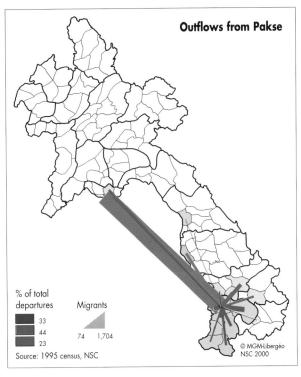

**Outflows from Pakse**

% of total
departures
- 33
- 44
- 23

Migrants
74    1,704

© MGM-Libergéo
NSC 2000

Source: 1995 census, NSC

*Atlas of Laos*

## Migration excluding Vientiane municipality (1985-1995)

The two maps shown here analyse other flows within or between provinces that are less well known. The migration balance between districts of the same province can be used to measure the power of attraction of the provincial capitals. This is generally low, even for the largest towns of the Mekong Valley, with the exception of Pakse, which attracts inflows from both sides of the river. However, the beginnings of polarisation are apparent around new towns like Phonsavan in Xiengkhuang bordering the Plain of Jars, Muong Xay at the junction of the main roads in the North, and Namtha, which controls border trade with China. The movements of the ethnic

minorities of the mountains towards the plains and valleys in the North and the Centre are of similar magnitude to those towards the towns. These movements are circular in Luangnamtha; westward in Xayabury, Xiengkhuang and Sekong; and towards the Mekong in the provinces of Vientiane and Borikhamxay, with the exception of Viengthong, which is also a gateway to Khamkeuth and the road leading to Vietnam.

Movements are sizeable in three provinces. In Luangphrabang, the villages have been shifted closer to Road 13 in the district of Phoukhoune, located at the fork that leads to the Plain of Jars. In Phongsaly and Oudomxay, villages have been established along the new road linking the two provincial capitals in the districts of Booneua, Boontai and Muong La. In Attapeu, the flow is

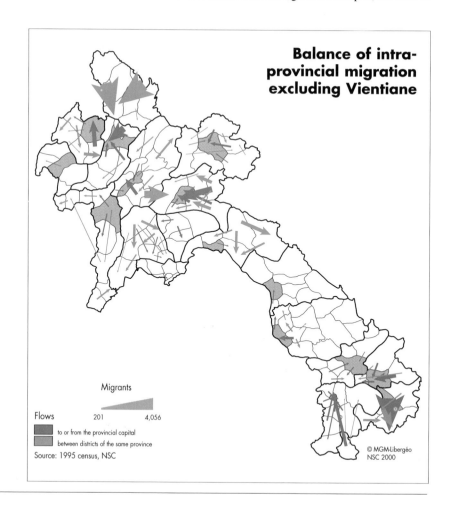

Balance of intra-provincial migration excluding Vientiane

Migrants

Flows          201        4,056

▮ to or from the provincial capital

▮ between districts of the same province

Source: 1995 census, NSC

© MGM-Libergéo
NSC 2000

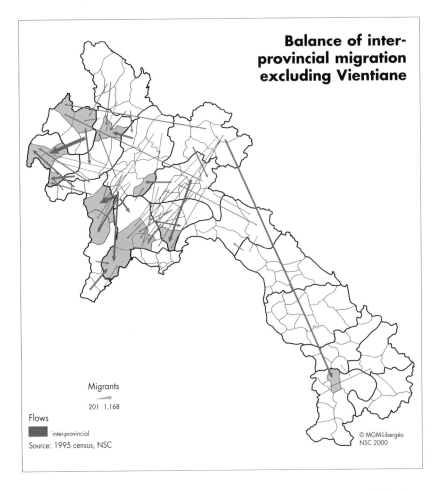

**Balance of inter-provincial migration excluding Vientiane**

Migrants

201  1,168

Flows

inter-provincial

Source: 1995 census, NSC

© MGM-Libergéo
NSC 2000

reversed: people are leaving the districts bordering the Sekong River for the mountainous district bordering the new town of Phouvong. The Laven villages of this district were resettled in the valley after 1975, but have not been able to adapt to flooded rice cultivation. They have therefore been authorised to return to their original district. Most of them, however, have settled near the new district capital established in 1992 in the foothills, linked by a 12-km road to the provincial capital.

The balance of migration flows between districts located in different provinces is only relevant to the northern half of the country, where four flows can be identified. The first, already mentioned, confirms on another scale the downward movement of population groups from Phongsaly province towards Oudomxay

province and, to a lesser extent, towards the neighbouring districts of Namtha and Nambak. The other three flows indicate the attraction exerted by the Mekong Valley. Bokeo province attracts the largest number from southern Luangnamtha and northern Xayabury. The town of Huoixai is not the only destination; so are the three neighbouring districts, which form the Laotian part of the northern economic development quadrangle. Xayabury is the next province that attracts population groups from southern Luangphrabang province. Lastly, Vientiane, both the province and the municipality, receives arrivals from the North-East, along the Vientiane–Xamneua axis. As in the northern economic development quadrangle, population flows precede the rehabilitation or construction of direct road links.

## Problems of accessibility due to unexploded ordnance

During the clandestine bombing raids carried out by the United States between 1964 and 1973, over two million tonnes of bombs were dropped on Laos—more than on the operation fields in Europe in the Second World War. A third of this ordnance remains unexploded and has caused long-term contamination of the territory. The distribution map of this contamination shows the main targets and therefore the main areas of damage. It also indicates problems of accessibility, which cannot be overlooked by territorial development policies. Only three of the 18 provinces were completely spared: Oudomxay, Bokeo and Xayabury, and only three others partly: the districts bordering China in Phongsaly, Vientiane municipality and the bank of the Mekong on Savannakhet Plain.

The Xiengkhuang Plateau, bombed because of its strategic location at the junction between the territories of the North and South controlled by the Pathet Lao, is one of the worst affected provinces. Next comes Huaphanh and its capital Xamneua, the headquarters of the Pathet Lao administration, which sheltered in caves to avoid the bombings. The Nam Ou, which governs access to Luangphrabang from the North-West and North-East is also clearly identifiable on this map. These eastern provinces of the North are populated by Lao, Khmu and Hmong.

The network of the Ho Chi Minh Trail in Laos, used by the Vietnamese army to supply its troops south of the 17th parallel, was another major target of the second Indochina War. It appears clearly on the map on page 18. This contaminated zone, the broadest, as it stretches from eastern Khammouane province to Attapeu province in the South, corresponds to the southern nucleus of Austro-Asiatic settlement. Other more scattered regions suffered from the jettisoning of unused bombs by US planes returning from their bombing raids in North Vietnam, and from the bombings carried out on the main fields of the operation in Laos.

The map of the location of casualties (those killed and injured) clearly shows the two worst affected regions: the Plain of Jars and the sections of the Ho Chi Minh Trail located on either side of the 17th parallel.

The map of the circumstances of accidents shows regional differentiation. In the North-East and in Luangphrabang and Luangnamtha, handling and playing with UXO are the major causes of accidents. On the Plain of Jars, extended by northern Vientiane province, handling and playing with UXO is as frequent a cause of accidents as travelling along roads or through the forest, and as farm or domestic work. In the South, the first two types of circumstance are also found, but their distribution is different. The main cause of accidents on the western fringe of the contaminated zone is handling and playing with UXO; while in the western part of Savannakhet Plain and the districts neighbouring Attapeu and Sekong, accidents mainly occur while travelling along roads or through the forest. Lastly, accidents occurring during farm and domestic work are the most common in Khammouane and Saravane provinces.

Unexploded cluster bombs (bombies) are by far the most common cause of accidents in the districts along the Vietnamese border in Savannakhet and Attapeu provinces in the South and Huaphanh and Xiengkhuang provinces in the Centre. Over a broad meridian belt bordering this first area to the west, cluster bombs and anti-personnel mines are scattered over the former demarcation line between the zones controlled by the royal government and the Neo Lao Haksat. This line gradually moved westward during the partition years. Grenades and mines only predominate in certain parts of the fringes of the contaminated zone: in north-western Luangnamtha, around Vientiane Plain and in the Mekong Valley in Champassack.

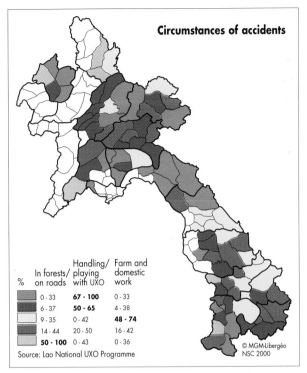

**Contamination by UXO**

| % | Low to moderate | High | Severe |
|---|---|---|---|
| | **91 - 100** | 0 - 9 | 0 |
| | **73 - 90** | 7 - 25 | 0 - 5 |
| | **58 - 68** | 26 - 36 | 0 - 9 |
| | **35 - 51** | **36 - 61** | 0 - 12 |
| | 28 - 29 | **28 - 51** | **20 - 44** |

Source: Lao National UXO Programme

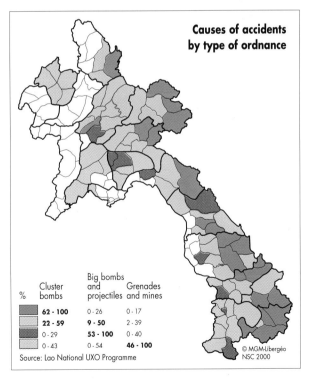

**Circumstances of accidents**

| % | In forests/ on roads | Handling/ playing with UXO | Farm and domestic work |
|---|---|---|---|
| | 0 - 33 | **67 - 100** | 0 - 33 |
| | 6 - 37 | **50 - 65** | 4 - 38 |
| | 9 - 35 | 0 - 42 | **48 - 74** |
| | 14 - 44 | 20 - 50 | 16 - 42 |
| | 50 - 100 | 0 - 43 | 0 - 36 |

Source: Lao National UXO Programme

© MGM-Libergéo
NSC 2000

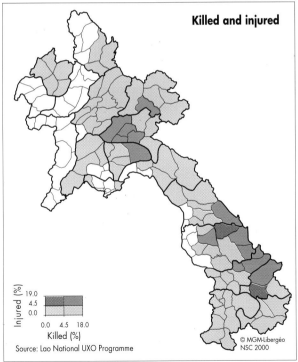

**Killed and injured**

Injured (%)
19.0
4.5
0.0

0.0   4.5   18.0
Killed (%)

Source: Lao National UXO Programme

© MGM-Libergéo
NSC 2000

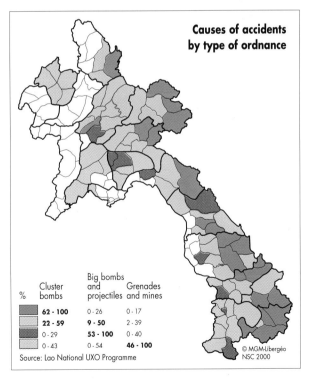

**Causes of accidents by type of ordnance**

| % | Cluster bombs | Big bombs and projectiles | Grenades and mines |
|---|---|---|---|
| | **62 - 100** | 0 - 26 | 0 - 17 |
| | **22 - 59** | **9 - 50** | 2 - 39 |
| | 0 - 29 | **53 - 100** | 0 - 40 |
| | 0 - 43 | 0 - 54 | **46 - 100** |

Source: Lao National UXO Programme

© MGM-Libergéo
NSC 2000

# Chapter 4.
# Level of education, activity and employment

Laos is sparsely populated compared with the neighbouring countries. Therefore, the characteristics of the population such as the age and sex structure, level of education, the ratio of the economically inactive to the economically active population, the breakdown of manpower by economic sector are some of the main constraints on economic and social development.

After 25 years of peace, the ratio of men to women is steadily increasing. It rose from 96.1 in 1985 to 97.7 in 1995; breakdown by sex is no longer a relevant criterion of spatial differentiation. With the post-war baby boom, Lao PDR has a young population: 44% are aged under 15 and 55% under 20, which explains the wider base of the population pyramid in 1995. The dissymmetry in the pyramid is also a clear sign of the legacy of the war: there are far fewer men than women in the 15-40 age group. The population has nevertheless begun to age with the demographic transition. In 2020, according to the most likely forecast, the proportion of people aged under 15 will have fallen from 44% to 34% of the population; that of adults (15-64 years) will have risen from 52% to 62%; and that of elderly people will have risen slightly from 3.7% to 4%. This will be reflected in a population pyramid with a narrower base.

With the increase in the proportion of adults, employment will be a major challenge for the future, both quantitatively and qualitatively. Raising the population's level of education is thus a priority development objective. The literacy rate for the country as a whole is 60%, but this figure masks strong inequalities. First, between the sexes, since nearly three-quarters of men are literate but only half of women (74% and 48% respectively). Then, between urban and rural people: 85% of town-dwellers are literate, compared with only 55% of rural-dwellers. Lastly, according to ethnic origin: 86% of the Lao are literate, compared with 60% of the Khmu (Austro-Asiatic family) and 46% of the Hmong (Miao-Yao family), taking into account only the dominant ethnic groups—i.e. the most advantaged—of each of the three main ethnolinguistic families. The most recent settlers are the least literate because of their isolated location on the mountain peaks.

The proportion of the Laotian population aged over 6 (the age at which primary education begins) that has never attended school is 38%, again with strong contrasts: 28% of men compared with 47% of women; 14% of town-dwellers compared with 43% of rural-dwellers; 23% of the Lao, compared with 56% of the Khmu and 67% of the Hmong. The level of education is low: 11% of the population have completed primary school, 4% junior secondary school, 2% senior secondary school and 2% higher education. This is partly a legacy of the war, since large numbers of educated people left the country in 1975, but it is also due to the delay in developing the road network, which has left some ethnic groups in the mountains isolated.

The base for the activity rate in the 1995 census is the population aged 10 years and over, i.e. 3.157 million people, or 69% of the total population. This group breaks down into an economically inactive population of 937,000 and an economically active population of 2,220,000, i.e. 30% and 70% of this population group. Some 69% of the economically inactive population are school or university students, 13% perform domestic tasks and 18% are retired or sick. Of the economically active population 97.6% are employed and 2.4%

unemployed, according to the census returns.

The female activity rate is slightly higher (71.2%) than the male (69.5% of the population aged 10 years and over). Ethnic origin accentuates this difference: the figures are 66% and 65.7% respectively for the Lao, compared with 77.8% and 74% for the Khmu, and 81.6% and 71.1% for the Hmong. The activity rate is lowest among the Lao (65.9%), who are better educated and comprise more retired people, and higher among the Khmu (75.9%) and the Hmong (76.4%), who are more isolated and engaged mainly in agricultural work.

The 1995 census preferred a classification by occupational groups to a breakdown of the economically active population by economic sector and branch according to the International Standard Industrial Classification (ISIC). To facilitate international comparisons, this atlas has processed the available data according to sectors and branches. In a highly agricultural country such as Laos, the primary sector accounts for 84.7% of the economically active population, of which 84.4% are engaged in agriculture, and only 0.3% in forestry and mining. Services come next with 10.3% of the economically active population, breaking down as 4.6% in market services and 5.7% in the public sector where the territorial administration, both civil and military, is ahead of education and health (3.1%, 2% and 0.5% respectively). Only 3.3% of the economically active population are employed in industry. These are low-wage industries: textiles and garments (1%) and timber and furniture (0.5%). The remainder of the economically active population (1.7%) is classified as "other, not specified".

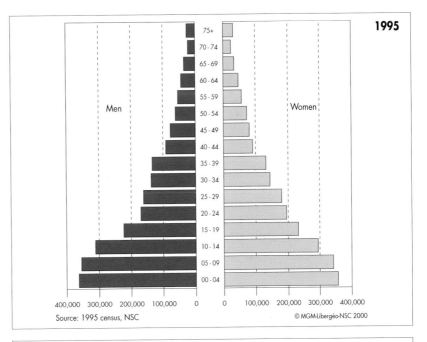

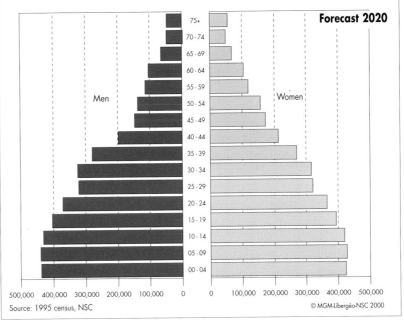

# Household characteristics

Household size, consisting on average of six people, varies with ethnic origin. In the north-eastern triangle populated by the Hmong, in the areas populated by the Katang in Savannakhet province, by the Taoey in Saravane province and by the Talieng in Attapeu province, i.e. in a section of the southern Austro-Asiatic nucleus of settlement, households comprise 6.5 to 8.1 people. The other Austro-Asiatics, notably the Khmu in the North, are around the national average, while the areas of Tai-Kadai and Tibeto-Burman settlement tend to be below it. The size of urban households is smallest in Vientiane city and municipality and in Luang-phrabang. Urban households are larger in the South and North, and are considerably larger in Savannakhet than in Pakse, and in Namtha than in Muong Xay.

The divorce rate, higher in the southern half of the country, could be linked to the Lao settlement in the Mekong Valley (except the southern part of Xayabury province), and the area of the Makong (Austro-Asiatic family) in Khammouane, but these correlations need to be verified by field surveys. There is a clear link between divorce and the size of the town. The cities of Vientiane and Pakse show higher divorce rates than Savannakhet, than the district capitals on Vientiane Plain and in the Mekong Valley upstream from it, and than the towns along the urban axis in the North. The towns in the eastern half of the country, which is not highly urbanised, have extremely low divorce rates.

For the population as a whole, as for the urban population, the mountainous regions that were the most severely affected by the bombings, particularly in the North-East, have the highest proportion of young people, which is a consequence of the post-war baby boom. The lowest proportions are found in the most populous zones of the Mekong Valley, particularly the towns.

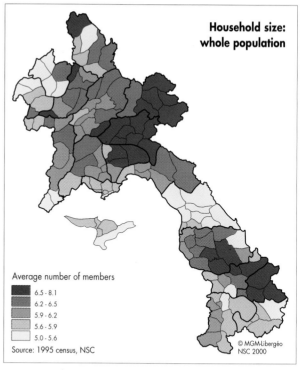

**Household size: whole population**

Average number of members
- 6.5 - 8.1
- 6.2 - 6.5
- 5.9 - 6.2
- 5.6 - 5.9
- 5.0 - 5.6

Source: 1995 census, NSC

© MGM-Libergéo
NSC 2000

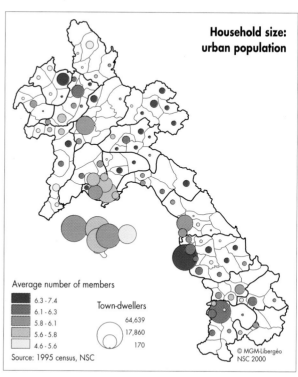

**Household size: urban population**

Average number of members
- 6.3 - 7.4
- 6.1 - 6.3
- 5.8 - 6.1
- 5.6 - 5.8
- 4.6 - 5.6

Town-dwellers
- 64,639
- 17,860
- 170

Source: 1995 census, NSC

© MGM-Libergéo
NSC 2000

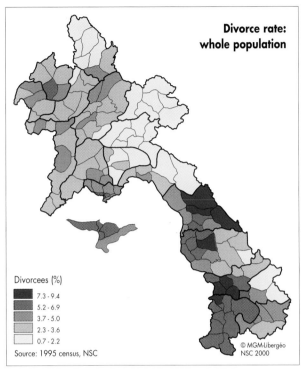

**Divorce rate:
whole population**

Divorcees (%)

- 7.3 - 9.4
- 5.2 - 6.9
- 3.7 - 5.0
- 2.3 - 3.6
- 0.7 - 2.2

Source: 1995 census, NSC

© MGM-Libergéo
NSC 2000

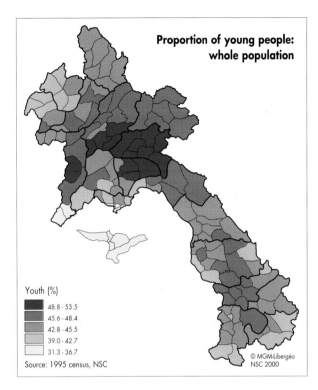

**Proportion of young people:
whole population**

Youth (%)

- 48.8 - 53.5
- 45.6 - 48.4
- 42.8 - 45.5
- 39.0 - 42.7
- 31.3 - 36.7

Source: 1995 census, NSC

© MGM-Libergéo
NSC 2000

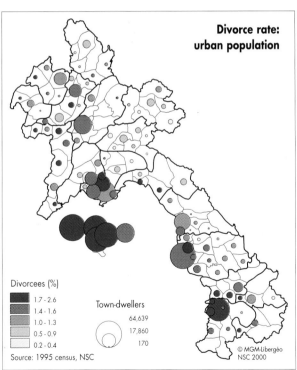

**Divorce rate:
urban population**

Divorcees (%)

- 1.7 - 2.6
- 1.4 - 1.6
- 1.0 - 1.3
- 0.5 - 0.9
- 0.2 - 0.4

Town-dwellers

64,639

17,860

170

Source: 1995 census, NSC

© MGM-Libergéo
NSC 2000

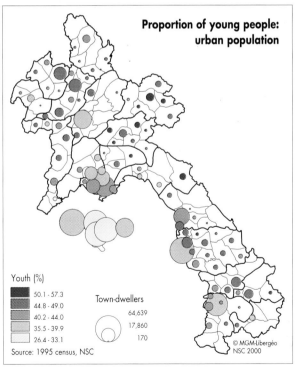

**Proportion of young people:
urban population**

Youth (%)

- 50.1 - 57.3
- 44.8 - 49.0
- 40.2 - 44.0
- 35.5 - 39.9
- 26.4 - 33.1

Town-dwellers

64,639

17,860

170

Source: 1995 census, NSC

© MGM-Libergéo
NSC 2000

*Atlas of Laos*

**63**

# Literacy

The distribution of literacy is similar to the population map on page 16, with rates above the national average (60%) in the corridor bordering the Mekong from Kenethao to the Cambodian border, and along the Vientiane–Xamneua axis. These two belts of high literacy rates are broader for men, with rates above the national male average of 74%. They are narrower for women, but rates remain above the national female average of 48%. Literacy by ethnic group resembles the map of the population by ethnolinguistic family (page 45), with one difference. The southern Austro-Asiatic group no longer includes the south-eastern corner of Savannakhet province, because the road network on the plain has reduced isolation there.

Literacy rates for young adults, aged between 15 and 35, most of whom are beyond school age, show a dissymmetry. The northern half of the country is more advanced (with rates over 66%), especially the northern economic development quadrangle and a broad ring around Vientiane, from Xayabury to Borikhamxay. The southern half lags behind (with rates below 64%), except for western Savannakhet province and, to a lesser extent, Champassack province. The lowest rates, below 62%, are found in a broad belt along the provinces bordering Vietnam, from Khammouane to Sekong.

Considering only the urban population, the five largest towns of the Mekong Valley, the most urbanised capitals of the districts neighbouring the capital—Xaythany and Hadxaifong—and the district capitals in Xayabury province show higher-than-average urban literacy rates (83%). In the North-West, Muong Xay and Namtha lag behind Phonsavan and Xamneua in the North-East, which were closer to the Pathet Lao administration during the war and benefited from better schooling. In the interior of the South, the former provincial capitals, Saravane and Attapeu, are ahead of the new capital, Lamarm, in Sekong province. Sepone, with its important trading and strategic location on Road 9 on the Vietnamese border, shows high rates.

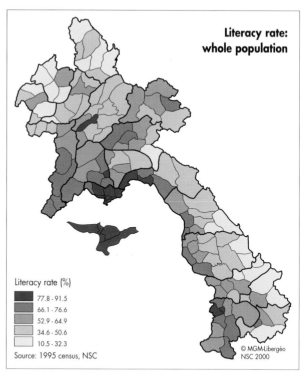

**Literacy rate: whole population**

Literacy rate (%)
- 77.8 - 91.5
- 66.1 - 76.6
- 52.9 - 64.9
- 34.6 - 50.6
- 10.5 - 32.3

Source: 1995 census, NSC

© MGM-Libergéo
NSC 2000

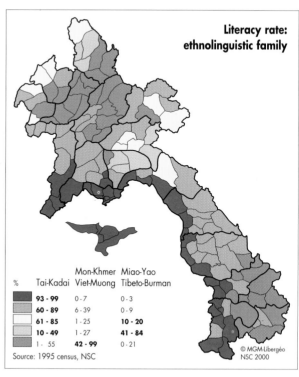

**Literacy rate: ethnolinguistic family**

| % | Tai-Kadai | Mon-Khmer Viet-Muong | Miao-Yao Tibeto-Burman |
|---|---|---|---|
| | 93 - 99 | 0 - 7 | 0 - 3 |
| | 60 - 89 | 6 - 39 | 0 - 9 |
| | 61 - 85 | 1 - 25 | 10 - 20 |
| | 10 - 49 | 1 - 27 | 41 - 84 |
| | 1 - 55 | 42 - 99 | 0 - 21 |

Source: 1995 census, NSC

© MGM-Libergéo
NSC 2000

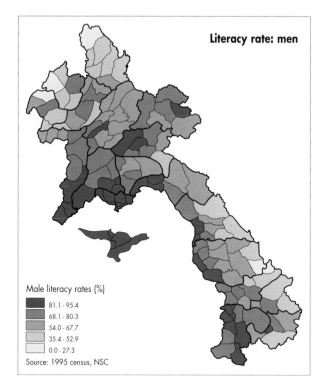

**Literacy rate: men**

Male literacy rates (%)
- 81.1 - 95.4
- 68.1 - 80.3
- 54.0 - 67.7
- 35.4 - 52.9
- 0.0 - 27.3

Source: 1995 census, NSC

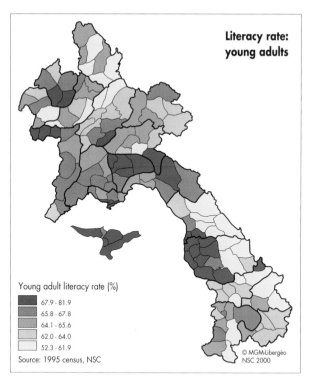

**Literacy rate: young adults**

Young adult literacy rate (%)
- 67.9 - 81.9
- 65.8 - 67.8
- 64.1 - 65.6
- 62.0 - 64.0
- 52.3 - 61.9

Source: 1995 census, NSC

© MGM-Libergéo
NSC 2000

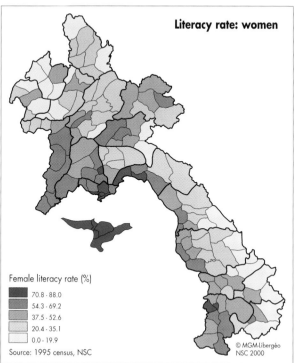

**Literacy rate: women**

Female literacy rate (%)
- 70.8 - 88.0
- 54.3 - 69.2
- 37.5 - 52.6
- 20.4 - 35.1
- 0.0 - 19.9

Source: 1995 census, NSC

© MGM-Libergéo
NSC 2000

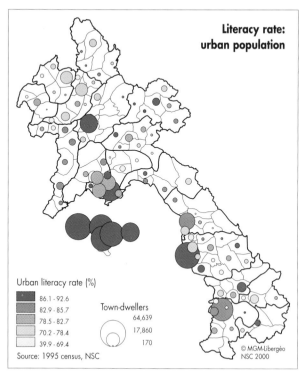

**Literacy rate: urban population**

Urban literacy rate (%)
- 86.1 - 92.6
- 82.9 - 85.7
- 78.5 - 82.7
- 70.2 - 78.4
- 39.9 - 69.4

Town-dwellers
- 64,639
- 17,860
- 170

Source: 1995 census, NSC

© MGM-Libergéo
NSC 2000

*Atlas of Laos*

## Level of education and economically inactive population

The distribution of population groups without primary education (38% for the country as a whole) follows the same basic structure of settlement in three belts that appeared for literacy. Two belts run lengthways: the Lao, the best educated, along the Mekong, and the other ethnolinguistic families, much less educated, along the land borders. The latter is crossed by the third, crossways belt, the north-eastern axis between Vientiane and Xamneua, which occupies an intermediate position.

In most of the country, more than three-quarters of the population have received only primary education at best. The provincial capitals, and sometimes the neighbouring districts, form pockets where these figures are lower and where more people have attended secondary school. Only in the capital and Pakse has a significant proportion of the population received higher education (5% to 16%). The region of Vientiane is the only privileged area of any size. Considering only the urban population, Vientiane, Savannakhet and Pakse, together with Huoixai, Phonsavan and Saravane, form the first class, where the proportion of the population that has attended secondary school is almost equal to the proportion that has attended primary school. All the other cities and district capitals on Vientiane Plain are in the second class, with a much less even ratio.

The map of the economically inactive population reflects the map of the ethnolinguistic families, with the Tibeto-Burmans and the Miao-Yao forming one group. The structure of the economically inactive population is organised into two meridian belts, with the north-eastern axis included in the first. There is a contrast between the areas populated by Tai-Kadai, where the proportion of school and university students is higher than the national average (69%), and the areas where the other ethnolinguistic families predominate, where the proportion is below the national average. For the urban population, the proportion of retired people is higher in the two upstream districts of the capital and in the two large towns of the South, while that of school and university students is the lowest in the two downstream districts of the capital and in the towns in the North and North-East.

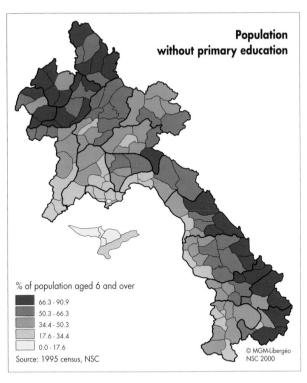

Population without primary education

% of population aged 6 and over

66.3 - 90.9
50.3 - 66.3
34.4 - 50.3
17.6 - 34.4
0.0 - 17.6

Source: 1995 census, NSC

© MGM-Libergéo
NSC 2000

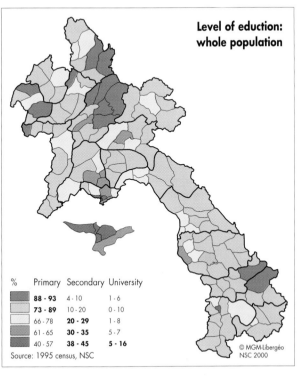

Level of eduction: whole population

| % | Primary | Secondary | University |
|---|---------|-----------|------------|
| | 88 - 93 | 4 - 10 | 1 - 6 |
| | 73 - 89 | 10 - 20 | 0 - 10 |
| | 66 - 78 | 20 - 29 | 1 - 8 |
| | 61 - 65 | 30 - 35 | 5 - 7 |
| | 40 - 57 | 38 - 45 | 5 - 16 |

Source: 1995 census, NSC

© MGM-Libergéo
NSC 2000

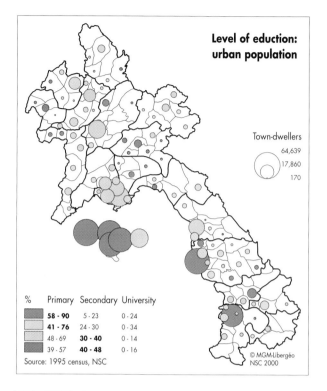

**Level of eduction:
urban population**

Town-dwellers

64,639
17,860
170

| % | Primary | Secondary | University |
|---|---|---|---|
| ■ | **58 - 90** | 5 - 23 | 0 - 24 |
| □ | **41 - 76** | 24 - 30 | 0 - 34 |
| □ | 48 - 69 | **30 - 40** | 0 - 14 |
| ■ | 39 - 57 | **40 - 48** | 0 - 16 |

Source: 1995 census, NSC

© MGM-Libergéo
NSC 2000

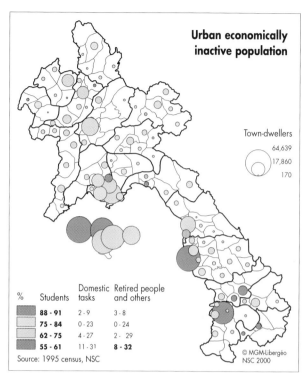

**Urban economically
inactive population**

Town-dwellers

64,639
17,860
170

| % | Students | Domestic tasks | Retired people and others |
|---|---|---|---|
| ■ | **88 - 91** | 2 - 9 | 3 - 8 |
| □ | **75 - 84** | 0 - 23 | 0 - 24 |
| □ | **62 - 75** | 4 - 27 | 2 - 29 |
| ■ | **55 - 61** | 11 - 31 | **8 - 32** |

Source: 1995 census, NSC

© MGM-Libergéo
NSC 2000

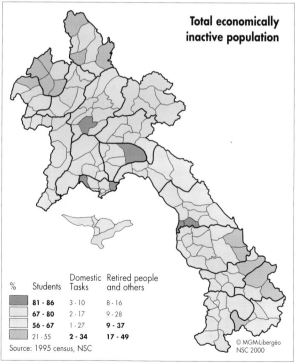

**Total economically
inactive population**

| % | Students | Domestic Tasks | Retired people and others |
|---|---|---|---|
| ■ | **81 - 86** | 3 - 10 | 8 - 16 |
| □ | **67 - 80** | 2 - 17 | 9 - 28 |
| □ | **56 - 67** | 1 - 27 | **9 - 37** |
| ■ | 21 - 55 | **2 - 34** | **17 - 49** |

Source: 1995 census, NSC

© MGM-Libergéo
NSC 2000

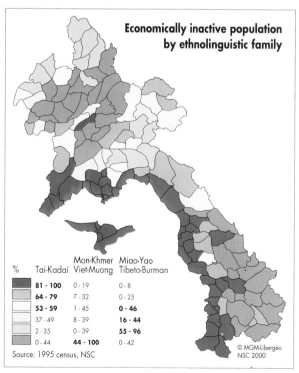

**Economically inactive population
by ethnolinguistic family**

| % | Tai-Kadai | Mon-Khmer Viet-Muong | Miao-Yao Tibeto-Burman |
|---|---|---|---|
| ■ | **81 - 100** | 0 - 19 | 0 - 8 |
| □ | **64 - 79** | 7 - 32 | 0 - 25 |
| □ | **53 - 59** | 1 - 45 | **0 - 46** |
| □ | 37 - 49 | 8 - 39 | **16 - 44** |
| ■ | 2 - 35 | 0 - 39 | **55 - 96** |
| ■ | 0 - 44 | **44 - 100** | 0 - 42 |

Source: 1995 census, NSC

© MGM-Libergéo
NSC 2000

*Atlas of Laos*

**67**

# Activity and unemployment rates

The activity rate is highest in the peripheral areas populated by the Tibeto-Burmans in the far North and the areas populated by the Austro-Asiatics in the South. This does not include the area populated by the Khmu (Austro-Asiatics of the North), nor that populated by the Miao-Yao, which shows rates closer to the Tai-Kadai in the southern half of the country. The municipality and province of Vientiane, plus Xayabury and Xiengkhuang provinces, have the lowest activity rates, because school enrolments there are the highest. This pattern is also reflected in the female activity rate, with a greater extension of the peripheral areas, particularly in the North. The activity rate for the urban population is lower in the four largest towns of the Mekong Valley and in the main towns on Vientiane Plain than in the capital. It is higher on the bank of the Mekong, in the South and the northern economic development quadrangle.

The unemployment rates declared by households in the census for the population as a whole and for the female population, as a percentage of the economically active population, show a similar distribution. The towns stand out clearly with rates considerably higher than the national average of 2.4%. Unemployment attains 16-18% in Pakse, 9-14% in the districts of the capital and 3-7% in the other towns, except the peripheral provincial capitals in the North and South, where the rate is closer to the national average. The map of urban unemployment is more detailed. Savannakhet, Pakse and the two districts upstream and downstream of Vientiane have rates between 12% and 18%. These areas are followed by the two central districts of Vientiane, Luangphrabang, Thakhek and Thoulakhom and Keo Oudom on Vientiane Plain, where unemployment ranges from 8% to 11%. The largest towns clearly show an urban unemployment problem, accentuated by the onset of the Asian crisis in summer 1997.

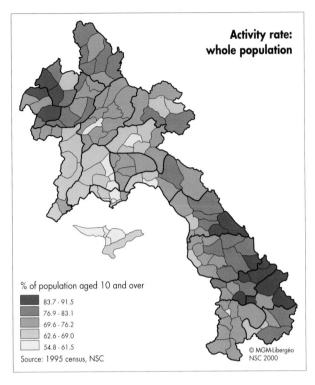

**Activity rate: whole population**

% of population aged 10 and over

- 83.7 - 91.5
- 76.9 - 83.1
- 69.6 - 76.2
- 62.6 - 69.0
- 54.8 - 61.5

Source: 1995 census, NSC

© MGM-Libergéo
NSC 2000

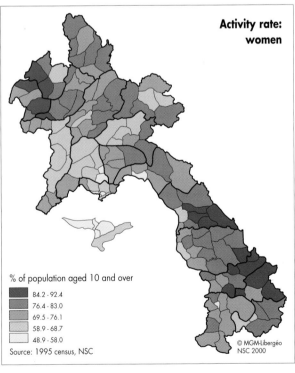

**Activity rate: women**

% of population aged 10 and over

- 84.2 - 92.4
- 76.4 - 83.0
- 69.5 - 76.1
- 58.9 - 68.7
- 48.9 - 58.0

Source: 1995 census, NSC

© MGM-Libergéo
NSC 2000

*Level of education, activity and employment*

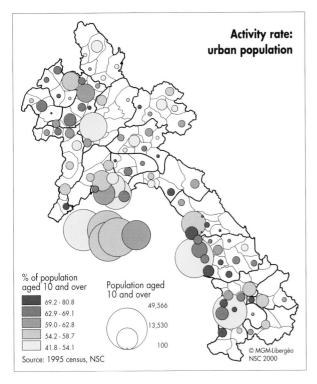

**Activity rate:
urban population**

% of population
aged 10 and over
- 69.2 - 80.8
- 62.9 - 69.1
- 59.0 - 62.8
- 54.2 - 58.7
- 41.8 - 54.1

Population aged
10 and over
- 49,566
- 13,530
- 100

Source: 1995 census, NSC

© MGM-Libergéo
NSC 2000

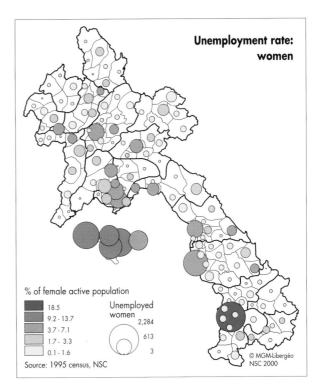

**Unemployment rate:
women**

% of female active population
- 18.5
- 9.2 - 13.7
- 3.7 - 7.1
- 1.7 - 3.3
- 0.1 - 1.6

Unemployed
women
- 2,284
- 613
- 3

Source: 1995 census, NSC

© MGM-Libergéo
NSC 2000

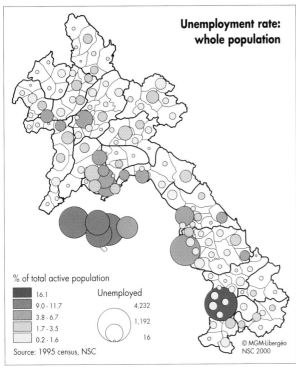

**Unemployment rate:
whole population**

% of total active population
- 16.1
- 9.0 - 11.7
- 3.8 - 6.7
- 1.7 - 3.5
- 0.2 - 1.6

Unemployed
- 4,232
- 1,192
- 16

Source: 1995 census, NSC

© MGM-Libergéo
NSC 2000

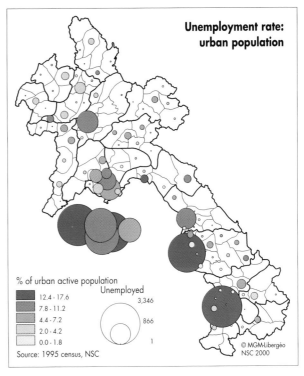

**Unemployment rate:
urban population**

% of urban active population
- 12.4 - 17.6
- 7.8 - 11.2
- 4.4 - 7.2
- 2.0 - 4.2
- 0.0 - 1.8

Unemployed
- 3,346
- 866
- 1

Source: 1995 census, NSC

© MGM-Libergéo
NSC 2000

*Atlas of Laos*

# Manpower by economic sector

The primary sector employs 84.7% of the total workforce, with agriculture accounting for 84.4%. This sector exceeds 92% in most of the country. It drops, however, to 70% around Pakse and on the Bolovens Plateau, in a large region around Vientiane, from Xayabury to Borikhamxay and along the north-eastern axis. Even for the urban population, agriculture is omnipresent except in two districts of Vientiane. In the other two districts of the capital and in Pakse, agriculture employs at least a quarter of the economically active population and more than half in the four other main cities.

The tertiary sector accounts for 10% of the total workforce. It is only predominant in the capital and in Pakse, and employs between a quarter and a third of the workforce in the four other largest towns. The tertiary sector employs similar proportions of the workforce in Hadxaifong, because of the bridge over the Mekong, in Keo Oudom, because of the dam on the Nam Ngum River, and in Phonsavan and the town of Attapeu. The secondary sector, 3.3% of the workforce, is much more concentrated. It exceeds 20% in the capital and ranges from 8% to 14% in the four other largest towns, in two peri-urban districts of Vientiane municipality and in Keo Oudom in Vientiane province.

For the urban population, the breakdown of manpower by economic sector shows the economic hierarchy of the towns. At the top of the list are the two central districts of the capital, followed by the two other districts, the four other large towns, then Phonsavan and Xamneua in the North-East, and Saravane and Attapeu in the South, where the tertiary sector is more important than the other two sectors. Agriculture is ahead of services in the main towns on Vientiane Plain and in Xayabury and, to a lesser extent, in Muong Xay and Namtha in the North. The breakdown of urban manpower by employer status shows a contrast between most of the northern half of the country, where family workers dominate, and Vientiane and the provincial capitals of the South, plus Xamneua and Phongsaly, the former bastions of support for the Pathet Lao administration in the North, where family workers are only slightly ahead of or equal to state-sector workers.

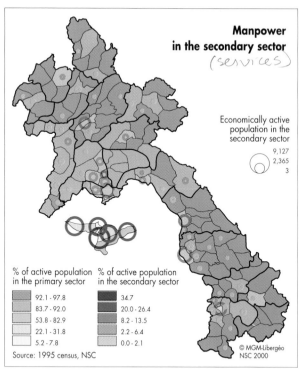

**Manpower in the secondary sector**
(services)

Economically active population in the secondary sector

9,127
2,365
3

% of active population in the primary sector
- 92.1 - 97.8
- 83.7 - 92.0
- 53.8 - 82.9
- 22.1 - 31.8
- 5.2 - 7.8

% of active population in the secondary sector
- 34.7
- 20.0 - 26.4
- 8.2 - 13.5
- 2.2 - 6.4
- 0.0 - 2.1

Source: 1995 census, NSC

© MGM-Libergéo
NSC 2000

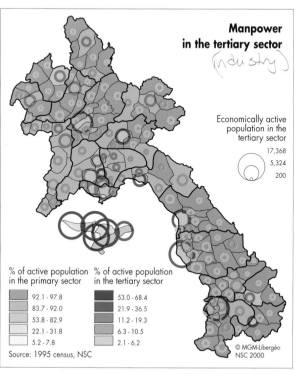

**Manpower in the tertiary sector**
(industry)

Economically active population in the tertiary sector

17,368
5,324
200

% of active population in the primary sector
- 92.1 - 97.8
- 83.7 - 92.0
- 53.8 - 82.9
- 22.1 - 31.8
- 5.2 - 7.8

% of active population in the tertiary sector
- 53.0 - 68.4
- 21.9 - 36.5
- 11.2 - 19.3
- 6.3 - 10.5
- 2.1 - 6.2

Source: 1995 census, NSC

© MGM-Libergéo
NSC 2000

*Level of education, activity and employment*

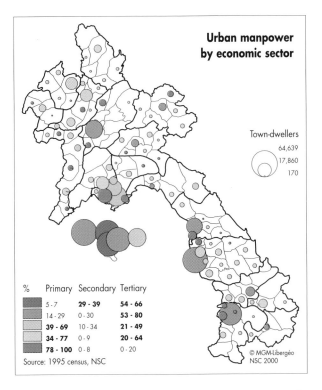

**Urban manpower by economic sector**

Town-dwellers
64,639
17,860
170

| % | Primary | Secondary | Tertiary |
|---|---|---|---|
| | 5 - 7 | 29 - 39 | 54 - 66 |
| | 14 - 29 | 0 - 30 | 53 - 80 |
| | 39 - 69 | 10 - 34 | 21 - 49 |
| | 34 - 77 | 0 - 9 | 20 - 64 |
| | 78 - 100 | 0 - 8 | 0 - 20 |

Source: 1995 census, NSC

© MGM-Libergéo
NSC 2000

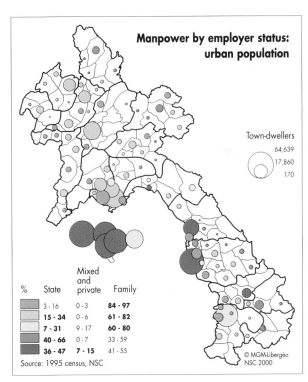

**Manpower by employer status: urban population**

Town-dwellers
64,639
17,860
170

| % | State | Mixed and private | Family |
|---|---|---|---|
| | 3 - 16 | 0 - 3 | 84 - 97 |
| | 15 - 34 | 0 - 6 | 61 - 82 |
| | 7 - 31 | 9 - 17 | 60 - 80 |
| | 40 - 66 | 0 - 7 | 33 - 59 |
| | 36 - 47 | 7 - 15 | 41 - 55 |

Source: 1995 census, NSC

© MGM-Libergéo
NSC 2000

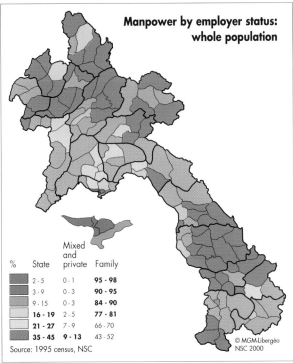

**Manpower by employer status: whole population**

| % | State | Mixed and private | Family |
|---|---|---|---|
| | 2 - 5 | 0 - 1 | 95 - 98 |
| | 3 - 9 | 0 - 3 | 90 - 95 |
| | 9 - 15 | 0 - 3 | 84 - 90 |
| | 16 - 19 | 2 - 5 | 77 - 81 |
| | 21 - 27 | 7 - 9 | 66 - 70 |
| | 35 - 45 | 9 - 13 | 43 - 52 |

Source: 1995 census, NSC

© MGM-Libergéo
NSC 2000

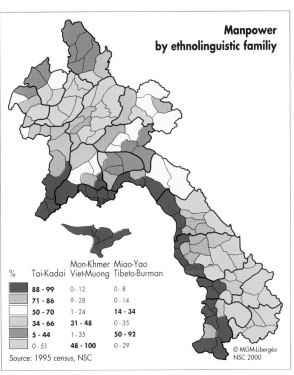

**Manpower by ethnolinguistic familiy**

| % | Tai-Kadai | Mon-Khmer Viet-Muong | Miao-Yao Tibeto-Burman |
|---|---|---|---|
| | 88 - 99 | 0 - 12 | 0 - 8 |
| | 71 - 86 | 9 - 28 | 0 - 14 |
| | 50 - 70 | 1 - 24 | 14 - 34 |
| | 34 - 66 | 31 - 48 | 0 - 35 |
| | 5 - 44 | 1 - 35 | 50 - 92 |
| | 0 - 51 | 48 - 100 | 0 - 29 |

Source: 1995 census, NSC

© MGM-Libergéo
NSC 2000

# Spatial structures of the population

The map of spatial structures, constructed on the basis of variables for the population as a whole in this chapter, reveals five classes, which can be organised into three groups. The first group (class 1), which contains only the capital, has the highest indicators of urbanisation, in terms of the proportion of the workforce employed in the secondary and tertiary sectors, manpower in the state sector, divorce rate, literacy, unemployment, and the lowest proportion of young people in the population, household size and activity rate.

At the other extreme, in the second group (classes 5 and 4), these indicators are the lowest and inverse in value, with family workers bolstering the activity rate. Class 5 comprises the peripheral districts populated by Austro-Asiatics and Tibeto-Burmans, which form a continuous group along the Vietnamese border, from Khammouane province to Sekong province in the southern half of the country, where urbanisation is low, and a discontinuous group in the northern half, interrupted by the provincial capitals. Class 4 covers these provincial capitals and most of the areas populated by Tai-Kadai and Miao-Yao, and is distinguished from class 5 by higher literacy and education rates. Class 4 covers the whole Mekong Valley, extended to the north-eastern triangle and the plateaux of the provinces on the Cambodian border.

The third group comes between the previous two in areas where urbanisation is emerging or consolidating. Class 3, characterised by a larger tertiary workforce but a low activity rate, comprises the emerging provincial capitals in the urban network, such as Phonsavan and Namtha, and older towns like Xayabury, as well as the districts on Vientiane Plain. Class 2 consists of the two most urbanised districts neighbouring Vientiane, the towns of the Mekong Valley, plus Thalat (Keo Oudom district) near the Nam Ngum dam, and Attapeu. This class is characterised by better literacy rates and levels of education.

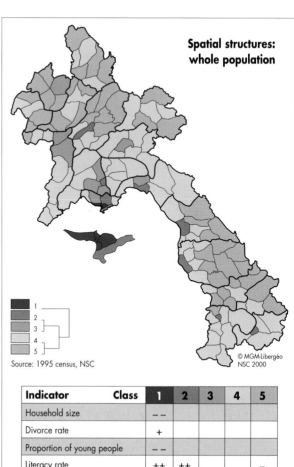

**Spatial structures: whole population**

1
2
3
4
5

Source: 1995 census, NSC

© MGM-Libergéo
NSC 2000

| Indicator / Class | 1 | 2 | 3 | 4 | 5 |
|---|---|---|---|---|---|
| Household size | – – | | | | |
| Divorce rate | + | | | | |
| Proportion of young people | – – | | | | |
| Literacy rate | ++ | ++ | | | – |
| Level of education | ++ | + | | | – |
| Economically inactive population | S+R | S+R | S+R | R+D | D+R |
| Economically active population | – – | – – | – | | + |
| Unemployment rate | + | | – | – | – – |
| Manpower in the secondary sector | ++ | | – | – – | – – |
| Manpower in the tertiary sector | ++ | + | | – | – – |
| Manpower by employer status | St++ | St+ | F+ | F++ | F+ |

S: Students, D: domestic tasks, R: retirees, St: state, F: family

The map of spatial structures of the urban population gives another picture of urbanisation. The first class comprises the three largest towns of the country, Vientiane, Savannakhet and Pakse, where the same indicators of urbanisation as in the previous classification are the highest. At the other extreme, classes 4 and 5 cover the smallest district capitals, where the indicators of urbanisation are at their lowest. The two classes are only distinguished by the low rates of unemployment, literacy and education for class 5, whose components are fairly scattered upstream and downstream from the Mekong, and by a slightly higher proportion of young people in class 4, which is more concentrated in the large north-eastern triangle. Xamneua is the only provincial capital to appear in this class, which indicates a lag in urbanisation. It is on the same level as Hadxaifong, a peri-urban district downstream from Vientiane, which is experiencing an acceleration of urbanisation due to the bridge over the Mekong.

Class 3, which shows similarities to class 4, is distinguished by a low divorce rate and smaller household size. This class covers the urbanising provincial capitals, particularly in the North-West, but also Phonsavan (Xiengkhuang) and Lamarm (Sekong), as well as some of the districts neighbouring Savannakhet and Pakse. Class 2 consists of the other provincial capitals bordering the Mekong, particularly middle-sized towns such as Luangphrabang and Thakhek, and smaller towns such as Huoixai, Xayabury and Saravane, as well as the district capitals on Vientiane Plain and, to a lesser extent, the district capitals in Xayabury and Saravane provinces on the rim of the Bolovens Plateau. The indicators of urbanisation in this class show average values, still far lower than those in class 1.

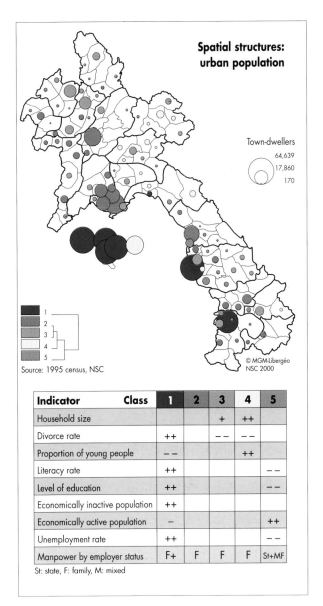

**Spatial structures: urban population**

Town-dwellers
64,639
17,860
170

Source: 1995 census, NSC

© MGM-Libergéo
NSC 2000

| Indicator                      Class | 1    | 2 | 3   | 4   | 5     |
|---------------------------------------|------|---|-----|-----|-------|
| Household size                        |      |   | +   | ++  |       |
| Divorce rate                          | ++   |   | – – | – – |       |
| Proportion of young people            | – –  |   |     | ++  |       |
| Literacy rate                         | ++   |   |     |     | – –   |
| Level of education                    | ++   |   |     |     | – –   |
| Economically inactive population      | ++   |   |     |     |       |
| Economically active population        | –    |   |     |     | ++    |
| Unemployment rate                     | ++   |   |     |     | – –   |
| Manpower by employer status           | F+   | F | F   | F   | St+MF |

St: state, F: family, M: mixed

# Chapter 5. Agriculture

The share of agriculture in the economy is huge, although it has begun to diminish slightly over the past few years. According to the 1995 census, 84.7% of the economically active population was engaged in agriculture and agriculture accounted for 54.3% of GDP. Between 1990 and 1996, its contribution fell from 60.7% to 52% of GDP, because of a surge in the contribution from the industrial sector, which rose from 14.4% to 20.6%, a trend halted by the Asian crisis since summer 1997. With forestry, agriculture accounted for 35.4% of exports by value in 1995 (25.4% for timber and 10% for crops). As a result of the crisis, the share of these two components has risen: in 1997, they increased to 41% of exports (26.7% for timber and 14.3% for crops), according to data from the Ministry of Trade, although these were only available for the six main items.

However, little is known about agriculture in Laos. The agricultural census conducted in 1999 was the first ever to be undertaken in the country. As the results are not yet available, the National Statistical Centre collected data at district level (1996b in the table opposite) for this atlas, since the Ministry of Agriculture only publishes provincial data (1996a). The difference between the two sources is mainly due to a lack of data at district level for the special zone of Xaysomboun. Despite this shortcoming, the atlas highlights the main territorial differentiations of agriculture in Laos, which the agricultural census will define more precisely in the near future.

The crop area—678,200 ha in 1996—accounts for only 2.9% of the total area. If we take into account the approximately ten years of fallow for the 172,600 ha of slash-and-burn cultivation, the area used for agriculture increases to 10% of the national territory. The crop area increased substantially after the war, from 581,400 ha in 1976 to 812,000 ha at the beginning of the 1980s. In the 1990s it declined and then stabilised within a range of 678,000 ha to 730,000 ha, depending on weather conditions. Some of the ricefields on the floodplains and on the upper terraces have been abandoned because of frequent flooding in the first case and drought in the second.

Since only 3% of the harvested area is irrigated in the dry season, there are wide variations in the crop area and agricultural output from one year to another because of strong inter-annual and intra-annual irregularities in rainfall. Vientiane, for example (see page 20), receives between 1,200 mm and 2,100 mm of rainfall a year, with an average of 1,700 mm, which is above the 1,500 mm required for rice cultivation in rain-fed areas. As a result, over a recent period of nine years, two years (1988 and 1993) were bad, because of a combination of floods and droughts, and output was only 230-250 kg of paddy per capita; three years (1991, 1995 and 1996) only just covered needs (286-310 kg), because floods destroyed 69,000 ha to 73,000 ha (i.e. 11% of the ricefields); but four years (1990, 1992, 1993 and 1994) were good, with output of 340-360 kg.

For seven years out of nine, therefore, Laos was self-sufficient at national level, although there were regional problems. The provinces with surpluses are in the South and the provinces with deficits in the North. The meridian structure of Laos and the difficulty of travelling within the country mean that it is often easier, and even more economical, to sell the South's surpluses to Thailand and make up the North's deficits by imports. This is why the flow of imports remains at around 5,000-7,000 t in good years and can reach 40,000 t in bad years, sometimes with a lag of a year to reconstitute stocks.

These figures are the result of a policy of self-sufficiency in food introduced in 1975. This policy boosted the share of rice, which, since 1988, has accounted for between 81% and 84% of the crop area. Rain-fed paddy accounts for more than half (48-55%) and swidden rice (ray) between a quarter and a third (25-31%). Other food crops account for between 10% and

| | 1988 | % | 1994 | % | 1996 a | % | 1996 b | % |
|---|---|---|---|---|---|---|---|---|
| **Cultivated area (ha 000s)** | 682.1 | 100.0 | 730.5 | 100.0 | 678.2 | 100.0 | 638.5 | 100.0 |
| **Total rice** | 524.8 | 81.0 | 611.0 | 83.6 | 553.7 | 81.6 | 535.4 | 83.9 |
|    Rain-fed rice | 311.3 | 48.0 | 380.9 | 52.1 | 363.1 | 53.5 | 354.4 | 55.5 |
|    Irrigated rice | 11.4 | 1.8 | 11.0 | 1.5 | 18.0 | 2.7 | 19.6 | 3.1 |
|    Swidden rice | 202.1 | 31.2 | 219.1 | 30.0 | 172.6 | 25.4 | 161.4 | 25.3 |
| **Other food crops** | 90.0 | 13.9 | 80.4 | 11.0 | 81.3 | 12.0 | 65.1 | 10.2 |
|    Root crops | 27.8 | 4.3 | 21.9 | 3.0 | 14.6 | 2.2 | 19.3 | 3.0 |
|    Maize | 37.8 | 5.8 | 28.1 | 3.8 | 37.4 | 5.5 | 27.4 | 4.3 |
|    Beans, soy and groundnuts | 14.8 | 2.3 | 13.9 | 1.9 | 14.7 | 2.2 | 10.8 | 1.7 |
|    Vegetables and other | 9.6 | 1.5 | 16.5 | 2.3 | 14.6 | 2.1 | 7.6 | 1.2 |
| **Cash crops** | 33.4 | 5.1 | 39.1 | 5.4 | 43.2 | 6.4 | 38.0 | 5.9 |
|    Tobacco | 7.1 | 1.1 | 7.3 | 1.0 | 7.2 | 1.1 | 3.6 | 0.6 |
|    Cotton | 6.6 | 1.0 | 7.2 | 1.0 | 9.1 | 1.3 | 7.2 | 1.1 |
|    Sugar cane | 3.9 | 0.6 | 2.8 | 0.4 | 3.4 | 0.5 | 3.4 | 0.5 |
|    Coffee | 15.5 | 2.4 | 20.0 | 2.7 | 23.1 | 3.4 | 20.0 | 3.1 |
|    Tea and other | 0.3 | 0.0 | 1.8 | 0.3 | 0.4 | 0.1 | 3.8 | 0.6 |
| **Output of paddy per capita (kg)** | 250.0 | | 340.0 | | 300.0 | | 286.0 | |
| **Rice imports (t 000s)** | 41.0 | | 16.4 | | 26.7 | | – | |

Sources: 1988, 1994 and 1996a, Ministry of Agriculture; 1996b, National Statistical Centre.

14% (particularly maize and root crops) and cash crops between 5% and 7% (about half of which is coffee).

It is now time to promote the diversification of agricultural produce to raise the living standards of farmers. This requires new priorities for agriculture, which public investment is beginning to turn into a reality. In 1996, a little over a fifth of public investment went to agriculture (17.7% to crops and 4.6% to rural development) and 44.4% to improving transport and communications. The development of extensive agriculture with low technical investment (consumption of fertilisers and selected seeds is extremely low) depends on extending the road network to enhance the distribution of inputs, the collection and processing of produce and the organisation of markets. Much remains to be achieved: only 1% of foreign investment between 1991 and 1997 went to agriculture and farmers received less than 10% of bank loans.

The era of large-scale irrigation projects involving major investment is over and the priority is on better use of existing agricultural land. According to an irrigation census carried out by the Ministry of Agriculture in 1996, only 22% of the area that can be irrigated in the wet season is used in the dry season. A study by the Asian Development Bank, cited in *Economic Development in Lao PDR: Horizon 2000*, showed that 50,000 tonnes of paddy could be produced by improving micro-irrigation during the wet season, which is equivalent to the deficit in the worst years, such as 1988. A further 30,000 tonnes could be produced if the irrigated areas were used to full capacity in the dry season. However, the only way to cover operating costs in these areas would be to diversify production in the dry season.

The diversification of mountain agriculture, by increasing dry fields and orchards, is the most urgent priority for the two-thirds of Laos located at altitudes of over 500 m. The diversification of agriculture will enable Laos to take advantage of two factors of production it has in plentiful supply, namely land and labour. With the Bolovens and Xiengkhuang Plateaux, Laos has the last "agricultural frontier" for cash cropping in the Indochinese Peninsula. Coffee from the Bolovens Plateau, tea plants exported from the Xiengkhuang Plateau to India during the colonial period, and temperate fruit and vegetables as well as cattle, previously exported from both areas to the delta towns, remain largely under-utilised resources. Their expansion could offset the decline of timber in exports (which fell from 32.5% to 21.4% between 1995 and 1997) and assist forest conservation. Since the Asian crisis has reduced the share of industry and electricity in exports, there is a risk that illegal logging will further deplete forest resources.

*Atlas of Laos*

# Crop systems and manpower in agriculture

The 1996 map of crop systems by area reveals a meridian structure. The western part of the country near the Mekong, interrupted only at Xayabury, is over 90% dominated by rice, while in the eastern mountainous part, other food crops account for up to a third of the total. Cash crops overtake rice on the Bolovens Plateau (coffee) and are equal to rice on its northern slope. In other areas, cash crops cover less than a fifth of the area under cultivation, and annual crops prevail over perennials along a meridian axis from the Nam Beng and the Nam Ou Rivers in the North to the Mekong Valley in Xayabury province.

The types of rice cultivation reflect the spatial structure of the ethnolinguistic families. Wet-season rice cultivation exceeds 80% of the crop area in the Mekong Valley from the capital to the Cambodian border, and accounts for between 41% and 78% in Xayabury and along the Vientiane–Xiengkhuang axis, as the share of swidden rice increases (15-60%). On both sides of this axis in the North and in the Austro-Asiatic settlement in the South, swidden rice exceeds two-thirds of the crop area. Irrigated rice is only really significant (28-50% of the total crop area) at the junction between the Se Bang Fai and the Mekong as well as in the capital.

The proportion of areas irrigated in the dry season exceeds three-quarters of the crop area in the lower Se Bang Fai Basin. It is between 45% and 70% on Vientiane Plain as a whole. The main type is pump irrigation, which is costly over large areas. Savannakhet province also uses reservoirs and diversified techniques to offset insufficient rainfall, which can be lower than 1,400 mm (see page 20). In other areas, small-scale supplemental irrigation during the wet season is the main type used, with traditional wooden dams in Vientiane province, and stone, cement and earth dams in Luangphrabang province and, more widely, in the North, the North-East and Saravane province where rainfall is not as low. Gabions are the most widely used technology for this small-scale irrigation.

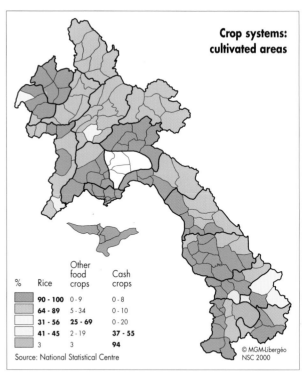

**Crop systems: cultivated areas**

| % | Rice | Other food crops | Cash crops |
|---|---|---|---|
| 90 - 100 | 0 - 9 | 0 - 8 |
| 64 - 89 | 5 - 34 | 0 - 10 |
| 31 - 56 | 25 - 69 | 0 - 20 |
| 41 - 45 | 2 - 19 | 37 - 55 |
| 3 | 3 | 94 |

Source: National Statistical Centre

© MGM-Libergéo NSC 2000

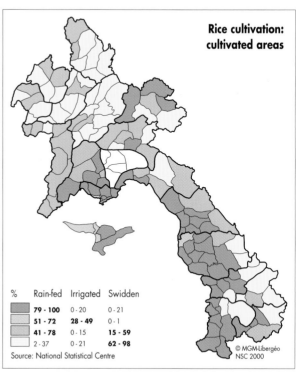

**Rice cultivation: cultivated areas**

| % | Rain-fed | Irrigated | Swidden |
|---|---|---|---|
| 79 - 100 | 0 - 20 | 0 - 21 |
| 51 - 72 | 28 - 49 | 0 - 1 |
| 41 - 78 | 0 - 15 | 15 - 59 |
| 2 - 37 | 0 - 21 | 62 - 98 |

Source: National Statistical Centre

© MGM-Libergéo NSC 2000

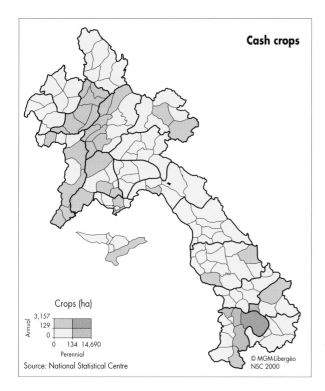

**Cash crops**

Crops (ha)

Annual
3,157
129
0

0   134  14,690
Perennial

Source: National Statistical Centre

© MGM-Libergéo
NSC 2000

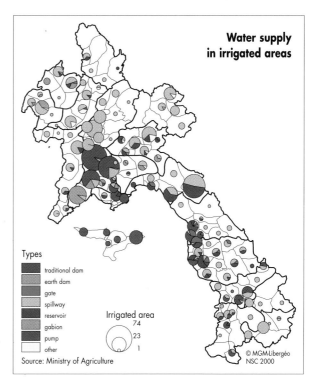

**Water supply
in irrigated areas**

Types

- traditional dam
- earth dam
- gate
- spillway
- reservoir
- gabion
- pump
- other

Irrigated area
74
23
1

Source: Ministry of Agriculture

© MGM-Libergéo
NSC 2000

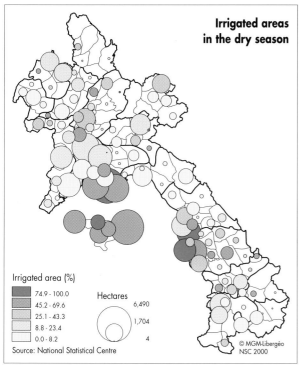

**Irrigated areas
in the dry season**

Irrigated area (%)

- 74.9 - 100.0
- 45.2 - 69.6
- 25.1 - 43.3
- 8.8 - 23.4
- 0.0 - 8.2

Hectares
6,490
1,704
4

Source: National Statistical Centre

© MGM-Libergéo
NSC 2000

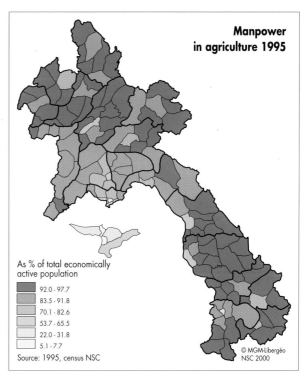

**Manpower
in agriculture 1995**

As % of total economically
active population

- 92.0 - 97.7
- 83.5 - 91.8
- 70.1 - 82.6
- 53.7 - 65.5
- 22.0 - 31.8
- 5.1 - 7.7

Source: 1995, census NSC

© MGM-Libergéo
NSC 2000

*Atlas of Laos*

# Rice cultivation

Since output of paddy is calculated by multiplying the area under cultivation by an average yield, the maps show only crop areas and actual yields, which are considerably lower than the figures published by the Ministry of Agriculture at provincial level, except for swidden rice (1.8 and 1.5 t/ha respectively in 1996).

The map of rain-fed rice (over half the area sown to rice) reproduces the map of rice cultivated areas on the previous page and extends the north-eastern axis to Huaphanh. The North exceeds the average yield (2.6 t/ha of paddy), with the best yields (over 3.4 t/ha) being located on the western fringe, where the crop areas are smaller, and in Huaphanh, where the crop areas are larger and have benefited from technical assistance since the partition period. Expert reports have raised doubts about the accuracy of such figures, given the low level of technical investment. The average area irrigated in the dry season (22% of the total irrigable area) and the average yield (3 t/ha of paddy) are only exceeded on Vientiane Plain, in the lower Se Bang Fai, in southern Luangphrabang province and in the district of Xiengkhor (Huaphanh); yields of 4 t/ha are recorded downstream from Vientiane and Thakhek.

Swidden rice (25% of the area sown to rice on average) occupies more than half the area sown to rice in the two areas of Austro-Asiatic settlement: that of the Khmu in the North and the area along Vietnamese border, including the Bolovens Plateau, in the South. In the Mekong Valley settled by Lao, and in Huaphanh province, it is below 11%, but still significant. Whenever possible, the Lao sow small areas to swidden rice, which is reputed to be more fragrant, on hillsides or in the foothills, alongside their rain-fed paddy fields on the plains and in the valleys. The yield is above the average (1.8 t/ha of paddy) in Xayabury province, in the heart of Khmu settlement (Luangphrabang), and in the districts populated by Leu and Nhuane (Tai-Kadai) bordering the Mekong in the North. These groups practise the most environmentally friendly type of swidden rice cultivation, as long as the population density remains low.

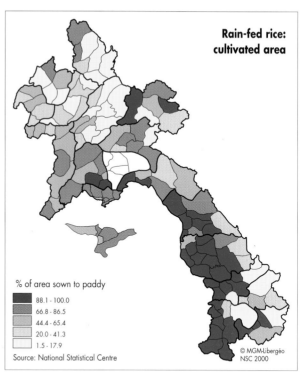

**Rain-fed rice: cultivated area**

% of area sown to paddy

- 88.1 - 100.0
- 66.8 - 86.5
- 44.4 - 65.4
- 20.0 - 41.3
- 1.5 - 17.9

Source: National Statistical Centre

© MGM-Libergéo
NSC 2000

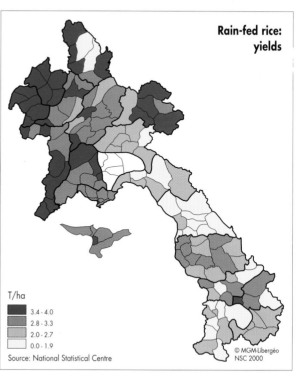

**Rain-fed rice: yields**

T/ha

- 3.4 - 4.0
- 2.8 - 3.3
- 2.0 - 2.7
- 0.0 - 1.9

Source: National Statistical Centre

© MGM-Libergéo
NSC 2000

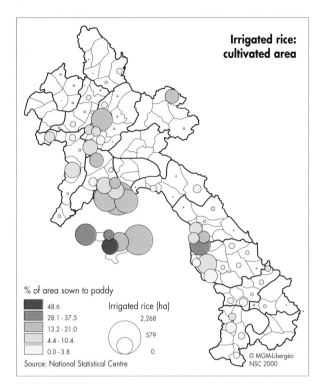

**Irrigated rice: cultivated area**

% of area sown to paddy

- 48.6
- 28.1 - 37.5
- 13.2 - 21.0
- 4.4 - 10.4
- 0.0 - 3.8

Irrigated rice (ha)

- 2,268
- 579
- 0

Source: National Statistical Centre

© MGM-Libergéo
NSC 2000

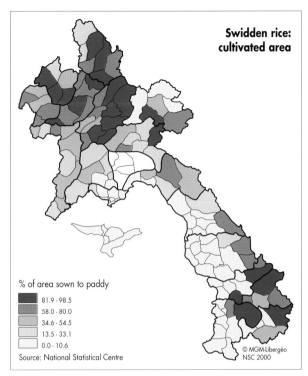

**Swidden rice: cultivated area**

% of area sown to paddy

- 81.9 - 98.5
- 58.0 - 80.0
- 34.6 - 54.5
- 13.5 - 33.1
- 0.0 - 10.6

Source: National Statistical Centre

© MGM-Libergéo
NSC 2000

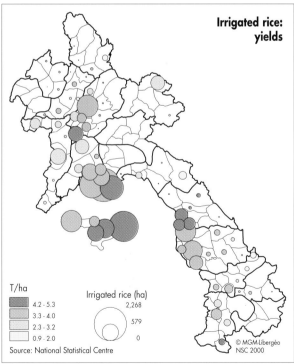

**Irrigated rice: yields**

T/ha

- 4.2 - 5.3
- 3.3 - 4.0
- 2.3 - 3.2
- 0.9 - 2.0

Irrigated rice (ha)

- 2,268
- 579
- 0

Source: National Statistical Centre

© MGM-Libergéo
NSC 2000

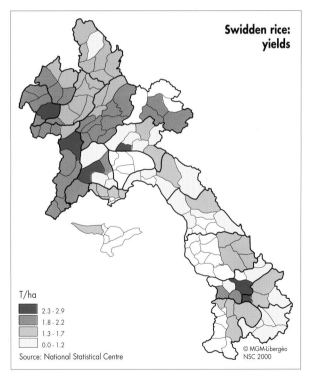

**Swidden rice: yields**

T/ha

- 2.3 - 2.9
- 1.8 - 2.2
- 1.3 - 1.7
- 0.0 - 1.2

Source: National Statistical Centre

© MGM-Libergéo
NSC 2000

*Atlas of Laos*

## Other food crops

Other food crops occupy only 10% of the area under cultivation, 8.4 times less than rice. Root crops—mainly sweet potato and cassava—account for 3%. These are mainly grown in regions with low rainfall: in a large northern triangle from Phongsaly to Xayabury and Huaphanh provinces, and in the eastern districts of Saravane and Sekong provinces. In these areas, they occupy between a third and two-thirds of the area sown to food crops other than rice. Root crops are also grown, to a lesser extent, in Khammouane and Savannakhet provinces. Their yields only exceed 9 t/ha in southern Luangphrabang province and in Vientiane municipality, where they only occupy small areas.

Maize, the next most widely grown crop after paddy (4.3% of the total crop area), is concentrated in the same northern triangle as root crops, where it generally occupies between half and three-quarters of the area sown to food crops other than rice. This proportion is only exceeded in northern Phongsaly province on the Chinese border, in Bokeo on the Myanmar border and in Borikhamxay on the Vietnamese border, and, to a lesser extent, along the Vietnamese border all the way to the south. Khammouane province has the best yields, followed by the axis between Nhot Ou (Phongsaly) and the Nam Beng, where yields surpass the average of 2 t/ha.

Beans, groundnuts and soy (1.7% of the total crop area) are more concentrated in the North (Oudomxay, Luangphrabang and Huaphanh provinces), where they rarely exceed 43% of the area sown to crops other than rice. This figure is largely exceeded in Champassack in the South. However, it is along the axis from Phongsaly to the Nam Beng and in southern Xayabury that groundnut yields are above the average (2.1 t/ha).

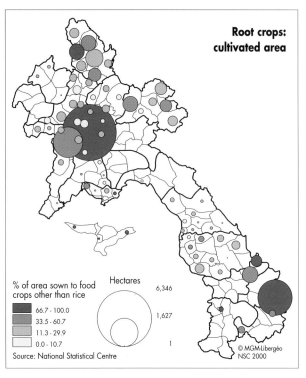

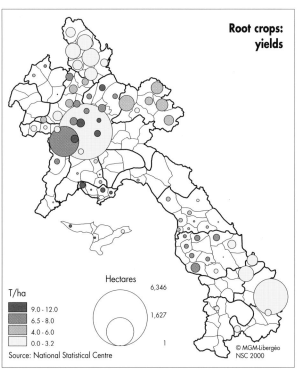

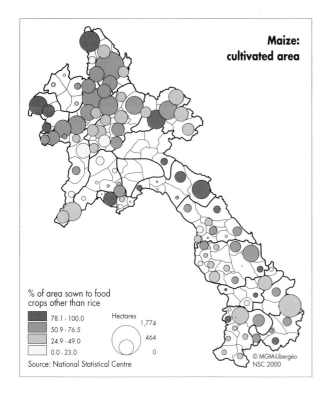

**Maize:**
**cultivated area**

% of area sown to food
crops other than rice

- 78.1 - 100.0
- 50.9 - 76.5
- 24.9 - 49.0
- 0.0 - 23.0

Hectares
1,774
464
0

Source: National Statistical Centre

© MGM-Libergéo
NSC 2000

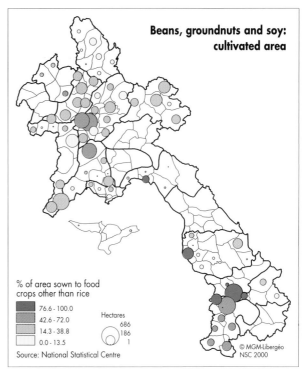

**Beans, groundnuts and soy:**
**cultivated area**

% of area sown to food
crops other than rice

- 76.6 - 100.0
- 42.6 - 72.0
- 14.3 - 38.8
- 0.0 - 13.5

Hectares
686
186
1

Source: National Statistical Centre

© MGM-Libergéo
NSC 2000

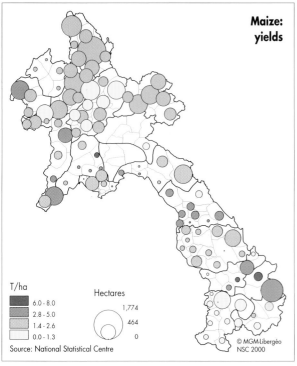

**Maize:**
**yields**

T/ha

- 6.0 - 8.0
- 2.8 - 5.0
- 1.4 - 2.6
- 0.0 - 1.3

Hectares
1,774
464
0

Source: National Statistical Centre

© MGM-Libergéo
NSC 2000

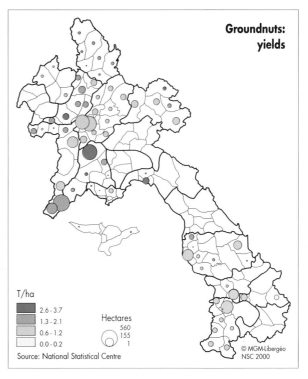

**Groundnuts:**
**yields**

T/ha

- 2.6 - 3.7
- 1.3 - 2.1
- 0.6 - 1.2
- 0.0 - 0.2

Hectares
560
155
1

Source: National Statistical Centre

© MGM-Libergéo
NSC 2000

*Atlas of Laos*

# Cash crops

Cash crops occupy only 6% of the total area under cultivation. Coffee, which accounts for half of this figure (3.1%), is concentrated on the Bolovens Plateau, where it occupies more than two-thirds of the area sown to cash crops, with an average yield of 0.5 t/ha. Cotton, 1% of the cultivated area, is mainly found in western Vientiane province (Xanakham) and in southern Xayabury province, where it accounts for over 80% of the area sown to cash crops. Cotton is also grown in the Nam Beng and Nam Ou Valleys. In these two regions, yields are between 0.8 t/ha and 1.5 t/ha.

Tobacco (0.6% of the crop area according to the data collected at district level, but 1.1% according to the Ministry of Agriculture) is mainly concentrated in Vientiane municipality, where the main cigarette factories are located and where it occupies more than 72% of the area sown to cash crops. Another tobacco-growing area consists of the districts bordering the Mekong in Savannakhet and Champassack in the South. Surprisingly enough, yields above 3.7 t/ha are found in Oudomxay in the North, where production has remained traditional.

Sugar cane occupies a limited area (0.5% of the crop area on average), but exceeds 80% of the area sown to cash crops in the district of Xaythany, neighbouring Vientiane, and in eastern Borikhamxay province connected to Vietnam. Yields are above the average (23.4 t/ha) there and in Luang-phrabang province, where cultivation is more traditional.

Thus, the provinces of Oudomxay and Luang-phrabang, where swidden rice occupies the largest areas, are also those with the most diversified agriculture, combining other food crops (maize and groundnuts) and cash crops (cotton, tobacco and sugar cane). They contrast with the districts that are more specialised in the production of cotton or tobacco, and particularly coffee on the Bolovens Plateau.

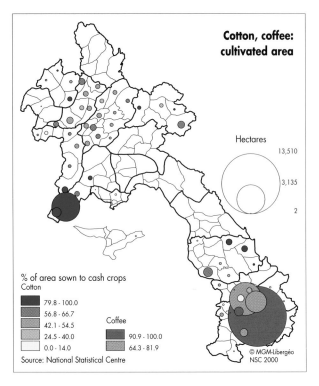

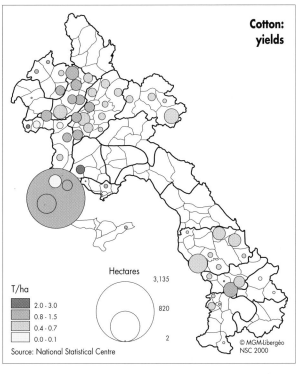

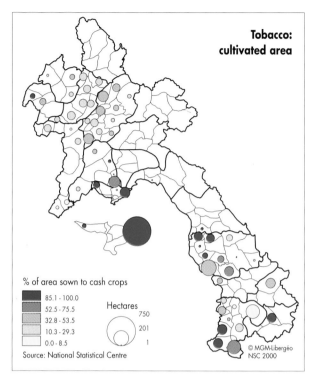

**Tobacco: cultivated area**

% of area sown to cash crops

- 85.1 - 100.0
- 52.5 - 75.5
- 32.8 - 53.5
- 10.3 - 29.3
- 0.0 - 8.5

Hectares
- 750
- 201
- 1

Source: National Statistical Centre

© MGM-Libergéo
NSC 2000

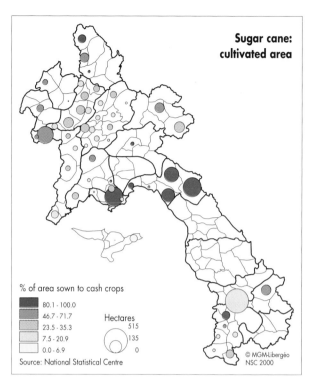

**Sugar cane: cultivated area**

% of area sown to cash crops

- 80.1 - 100.0
- 46.7 - 71.7
- 23.5 - 35.3
- 7.5 - 20.9
- 0.0 - 6.9

Hectares
- 515
- 135
- 0

Source: National Statistical Centre

© MGM-Libergéo
NSC 2000

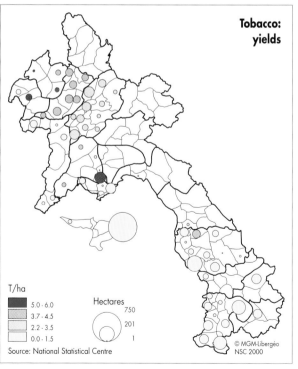

**Tobacco: yields**

T/ha
- 5.0 - 6.0
- 3.7 - 4.5
- 2.2 - 3.5
- 0.0 - 1.5

Hectares
- 750
- 201
- 1

Source: National Statistical Centre

© MGM-Libergéo
NSC 2000

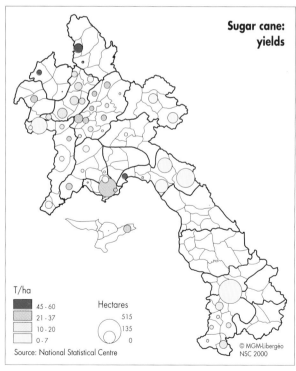

**Sugar cane: yields**

T/ha
- 45 - 60
- 21 - 37
- 10 - 20
- 0 - 7

Hectares
- 515
- 135
- 0

Source: National Statistical Centre

© MGM-Libergéo
NSC 2000

*Atlas of Laos*

**83**

## Livestock

In general, there is no direct correlation between the distribution of rain-fed ricefields and that of water buffalo, although these animals are used for ploughing and harrowing. The crop area in Laos is small, and large areas of grassland and dry dipterocarp forest close to populated regions are used for grazing. This atlas therefore relates the density of herds to population, expressing it in number of head of livestock per 100 persons.

With the exception of Savannakhet Plain, the regions with the highest density of buffalo are not the rice-growing plains but the surrounding areas: Khammouane province for Savannakhet, Attapeu province for Champassack and, to a lesser extent, the districts around Vientiane Plain. There is a closer link between the density of oxen and the plains from Savannakhet to Champassack in the South. Vientiane Plain is an exception. In the northern half of the country, high densities of oxen are linked to the area of Miao-Yao settlement (see page 45), particularly in Xiengkhuang, where the Hmong hold bullfights to celebrate the new year. Lastly, the Xiengkhuang and Bolovens Plateaux were major ox-breeding regions during the colonial period. Caravans of pack oxen left from there and were sold on arrival in the large delta towns.

Pig-breeding is characteristic of the highlands, where animist population groups, who sacrifice pigs, predominate. Goats and sheep were introduced during the war, which explains their relatively low densities; their distribution is similar to that of the Austro-Asiatic settlement, with two distinct groups in the North and the South of the country. The distribution of horses is concentrated along two axes: a meridian axis from Phongsaly to the Mekong in the North, and another from Xamneua to Xaysomboun in the North-East, which correspond respectively to the Tibeto-Burman and Hmong settlements (see page 45). Today, horses are used to transport goods to roads suitable for motorised vehicles. Lastly, elephants are found mainly in Luangphrabang province in the North and on the Bolovens Plateau in the South.

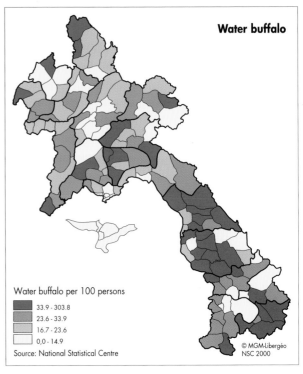

**Water buffalo**

Water buffalo per 100 persons

- 33.9 - 303.8
- 23.6 - 33.9
- 16.7 - 23.6
- 0.0 - 14.9

Source: National Statistical Centre

© MGM-Libergéo
NSC 2000

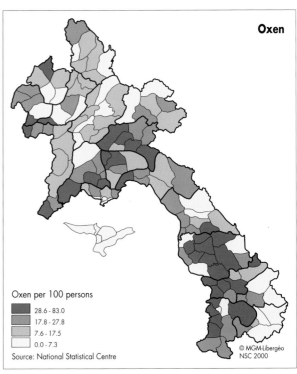

**Oxen**

Oxen per 100 persons

- 28.6 - 83.0
- 17.8 - 27.8
- 7.6 - 17.5
- 0.0 - 7.3

Source: National Statistical Centre

© MGM-Libergéo
NSC 2000

*Agriculture*

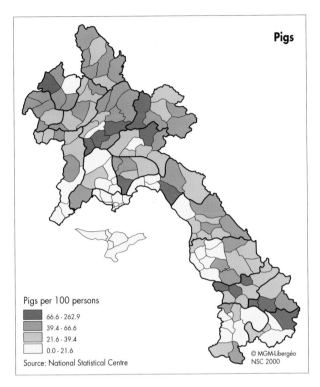

**Pigs**

Pigs per 100 persons

- 66.6 - 262.9
- 39.4 - 66.6
- 21.6 - 39.4
- 0.0 - 21.6

Source: National Statistical Centre

© MGM-Libergéo
NSC 2000

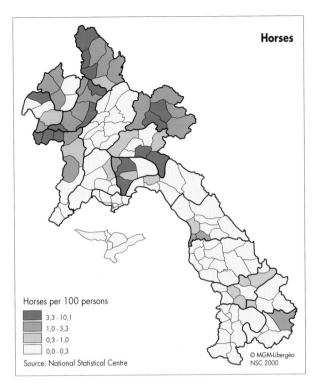

**Horses**

Horses per 100 persons

- 3,3 - 10,1
- 1,0 - 3,3
- 0,3 - 1,0
- 0,0 - 0,3

Source: National Statistical Centre

© MGM-Libergéo
NSC 2000

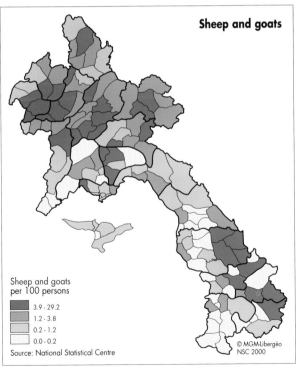

**Sheep and goats**

Sheep and goats
per 100 persons

- 3.9 - 29.2
- 1.2 - 3.8
- 0.2 - 1.2
- 0.0 - 0.2

Source: National Statistical Centre

© MGM-Libergéo
NSC 2000

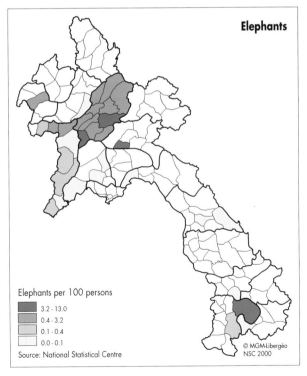

**Elephants**

Elephants per 100 persons

- 3.2 - 13.0
- 0.4 - 3.2
- 0.1 - 0.4
- 0.0 - 0.1

Source: National Statistical Centre

© MGM-Libergéo
NSC 2000

*Atlas of Laos*

# Food balances and forestry

The availability of food products per capita in 1996 just meets the standard defined by the Food and Agriculture Organisation (FAO): 300 kg of paddy equivalent (i.e. 180 kg of husked rice), according to the statistics from the Ministry of Agriculture. It is considerably below this standard (at 286 kg of paddy equivalent) according to the data collected by the National Statistical Centre used in this atlas. This standard is reached in the provinces bordering the Mekong from Bokeo to Vientiane in the North, and in the western half of Saravane and Savannakhet in the South, where rice cultivation is combined with other food crops. Rice alone rarely attained the threshold of 300 kg in 1996. The deficit provinces are located in the east of the country, in the highlands from Xiengkhuang to the Cambodian border. This group also includes Champassack province, the country's second biggest rice-producing region, hit by floods in 1996.

Indicators of factors of production are rare. The 1997-1998 Lao expenditure and consumption survey gives some idea of mechanisation, but only at provincial level. Between 16% and 25% of households own a tractor or a motorised cultivator in Vientiane municipality and the provinces bordering the Mekong upstream and downstream from the capital. This is related to the importance of the capital, to a high rate of rice cultivation and to the proximity of Thailand, since rates of mechanisation in the interior provinces are extremely low.

The distribution of sawmills is also concentrated in the provinces bordering the Mekong from Xayabury to the Cambodian border, where the forests are more accessible and exporting easier. Official output of undressed timber confirms this distribution. It is generally limited, except for three sites that concentrate 82% of felling and where hydroelectric dams are under construction. The clearing of the Nam Theun reservoir, in Khammouane province, provides 64% of the total and was completed before construction. The felling of trees submerged in the Nam Ngum reservoir is continuing (11%) and the Houay Ho reservoir in the South is being prepared. Plantation forest exists only in these three provinces.

*Agriculture*

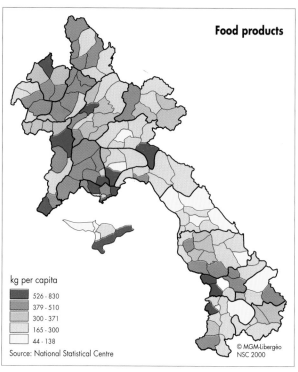

Food products

kg per capita
- 526 - 830
- 379 - 510
- 300 - 371
- 165 - 300
- 44 - 138

Source: National Statistical Centre

© MGM-Libergéo
NSC 2000

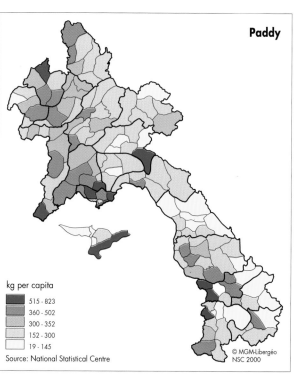

Paddy

kg per capita
- 515 - 823
- 360 - 502
- 300 - 352
- 152 - 300
- 19 - 145

Source: National Statistical Centre

© MGM-Libergéo
NSC 2000

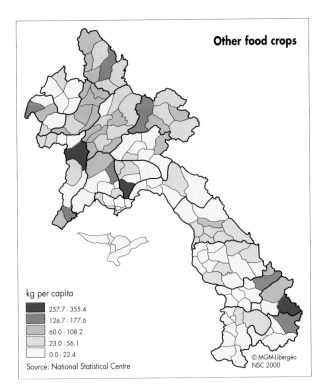

## Other food crops

kg per capita
- 257.7 - 355.4
- 126.7 - 177.6
- 60.0 - 108.2
- 23.0 - 56.1
- 0.0 - 22.4

Source: National Statistical Centre

© MGM-Libergéo
NSC 2000

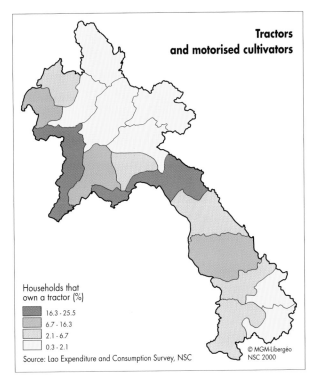

## Tractors and motorised cultivators

Households that
own a tractor (%)
- 16.3 - 25.5
- 6.7 - 16.3
- 2.1 - 6.7
- 0.3 - 2.1

Source: Lao Expenditure and Consumption Survey, NSC

© MGM-Libergéo
NSC 2000

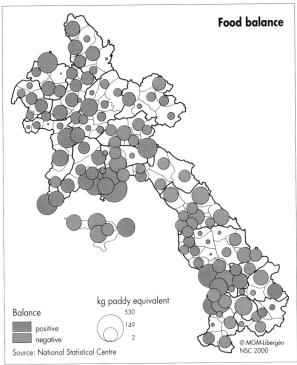

## Food balance

Balance
- positive
- negative

kg paddy equivalent
- 530
- 149
- 2

Source: National Statistical Centre

© MGM-Libergéo
NSC 2000

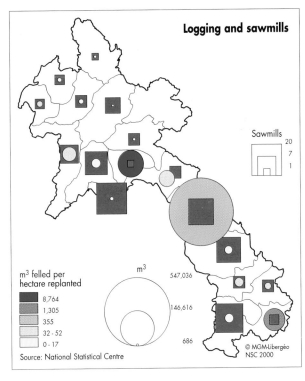

## Logging and sawmills

Sawmills
- 20
- 7
- 1

m³ felled per
hectare replanted
- 8,764
- 1,305
- 355
- 32 - 52
- 0 - 17

m³
- 547,036
- 146,616
- 686

Source: National Statistical Centre

© MGM-Libergéo
NSC 2000

*Atlas of Laos*

## Spatial structures of agriculture and livestock

The spatial structure of crops refines the pattern shown in the first three maps in this chapter (crop systems, rice cultivation and cash crops) and reveals a strong correlation with the map of settlement according to ethnolinguistic family (see page 45).

In the first class, notably along a meridian axis from Phongsaly to Luangphrabang, swidden rice is considerably more widespread than rain-fed rice, with root crops occupying an inversely proportionate share to that of rain-fed rice. The domination of swidden rice is also found in the second class, where maize and cotton stand out clearly, mainly in the Nam Beng Valley (Oudomxay). These two classes cover the two areas of Austro-Asiatic settlement, and link them with a discontinuous belt along the Vietnamese border at Borikhamxay and Khammouane. In the third class, formed by Xayabury and the axis from Vientiane to Huaphanh provinces, where the Tai-Kadai are more numerous than the Austro-Asiatics, all crops are around the national average. Rain-fed rice nevertheless prevails over swidden rice in these two areas, combined with cotton in Xayabury and maize on the Vientiane–Huaphanh axis. The last two classes correspond to the areas populated by the Lao. In the fourth class, rain-fed rice is combined with a minority component of swidden rice, grown for its fragrant flavour. In the hatched section of the fifth class, irrigated rice is predominant and, in the other section, irrigated rice appears alongside various cash crops.

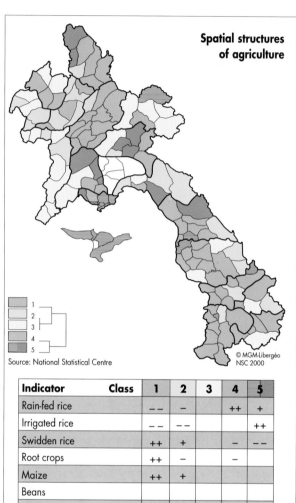

**Spatial structures of agriculture**

1
2
3
4
5

Source: National Statistical Centre

© MGM-Libergéo
NSC 2000

| Indicator          Class | 1 | 2 | 3 | 4 | 5 |
|--------------------------|----|----|----|----|----|
| Rain-fed rice | – – | – | | ++ | + |
| Irrigated rice | – – | – – | | | ++ |
| Swidden rice | ++ | + | | – | – – |
| Root crops | ++ | – | | – | |
| Maize | ++ | + | | | |
| Beans | | | | | |
| Tobacco | | | | + | |
| Cotton | | + | | | |
| Sugar cane | | + | | | |

The spatial structure of livestock breeding reveals three different types, each consisting of two classes. The first type comprises the districts characterised by elephants: the Bolovens Plateau, the main area of capture, and two districts neighbouring Luangphrabang, as the old royal palace maintains its own herd. In the second class, covering the rest of Luangphrabang province and its extensions, elephants are joined by pigs, sheep and goats, which have their highest densities here. The next two classes comprise the Mekong Valley. The third class, located mainly in Xayabury province, represents an average type for all kinds of livestock. The fourth class, where oxen and buffalo prevail over pigs, sheep and goats, of which there are few, covers western Savannakhet and Champassack provinces, which are the main rice-growing regions of Laos. Mountain livestock raising constitutes the last two classes, which are distinguished by the presence of horses in the provinces around Luangphrabang, where the Miao-Yao and Tibeto-Burman ethnolinguistic families are well established, and by the absence of horses in the areas where the Austro-Asiatics and the rest of the Tai-Kadai predominate.

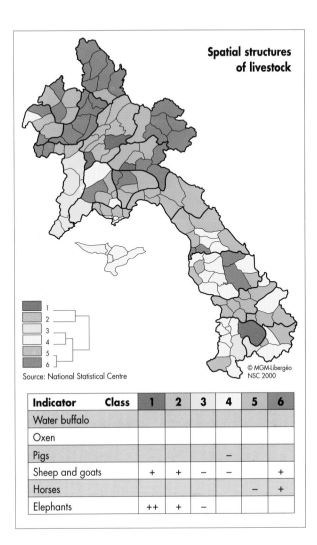

**Spatial structures of livestock**

1
2
3
4
5
6

Source: National Statistical Centre

© MGM-Libergéo
NSC 2000

| Indicator          Class | 1 | 2 | 3 | 4 | 5 | 6 |
|---|---|---|---|---|---|---|
| Water buffalo |   |   |   |   |   |   |
| Oxen |   |   |   |   |   |   |
| Pigs |   |   |   | − |   |   |
| Sheep and goats | + | + | − | − |   | + |
| Horses |   |   |   |   | − | + |
| Elephants | ++ | + | − |   |   |   |

# Chapter 6.
# Industry, mining and energy

The industrial sector, which also includes mining and energy, accounted for 17.4% of GDP in 1993, ranking just after services (24.3%) and agriculture (55.7%). This sector employed only 3.3% of the economically active population in 1995 (11.1% for services and 85.6% for agriculture) and 24.3% of the economically active population excluding agriculture. The data used here do not distinguish between output of undressed and dressed timber, which are both included in the industrial sector.

Industrial exports were multiplied by 3.6 between 1991 and 1995 on the strength of diversification of industrial output. The branches based on natural resources fell by half in relative value (from 65% in 1991 to 48% in 1995), with a bigger decline for hydroelectricity (from 22% to 9%), previously dominant, than for timber (from 42% to 39%). Diversification has bolstered the textile and garment industry (whose share rose from 15% to 20%). This branch has nevertheless been jeopardised by two events: the imposition of more restrictive quotas by the European Union; and the Asian crisis, which has restored the competitiveness of Thai businesses. However, motorcycle assembly (Suzuki and Honda) is a form of substitution for imports from Thailand.

The trend of foreign investment over the periods 1988-1992 and 1991-1997 is somewhat different, despite a sharp rise in the industrial sector's share from 52% to 84%. Since the new manufacturing industries are not capital-intensive, foreign investment has concentrated on hydroelectricity (72%). The opening of this sector to foreign financing, in the form of joint-ventures and Build-Own-Operate-Transfer (BOOT) financing, is a clearer sign of the transition towards a market economy.

Factories with Thai capital operating in the export sector are fragile. Some were closed down at the onset of the crisis and re-established in Bangkok to take advantage of reduced labour costs and economic services that gave them easier access to the international market. The industries that have positioned themselves in import substitution face competition from China for bottom-of-the-range products, much appreciated by consumers in the districts, and from Thailand for more elaborate products, suited to demand from the urban population. The limited extension of privatisation between 1989 and 1994 (the third of centrally managed, state-owned enterprises "privatised" were in fact rented, not sold, in 75% of cases); the problem of transport; and the sectioning off of the country into three small markets of one million consumers each (Vientiane, Luangphrabang and Savannakhet-Pakse), are the main impediments to industrial development, which is confined to the capital and the towns of the Mekong Valley.

The industries based on natural resources show strong potential for development, but require considerable investment. The mining sector is strengthening. In addition to tin from the Nam Pathene Valley in Khammouane (134,000 t of reserves, but only 720 t produced), redirected to the Phuket refinery in Thailand after the termination of the barter agreements with the Soviet Union, there is limestone quarrying for the new cement works in Vangvieng (province of Vientiane), and the production of 100,000 t of gypsum in Dong Hen (Savannakhet province), exported to cement works in Vietnam. Coal mining in Vientiane province has only just begun; lignite mining in Hongsa (northern Xayabury) has been delayed by the Thai crisis; and potassium mining on Vientiane Plain (50 billion t of reserves) will depend on a factory planned by ASEAN in Thailand. In the longer term, the main mineral resource will be iron from Xiengkhuang (Phou Nhuan and Phou Lek). This high iron content (60-70%) deposit of a billion tonnes can be accessed by open-cut mine. It requires investment estimated in 1975 at $245 million for the mine and $265 million for transporting the iron ore to the South China Sea.

Laos occupies only 26% of the area of the Mekong River Basin, but owns 81% of the hydroelectric potential of the tributaries of the lower basin (excluding China and Myanmar), estimated before 1975 at 16,000 MW by the Mekong Committee, with Vietnam and Thailand sharing less than a fifth (16% and 3%). The potential of Laos is currently estimated at 18,000 MW. As its current consumption is 60 MW, while its two large neighbours have a shortage, electricity is one of Lao PDR's main resources, which attracted 72% of foreign investment between 1991 and 1997.

The installed capacity at end 1999 was 615 MW, i.e. 3.4% of the identified potential, and 67% of output is exported under medium-term sales contracts signed with the Electricity Generating Authority of Thailand (EGAT) before the crisis. The Nam Ngum dam near Vientiane, which began production in 1972, has a capacity of 150 MW, and the Xe Xet dam (Saravane) added 45 MW in 1991. In 1998 the 210 MW of the Nam Theun-Hinboon dam (Khammouane) doubled capacity and introduced two innovations. It was the first dam co-financed by private investors under a BOOT contract (20% Norwegian and Swedish investment, 20% Thai investment and 60% Électricité du Laos) at a cost of $280 million. It was also the first high-head dam of this scale to use a pressure tunnel to divert the flow of the Nam Theun River to the Nam Hinboon. In 1999 an extra 150 MW were provided by Houay Ho (Attapeu) (60% Daewoo, 20% Thailand and 20% EDL) at a cost of $235 million; and 60 MW by the Nam Leuk, near the Nam Ngum, at a cost of $96.6 million financed partly by the Asian Development Bank.

A study carried out in December 1997 as part of the Nam Theun 2 project, *Prospects for Lao Power Export* (Lahmeyer International, Worley International, 1997) estimated Thailand's new needs at 27,000 MW by 2010. Thailand is expected to limit its imports to 5,700 MW and diversify its suppliers. 3,000 MW would come from Laos, 1,500 MW from Myanmar because gas is highly competitive, and 1,200 MW from the Dachaoshan dam near Jinghong in Yunnan. Prospects for Laotian exports for 2006-2010 were estimated at 4,500 MW: 3,000 MW to Thailand and 1,500 MW to central Vietnam. However, with the crisis, they could be reduced to between 3,200 MW and 2,770 MW in 2010: 600 MW from the lignite-fired plant in Hongsa (Xayabury), 450 MW from Nam Ngum 3, between 615 MW and 450 MW from Nam Ngum 2, 680 MW from Nam Theun 2, 390 MW from Xe Piang-Xe Nam Noi (Attapeu) and between 470 MW and 200 MW from Xe Kaman 1 (Attapeu). The Nam Theun 2 project, the third major high-head dam, where the Nam Theun reservoir level is 350 m higher than the Se Bang Fai, will given the highest return of all the dams in the Mekong Basin on its investment cost of $1.2 billion.

| Exports ($ m) | 1991a 96.6 | 1993a 240.6 | 1996a 322.6 |
|---|---|---|---|
| Timber and timber products | 42.3 | 27.5 | 38.6 |
| Textiles and garments | 15.7 | 20.4 | 19.9 |
| Other manufactured goods | 13.0 | 15.8 | 8.6 |
| Electricity | 22.1 | 8.1 | 9.2 |
| Motorcycle assembly | – | 15.0 | 3.9 |
| Agricultural products (incl. coffee) | 6.9 | 5.5 | 13.2 |
| Re-exported goods (cars, gold), other | – | 7.7 | 6.6 |
| Total | 100 | 100 | 100 |

| Industry by branch | Investment 1988-1992b | Foreign 1991-1997c | GDP 1993b | Manpower* 1995d |
|---|---|---|---|---|
| Electricity | 2.2 | 71.8 | 1.3 | 1.2 |
| Manufacturing | 19.2 | 7.4 | 12.8 | 3.7 |
| Mining | 14.3 | 1.2 | – | 1.3 |
| Timber and timber products | 9.4 | 2.5 | – | 4.0 |
| Textiles and garments | 6.6 | 1.0 | – | 6.8 |
| Construction | – | 0.6 | 3.1 | 6.8 |
| **Total industry** | **51.7** | **84.5** | **17.4** | **23.8** |

Sources: a. *Economic and Financial Sector Statistics*, Bank of Lao PDR 1997; b. *Laos' Dilemmas and Options*, 1997; c. Committee for Investment and Foreign Economic Cooperation; d. 1995 census, NSC. * Percentage of the non-farm workforce.

*Atlas of Laos*

# Industry

Industry, which employs 76,250 people (3.3% of the economically active population), is mainly urban. Distortions in the data, which mostly come from the register of industrial enterprises at provincial level, can be corrected by the data on manpower taken from the census. In Vientiane, this sector employs over 20% of the non-farm workforce. The share in the four other towns of the valley ranges from 8% to 14%. The private sector is exclusive along the axis from Vientiane province to Huaphanh province. The proportion of privately owned enterprises is extremely high for the capital (95%) and only decreases significantly in Thakhek (86%) and especially in Luangnamtha (67%).

In 1996 enterprises with large average capital were concentrated in Vientiane (219 million kip), followed a long way behind by Thakhek, on the strength of the mining sector, and Pakse, which benefits from the Thai railway that arrives in Ubon. These two towns are surpassed by Vientiane province, which profits from proximity to the capital. The average number of employees per enterprise reflects the low level of industrial development, with figures of only 25 in Vientiane, 10 in Thakhek and 6 in Savannakhet. Many "factories" are in fact cottage industries. According to these indicators, the North seems to have no industry, an observation that can be qualified by the 1994 data on the size of enterprises.

According to the distribution of capital at that date, Vientiane, Thakhek and Savannakhet had large enterprises (more than 100 employees) and medium-sized enterprises (between 10 and 99 employees). There were more medium-sized enterprises than small enterprises in Pakse and along a transverse axis in the North between Bokeo in the northern economic development quadrangle and Borikhamxay, via Xiengkhuang. According to the distribution of manpower, large enterprises predominate in Vientiane and Thakhek and medium-sized enterprises in Luangnamtha on the Chinese border. Medium-sized enterprises are ahead of small enterprises in Savannakhet and Pakse, and on the transverse axis in the North, although these are smaller in absolute value.

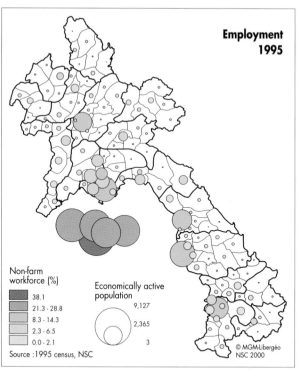

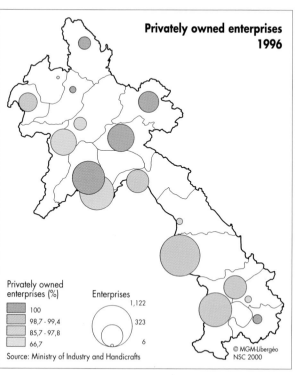

*Industry, mining and energy*

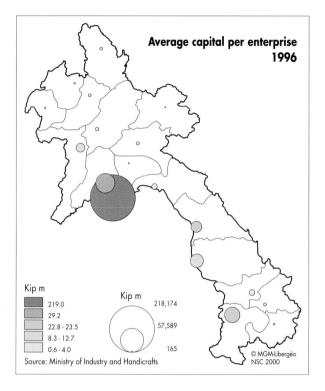

**Average capital per enterprise 1996**

Kip m
- 219.0
- 29.2
- 22.8 - 23.5
- 8.3 - 12.7
- 0.6 - 4.0

Kip m
- 218,174
- 57,589
- 165

Source: Ministry of Industry and Handicrafts

© MGM-Libergéo
NSC 2000

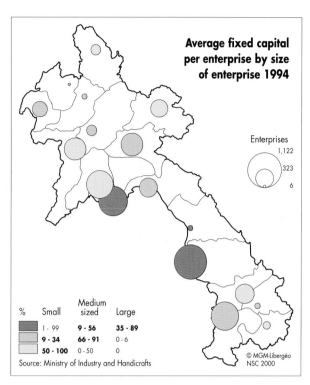

**Average fixed capital per enterprise by size of enterprise 1994**

Enterprises
- 1,122
- 323
- 6

| % | Small | Medium sized | Large |
|---|---|---|---|
| | 1 - 99 | 9 - 56 | 35 - 89 |
| | 9 - 34 | 66 - 91 | 0 - 6 |
| | 50 - 100 | 0 - 50 | 0 |

Source: Ministry of Industry and Handicrafts

© MGM-Libergéo
NSC 2000

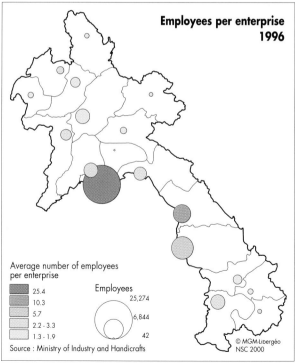

**Employees per enterprise 1996**

Average number of employees per enterprise
- 25.4
- 10.3
- 5.7
- 2.2 - 3.3
- 1.3 - 1.9

Employees
- 25,274
- 6,844
- 42

Source : Ministry of Industry and Handicrafts

© MGM-Libergéo
NSC 2000

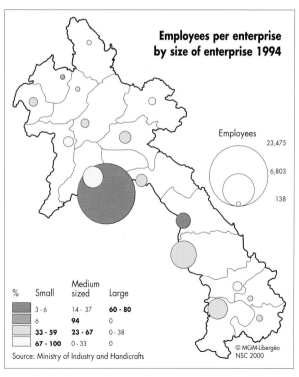

**Employees per enterprise by size of enterprise 1994**

Employees
- 23,475
- 6,803
- 138

| % | Small | Medium sized | Large |
|---|---|---|---|
| | 3 - 6 | 14 - 37 | 60 - 80 |
| | 6 | 94 | 0 |
| | 33 - 59 | 23 - 67 | 0 - 38 |
| | 67 - 100 | 0 - 33 | 0 |

Source: Ministry of Industry and Handicrafts

© MGM-Libergéo
NSC 2000

*Atlas of Laos*

# Agro-processing, textiles and garments

The agro-processing industry is better distributed across the whole territory because of the large number of very small-scale enterprises outside of the capital. Average fixed capital per enterprise in Vientiane municipality reaches 63 million kip, seven times higher than in Vientiane province, and 30 times higher than in Savannakhet and Pakse! The average number of employees per enterprise in Vientiane municipality is nine times higher than in the capitals of the neighbouring provinces and in Xiengkhuang, which has many advantages despite its relative isolation and which is ahead of far more populous Savannakhet and Pakse. The manpower employed in the agro-processing industry (4,800 employees) is concentrated in the two peri-urban districts of the capital. In Hadxaifong, the road leading to the bridge over the Mekong is lined with beer, soft-drink and condiment factories and the branch employs 7% of non-farm workers. Other factories and rice mills are located in Xaythany, and Pakse is a long way ahead of Savannakhet.

Textiles and garments (22,600 employees), low-wage industries in the export sector, are highly concentrated in the two largest towns. In Vientiane municipality, average fixed capital is seven times higher than in Savannakhet, and the average number of employees per enterprise is five times higher. With respective averages of around 100 workers in Vientiane and 20 in Savannakhet, these enterprises are real factories, on the scale of the local industrial landscape, employing between 20% and 12% of the non-farm workforce. In Vientiane, manpower in this sector is scattered over the four urbanised districts and the two most industrialised peri-urban districts. This can be explained by the availability of land held by Laotian entrepreneurs in partnership with Thai investors. It would be of interest to know the distribution of factories that have closed down and returned to Bangkok since the crisis.

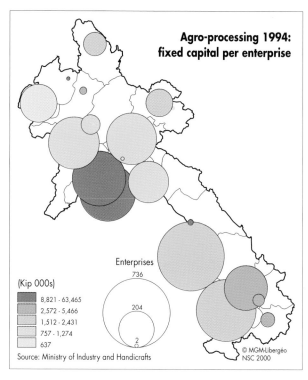

**Agro-processing 1994: fixed capital per enterprise**

Enterprises
736
204
2

(Kip 000s)
- 8,821 - 63,465
- 2,572 - 5,466
- 1,512 - 2,431
- 757 - 1,274
- 637

Source: Ministry of Industry and Handicrafts

© MGM-Libergéo
NSC 2000

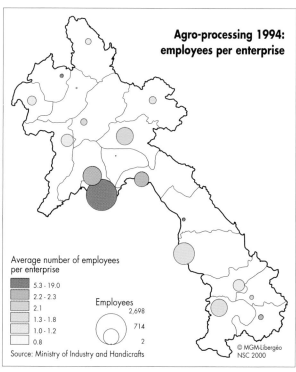

**Agro-processing 1994: employees per enterprise**

Average number of employees per enterprise
- 5.3 - 19.0
- 2.2 - 2.3
- 2.1
- 1.3 - 1.8
- 1.0 - 1.2
- 0.8

Employees
2,698
714
2

Source: Ministry of Industry and Handicrafts

© MGM-Libergéo
NSC 2000

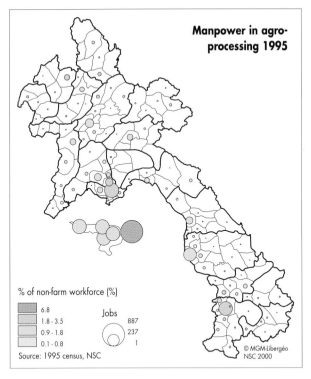

**Manpower in agro-processing 1995**

% of non-farm workforce (%)

- 6.8
- 1.8 - 3.5
- 0.9 - 1.8
- 0.1 - 0.8

Jobs
- 887
- 237
- 1

Source: 1995 census, NSC

© MGM-Libergéo
NSC 2000

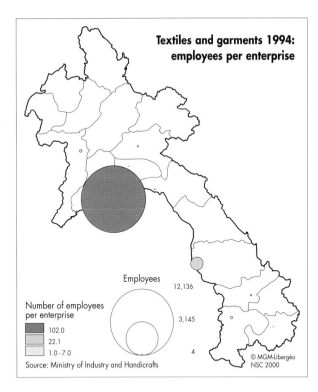

**Textiles and garments 1994: employees per enterprise**

Employees
- 12,136
- 3,145
- 4

Number of employees per enterprise
- 102.0
- 22.1
- 1.0 - 7.0

Source: Ministry of Industry and Handicrafts

© MGM-Libergéo
NSC 2000

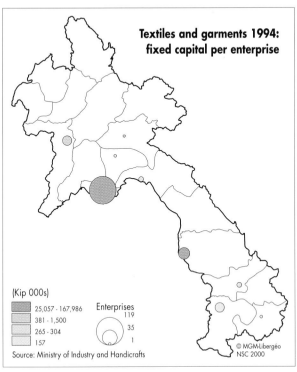

**Textiles and garments 1994: fixed capital per enterprise**

(Kip 000s)
- 25,057 - 167,986
- 381 - 1,500
- 265 - 304
- 157

Enterprises
- 119
- 35
- 1

Source: Ministry of Industry and Handicrafts

© MGM-Libergéo
NSC 2000

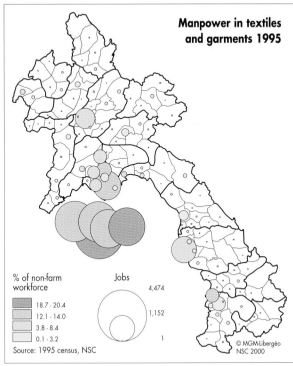

**Manpower in textiles and garments 1995**

% of non-farm workforce
- 18.7 - 20.4
- 12.1 - 14.0
- 3.8 - 8.4
- 0.1 - 3.2

Jobs
- 4,474
- 1,152
- 1

Source: 1995 census, NSC

© MGM-Libergéo
NSC 2000

## Timber and furniture, chemicals and plastics

The timber and furniture industry (12,900 employees) is located along the Mekong Valley from Vientiane to the Cambodian border, because its main market is Thailand. Average fixed capital per enterprise is higher in the southern towns than in Vientiane although the capital city is a long way ahead in terms of the average number of employees (42), surpassing Pakse (27), Savannakhet and Vientiane province (16 to 20). The distribution of employees fills in a gap in the data: the highest proportions (14% and 9% of non-farm workers respectively) are found in Thakhek, where a military-owned company exports timber to Vietnam, and Hadxaifong, a peri-urban district of the capital, together with two northern districts on the plain in Vientiane province. With the exception of Xayabury, the North is under-represented because there is more unstocked and bamboo forest there (see page 20).

The chemicals and plastics branch, which employs a small workforce (3,500 employees), is located along the Mekong Valley, particularly south of Vientiane, and the role of the capital is not predominant. Thakhek is ahead of the capital city in terms of average fixed capital (410 million kip compared with 177 million kip) and average number of employees (83 compared with 47). This branch only employs a significant proportion of non-farm workers (12-15%) in districts with salt wells—where brackish water is pumped from underground and the salt recovered after boiling—in Thoulakhom in Vientiane province and in the district of Vilabuly north of Road 9 in Savannakhet province.

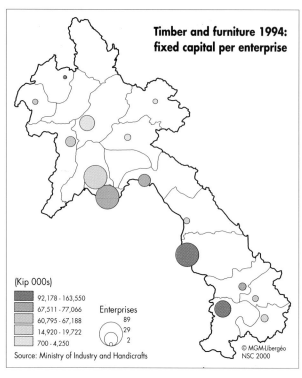

**Timber and furniture 1994: fixed capital per enterprise**

(Kip 000s)

- 92,178 - 163,550
- 67,511 - 77,066
- 60,795 - 67,188
- 14,920 - 19,722
- 700 - 4,250

Enterprises
89
29
2

Source: Ministry of Industry and Handicrafts

© MGM-Libergéo
NSC 2000

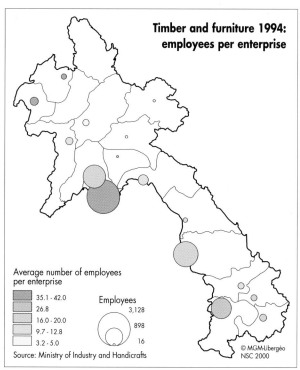

**Timber and furniture 1994: employees per enterprise**

Average number of employees per enterprise

- 35.1 - 42.0
- 26.8
- 16.0 - 20.0
- 9.7 - 12.8
- 3.2 - 5.0

Employees
3,128
898
16

Source: Ministry of Industry and Handicrafts

© MGM-Libergéo
NSC 2000

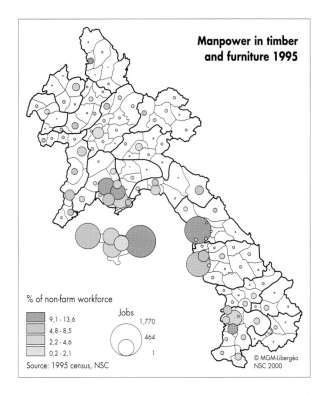

**Manpower in timber and furniture 1995**

% of non-farm workforce

Jobs
- 9,1 - 13,6
- 4,8 - 8,5
- 2,2 - 4,6
- 0,2 - 2,1

1,770
464
1

Source: 1995 census, NSC

© MGM-Libergéo
NSC 2000

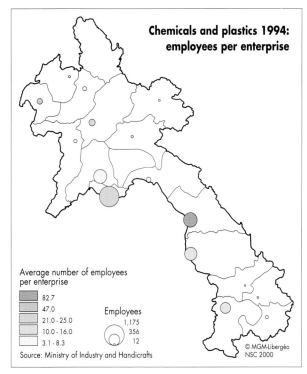

**Chemicals and plastics 1994: employees per enterprise**

Average number of employees per enterprise

- 82.7
- 47.0
- 21.0 - 25.0
- 10.0 - 16.0
- 3.1 - 8.3

Employees
1,175
356
12

Source: Ministry of Industry and Handicrafts

© MGM-Libergéo
NSC 2000

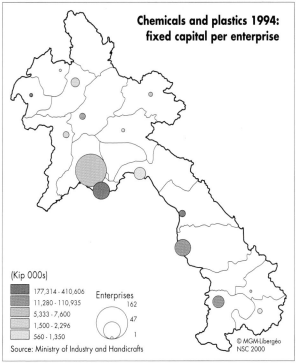

**Chemicals and plastics 1994: fixed capital per enterprise**

(Kip 000s)

Enterprises
- 177,314 - 410,606
- 11,280 - 110,935
- 5,333 - 7,600
- 1,500 - 2,296
- 560 - 1,350

162
47
1

Source: Ministry of Industry and Handicrafts

© MGM-Libergéo
NSC 2000

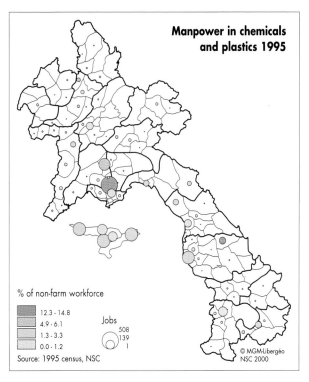

**Manpower in chemicals and plastics 1995**

% of non-farm workforce

- 12.3 - 14.8
- 4.9 - 6.1
- 1.3 - 3.3
- 0.0 - 1.2

Jobs
508
139
1

Source: 1995 census, NSC

© MGM-Libergéo
NSC 2000

# Machinery and vehicles, public works and construction

Metallurgy, machinery and vehicle assembly (motorcycles and motorised tricycles) form the smallest industrial branch with fewer than 2,900 employees. This branch is also highly concentrated in the three largest towns, and on an extremely small scale, with the exception of the two motorcycle assembly factories. Savannakhet is slightly ahead of Vientiane. In the North, but on a much lower scale, Muong Xay is ahead of Luangphrabang, in terms of both average fixed capital and average number of employees. The distribution of employment in the branch restores the urban hierarchy, with Vientiane surpassing the regional capitals of North and South, which come ahead of Savannakhet.

The construction branch, with 21,900 employees, is the biggest industrial branch, just ahead of textiles and garments. It is managed by the Ministry of Trade, which does not have data on the average number of employees per enterprise. However, the statistics on average fixed capital make it possible to separate construction from public works and irrigation. In terms of the number of enterprises, construction follows the urban hierarchy, with one exception: Luangphrabang is ahead of Pakse because of the development of tourism since the old royal capital was listed as a World Heritage site. The average fixed capital of enterprises is higher in the peripheral provinces of the North and North-East, where infrastructure in the provincial capitals is still being built. Public works and irrigation are more concentrated around the capital, particularly in Xaysetha, as well as in Luangnamtha and Xiengkhuang provinces.

The workforce of the construction and public works sector as a whole is better distributed across the whole territory, with the exception of the most peripheral provinces: Phongsaly in the North, and Sekong and Attapeu in the South. In the other provincial capitals and in many of the districts bordering the Mekong, this branch accounts for between 7% and 11% of non-farm workers. It accounts for as many as 13% in the peri-urban district of Xaythany in Vientiane, and 20% in Paksong on the Bolovens Plateau.

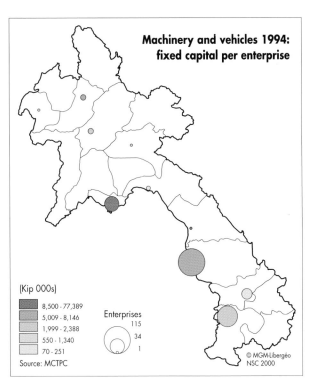

Machinery and vehicles 1994: fixed capital per enterprise

(Kip 000s)
- 8,500 - 77,389
- 5,009 - 8,146
- 1,999 - 2,388
- 550 - 1,340
- 70 - 251

Enterprises
115
34
1

Source: MCTPC

© MGM-Libergéo
NSC 2000

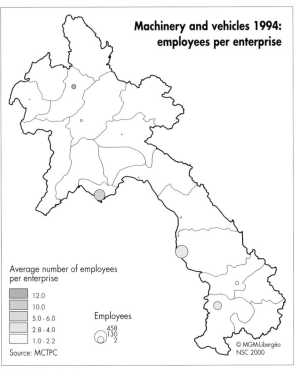

Machinery and vehicles 1994: employees per enterprise

Average number of employees per enterprise
- 12.0
- 10.0
- 5.0 - 6.0
- 2.8 - 4.0
- 1.0 - 2.2

Employees
458
130
2

Source: MCTPC

© MGM-Libergéo
NSC 2000

*Industry, mining and energy*

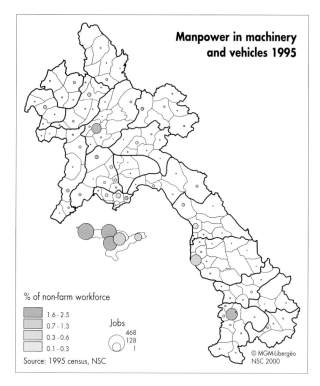

**Manpower in machinery and vehicles 1995**

% of non-farm workforce
- 1.6 - 2.5
- 0.7 - 1.3
- 0.3 - 0.6
- 0.1 - 0.3

Jobs
- 468
- 128
- 1

Source: 1995 census, NSC

© MGM-Libergéo
NSC 2000

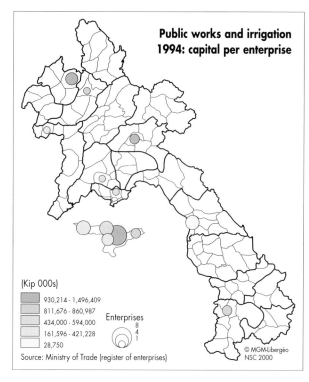

**Public works and irrigation 1994: capital per enterprise**

(Kip 000s)
- 930,214 - 1,496,409
- 811,676 - 860,987
- 434,000 - 594,000
- 161,596 - 421,228
- 28,750

Enterprises
- 8
- 4
- 1

Source: Ministry of Trade (register of enterprises)

© MGM-Libergéo
NSC 2000

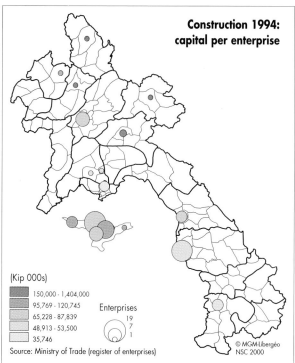

**Construction 1994: capital per enterprise**

(Kip 000s)
- 150,000 - 1,404,000
- 95,769 - 120,745
- 65,228 - 87,839
- 48,913 - 53,500
- 35,746

Enterprises
- 19
- 7
- 1

Source: Ministry of Trade (register of enterprises)

© MGM-Libergéo
NSC 2000

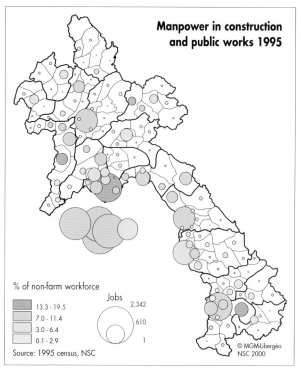

**Manpower in construction and public works 1995**

% of non-farm workforce
- 13.3 - 19.5
- 7.0 - 11.4
- 3.0 - 6.4
- 0.1 - 2.9

Jobs
- 2,342
- 610
- 1

Source: 1995 census, NSC

© MGM-Libergéo
NSC 2000

*Atlas of Laos*

# Mining, electricity and water

The main mining areas are: Khammouane province, which has tin mines and limestone quarries; the Vangvieng Basin, where the first cement works in the country is located, and also in Vientiane province, in Muong Feuang, where coal mining has begun. Dong Hen, in the province of Savannakhet, is the fourth site for mining output, with exports of gypsum to Vietnam. There are also scattered deposits in the North: coal in Viengphoukha and lignite in Hongsa. In the Xe Done Valley (Saravane) and eastern Xiengkhuang province, prospecting for coal has begun. The North–South imbalance is particularly evident in the area given over to mining concessions: Luangnamtha and Luangphrabang provinces, where prospecting is financed by foreign companies, are clearly ahead. Activity remains limited, however, with only 4,200 employees. Only in the tin district (Hinboon) are 26% of non-farm workers employed in the mining sector.

The energy, water and sanitation branch employs only 3,700 people and is much more concentrated in the towns. The number of installations can give a misleading picture. In Xiengkhuang and Huaphanh, the delay in public infrastructure has led to the use of private or village generators, which explains their low average capital and small average number of employees. The capitals bordering the Mekong are at an advantage in terms of average capital. In terms of average number of employees, this branch only attains a significant size in Vientiane. Manpower in the branch reflects the urban hierarchy, with one exception, as Pakse comes ahead of Savannakhet. On the sites of the two hydroelectric plants existing in 1995—Nam Ngum in Vientiane province and Xe Xet in Saravane province—this branch accounts for more than 3% of non-farm jobs.

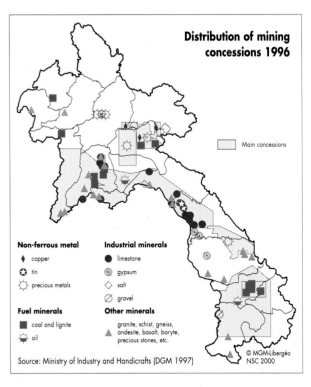

Distribution of mining concessions 1996

Main concessions

**Non-ferrous metal**
- copper
- tin
- precious metals

**Fuel minerals**
- coal and lignite
- oil

**Industrial minerals**
- limestone
- gypsum
- salt
- gravel

**Other minerals**
- granite, schist, gneiss, andesite, basalt, baryte, precious stones, etc.

Source: Ministry of Industry and Handicrafts (DGM 1997)

© MGM-Libergéo NSC 2000

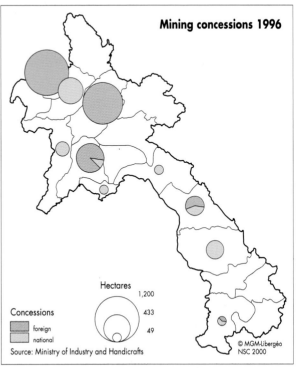

Mining concessions 1996

Hectares
1,200
433
49

**Concessions**
- foreign
- national

Source: Ministry of Industry and Handicrafts

© MGM-Libergéo NSC 2000

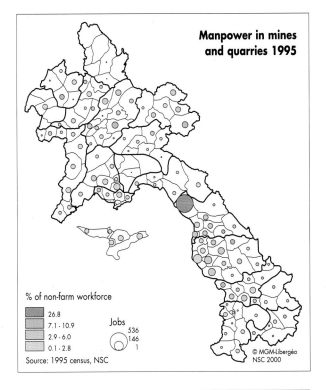

**Manpower in mines
and quarries 1995**

% of non-farm workforce

- 26.8
- 7.1 - 10.9
- 2.9 - 6.0
- 0.1 - 2.8

Jobs
536
146
1

Source: 1995 census, NSC

© MGM-Libergéo
NSC 2000

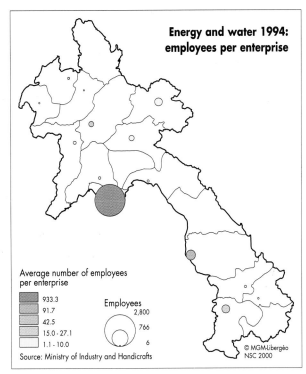

**Energy and water 1994:
employees per enterprise**

Average number of employees
per enterprise

- 933.3
- 91.7
- 42.5
- 15.0 - 27.1
- 1.1 - 10.0

Employees
2,800
766
6

Source: Ministry of Industry and Handicrafts

© MGM-Libergéo
NSC 2000

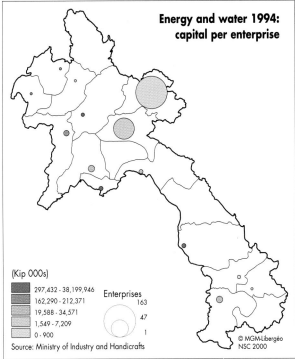

**Energy and water 1994:
capital per enterprise**

(Kip 000s)

- 297,432 - 38,199,946
- 162,290 - 212,371
- 19,588 - 34,571
- 1,549 - 7,209
- 0 - 900

Enterprises
163
47
1

Source: Ministry of Industry and Handicrafts

© MGM-Libergéo
NSC 2000

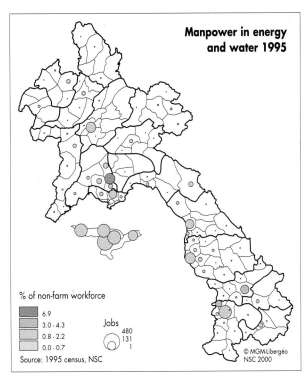

**Manpower in energy
and water 1995**

% of non-farm workforce

- 6.9
- 3.0 - 4.3
- 0.8 - 2.2
- 0.0 - 0.7

Jobs
480
131
1

Source: 1995 census, NSC

© MGM-Libergéo
NSC 2000

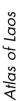

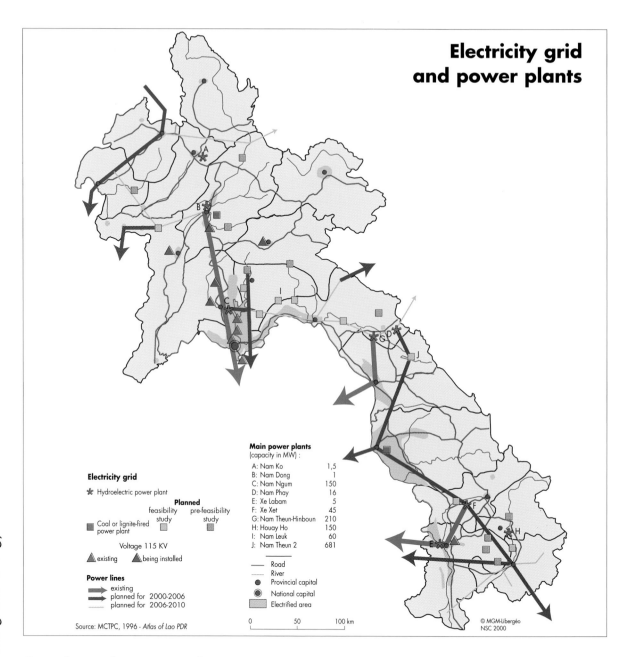

# Electricity grid and power plants

**Electricity grid**

✳ Hydroelectric power plant

**Planned**

| | feasibility study | pre-feasibility study |

◼ Coal or lignite-fired power plant

**Voltage 115 KV**

▲ existing ▲ being installed

**Power lines**

→ existing
→ planned for 2000-2006
→ planned for 2006-2010

Source: MCTPC, 1996 - Atlas of Lao PDR

**Main power plants**
(capacity in MW) :

| | |
|---|---|
| A: Nam Ko | 1,5 |
| B: Nam Dong | 1 |
| C: Nam Ngum | 150 |
| D: Nam Phay | 16 |
| E: Xe Labam | 5 |
| F: Xe Xet | 45 |
| G: Nam Theun-Hinboun | 210 |
| H: Houay Ho | 150 |
| I: Nam Leuk | 60 |
| J: Nam Theun 2 | 681 |

— Road
— River
● Provincial capital
◎ National capital
◼ Electrified area

0    50    100 km

© MGM-Libergéo
NSC 2000

*Industry, mining and energy*

## Supply and consumption of electricity and water

The current electricity transmission network is entirely outward bound. Its main function is to export electricity from the four large existing plants, Nam-Ngum, Xe Xet, Nam Theun-Hinboon and Houay Ho, around which regional distribution networks are beginning to form. Power interconnection only exists between Vientiane and Luangphrabang, supplying the cement works in Vangvieng along the way. Until 2006, the development of the network will continue to be mainly outward, with a diversification of the electricity lines for export from the planned hydroelectric plants and the lignite-fired plant (Hongsa).

**102**

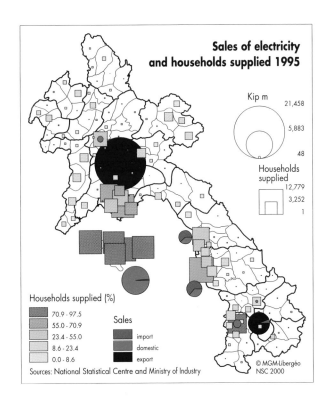

**Sales of electricity and households supplied 1995**

Kip m
21,458
5,883
48

Households supplied
12,779
3,252
1

Households supplied (%)
- 70.9 - 97.5
- 55.0 - 70.9
- 23.4 - 55.0
- 8.6 - 23.4
- 0.0 - 8.6

Sales
- import
- domestic
- export

Sources: National Statistical Centre and Ministry of Industry
© MGM-Libergéo NSC 2000

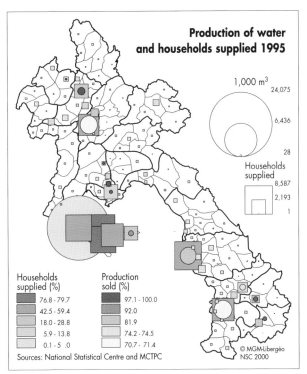

**Production of water and households supplied 1995**

1,000 m³
24,075
6,436
28

Households supplied
8,587
2,193
1

Households supplied (%)
- 76.8 - 79.7
- 42.5 - 59.4
- 18.0 - 28.8
- 5.9 - 13.8
- 0.1 - 5 .0

Production sold (%)
- 97.1 - 100.0
- 92.0
- 81.9
- 74.2 - 74.5
- 70.7 - 71.4

Sources: National Statistical Centre and MCTPC
© MGM-Libergéo NSC 2000

A transit line will also cross the northern economic development quadrangle to export electricity from Yunnan to Thailand. New lines making it possible to export to Vietnam will not be installed before 2010.

In 1995, Laos consumed only a third of the 1,000 GWh of electricity generated, and only a quarter of its output by value ($33.3 million). Because of the lack of interconnection in the southern half of the country and until Nam Theun-Hinboon became productive, in 1995 Laos also imported $2.5 million worth of electricity from Thailand, i.e. 10% of its exports and 7% of its output. Electrification in Laos is still a marker of urbanisation in most of the country. The exceptions, however, are the districts on the bank of the Mekong: on Vientiane Plain, between Thakhek and Savannakhet and around Pakse. Even in the towns, the progress of electrification is uneven. In Vientiane and Pakse, more than 70% of the population is connected and supplied by the Nam Ngum and Xe Xet plants. In Savannakhet and on Vientiane Plain, the proportion is over 50%, and in Luangphrabang and Thakhek, it is between a quarter and half. Four provinces lag a long way behind due to their isolation: Phongsaly in the North, Sekong and Attapeu in the South, and the special zone of Xaysomboun.

Production of drinking water and the proportion of households serviced reflect the urban hierarchy of the four main towns of the Mekong Valley. Thereafter, the pattern is different: in the northern half of the country, Muong Xay, the road node of the North was equipped before Namtha and Phonsavanh (Xiengkhuang); and in the South, the proportion of households serviced is higher in Lamarm and Attapeu than in Saravane. Although it is the fifth-largest town, Thakhek appears neglected, and is on the same level as the provinces bordering the Mekong upstream from Vientiane. The water conveyances in the four large towns of the Mekong Valley are in bad repair, which explains the low proportion of output sold, with losses on the network ranging from 18% to 29%.

*Atlas of Laos*

## Spatial structures of industry, mining and energy

Two groups, following a meridian pattern, can be distinguished according to the average capital of industrial enterprises. The first group, consisting of the first three classes, covers the peripheral mountainous provinces and two provinces—Borikhamxay and Saravane—that are open to both Thailand and Vietnam. The latter two provinces make up the first class, which has a low level of industrialisation: only timber and furniture are of significance. The second class, including the largest number of provinces, consists chiefly of the axis between Vientiane province and Xamneua and secondarily of the peripheral provinces in the North and South, plus two districts—one urban and one peri-urban—neighbouring Vientiane to the east. Rates of capitalisation are average or variable there for output of basic goods with low value added. The third class is only distinguished from the second by the greater significance of the energy, water and sanitation branch, because the infrastructure in the provincial capitals of Xayabury and Bokeo was recently built or modernised.

The second group, the most industrialised, is made up of the five main towns of the Mekong Valley. The fourth class comprises Savannakhet, Pakse and Luangphrabang, which have regional functions, and Xaythany, a peri-urban district to the north of Vientiane, where output is more diversified and on a larger scale. Chemicals and plastics are the leading branches, while construction and public works are the least important. The fifth class, comprising Vientiane and Thakhek, has a wide range of export industries (timber and furniture in Thakhek, textiles and garments in Vientiane) and delivers more elaborate products to the domestic market, with a concentration of agro-processing and machinery, construction and public works; the district of Xienghone (Xayabury) makes a modest contribution to this class through its civil engineering works for irrigation.

Three groups can be identified according to the distribution of industrial manpower. The first group, formed by the vast majority of districts, has no factories. The second group, consisting of the following three classes, shows varying degrees of emerging industry with rates close to average. The second class, which covers the branches of timber and furniture, machinery and vehicles, comprises the five main towns of the Mekong Valley and most of Vientiane Plain, which profits from the proximity of the capital city. In rural areas, this class also includes the border districts of the North and mining districts: limestone in Vangvieng (Vientiane province) and tin in Hinboon (Khammouane).

The third class is distinguished from the second by construction and public works, connected to specific projects, notably in Paksong on the Bolovens Plateau (Champassack) and in Muong Phiang (Xayabury). The fourth class is distinguished by the share of chemicals, since two districts have salt extraction plants: Thoulakhom (Vientiane province) and Vilabuly (Savannakhet). The processing of natural resources explains the rural nature and the fragmented distribution of these two classes. The third group (fifth class), the only really industrial class in terms of workforce, comprises only the district of Hadxaifong, located downstream from Vientiane in the direction of the bridge over the Mekong, which has highly diversified activities. This map differs strongly from the previous one, where three districts of the capital are ahead with more specialised, more capitalised industries.

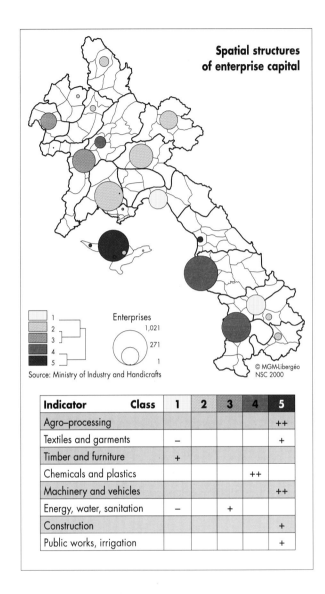

**Spatial structures of enterprise capital**

Enterprises
1,021
271
1

Source: Ministry of Industry and Handicrafts

© MGM-Libergéo
NSC 2000

| Indicator          Class | 1 | 2 | 3 | 4 | 5 |
|--------------------------|---|---|---|---|---|
| Agro–processing          |   |   |   |   | ++ |
| Textiles and garments    | – |   |   |   | + |
| Timber and furniture     | + |   |   |   |   |
| Chemicals and plastics   |   |   |   | ++ |   |
| Machinery and vehicles   |   |   |   |   | ++ |
| Energy, water, sanitation| – |   | + |   |   |
| Construction             |   |   |   |   | + |
| Public works, irrigation |   |   |   |   | + |

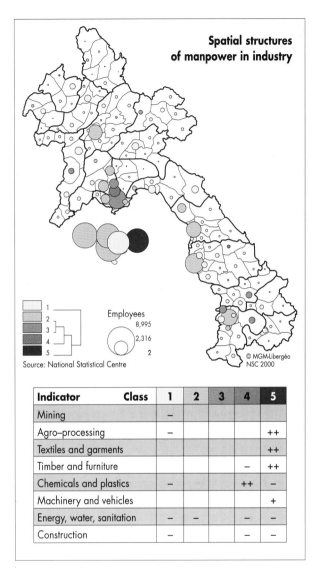

**Spatial structures of manpower in industry**

Employees
8,995
2,316
2

Source: National Statistical Centre

© MGM-Libergéo
NSC 2000

| Indicator          Class | 1 | 2 | 3 | 4 | 5 |
|--------------------------|---|---|---|---|---|
| Mining                   | – |   |   |   |   |
| Agro–processing          | – |   |   |   | ++ |
| Textiles and garments    |   |   |   |   | ++ |
| Timber and furniture     |   |   |   | – | ++ |
| Chemicals and plastics   | – |   |   | ++ | – |
| Machinery and vehicles   |   |   |   |   | + |
| Energy, water, sanitation| – | – |   | – | – |
| Construction             | – |   |   | – | – |

# Chapter 7. Transport, post and telecommunications

In a country with a meridian spatial structure that stretches over 1,755 km of road from Ban Lantui on the Chinese border (Phongsaly) to Khinak on the Cambodian border (Champassack), transport is one of the main constraints on economic development and territorial planning. Distance is also a factor in transverse links. While it has little impact in the southern half of the country, which is only 100 km wide between Ban Lao and the Keo Neua Pass (Khammouane) and no more than 250 km wide at Savannakhet and Pakse, it is much more significant in the North. More than 800 km of mountainous terrain separate Huoixai (Bokeo) on the Thai border in the west from Taichang (Huaphanh) on the Vietnamese border. Although the capital was moved from Luangphrabang to Vientiane in 1553 to occupy a more central position, it is still 650-890 km from the four provincial capitals of the North and 680-840 km from the four provincial capitals of the South.

The road network, mainly built in the 1930s and 1940s, was only partially modernised in the post-colonial period during the two decades of war. In the zone controlled by the royal government, Road 13 between Vientiane and Luangphrabang and the side road leading to the American bases of Long Cheng and Samthong on the western edge of the Xiengkhuang Plateau were rebuilt but not paved. In the zone controlled by the Neo Lao Haksat, priority was also given to strategic objectives, such as the transverse road linking Xamneua to Namtha, the road built with Chinese assistance along the Nam Beng towards Thailand, and the Ho Chi Minh Trail, which ran from the Mugia Pass (Khammouane) to the southern plateaux (Sekong and Saravane) and South Vietnam.

During the first decade after reunification in 1975, traffic was restored on the main roads and Road 9 was opened, with assistance from the socialist countries, as an alternative route to Vietnam via Thailand. At the start of the 1990s the government began gradual reconstruction of the network. Under the 1991-1995 plan, it earmarked 273.5 billion kip ($380 million) for the transport and telecommunications sector, i.e. more than half (51.2%) of all investment (i.e. $83 per capita), 21% of which came from the national budget and 79% from foreign assistance (see State Planning Committee 1996). In the 1996 plan, the sector accounted for 46% of the $181 million invested (see Chi Do Pham, IMF, 1994, p. 115), which broke down as 33% for transport, 6.4% for telecommunications and 6.6% for other infrastructure. In 1995, the sector, the government's main priority during the current transition towards a market economy, employed nearly 6% of the non-farm workforce, with other market services accounting for 31%.

Despite this effort, the road network remains a hindrance to development. The 21,500 km of roads existing in 1997 would be adequate if they were all in good condition. However, as the table opposite shows, paved roads account for only 16.5% of the total. Even combined with gravelled roads, fewer than half (44.6%) are usable all year round. More than three-quarters of national highways are either paved or gravelled, but only a third of provincial roads, which provide access to the districts!

The deficiency in the road network, combined with low income, explain the small size of the vehicle fleet (170,000, i.e. 0.04 per capita) and its uneven distribution: almost 55% of vehicles are concentrated in Vientiane municipality. These two factors also explain the fleet's composition: 75% are motorcycles, 6.3% are cars, and 18% are vehicles for transporting passengers and goods. Vientiane is mainly distinguished by the proportion of cars (74% of the national total) and buses (66%), and, to a lesser extent, by that of motorised tricycles (40%). The poor

| Roads 1997 | Total km | % Types | National | Provincial | District |
|---|---|---|---|---|---|
| Total km | 21,534 | | 6,442 | 7,132 | 7,960 |
| Paved | 3,544 | 16.5 | 47.1 | 1.6 | 5.0 |
| Gravelled | 6,050 | 28.1 | 29.7 | 32.6 | 22.8 |
| Earth | 11,940 | 55.4 | 23.2 | 65.8 | 72.2 |
| | | 100 | 100 | 100 | 100 |

| Vehicles 1996 | Number | % Motorcycles | % Motorised tricycles | % Cars | % Pickups | % Buses | %Lorries | Total |
|---|---|---|---|---|---|---|---|---|
| National total | 169,914 | 76.1 | 3.5 | 6.3 | 6.9 | 1.5 | 5.7 | 100 |
| o/w Vientiane municipality | 90,091 | 74.6 | 2.6 | 8.6 | 7.0 | 1.9 | 5.3 | 100 |
| Vientiane as % of total | 54.6 | 53.4 | 40.4 | 74.3 | 56.1 | 66.4 | 52.5 | |

| Transport 1996 | Total | % Road | % Water | % Air | Total/km | % Road | % Water | % Air |
|---|---|---|---|---|---|---|---|---|
| Passengers (m persons) | 19,032 | 92.2 | 6.6 | 1.2 | 1,021,6 | 91.0 | 2.7 | 6.3 |
| Goods (m t) | 1,516 | 64.5 | 35.4 | 0.1 | 94,7 | 75.8 | 23.8 | 0.4 |

| Telephone 1996 | Total | Vientiane | Provinces | %Vientiane |
|---|---|---|---|---|
| Telephone lines | 18,139 | 13,019 | 5,170 | 71.7 |
| Local urban (m mins.) | 47.7 | 39.7 | 8.0 | 83.2 |
| Inter-city (m mins.) | 10.7 | 4.4 | 6.3 | 41.1 |
| International (m mins.) | 6.2 | 4.9 | 1.3 | 79.0 |

Sources: Atlas data 1996, Ministry of Communication, Transport, Post and Construction.

condition of the road network is all the more detrimental as road accounts for 91% of passenger traffic and 76% of goods traffic. The Mekong and its tributaries are used principally for goods (24%) and air for passengers (6%).

However, major work has been undertaken to improve road infrastructure under the 1996-2000 plan, even if the Asian crisis has slowed this since summer 1997. The first project is the reconstruction of Road 13, which is nearing completion in the North (providing the link with the Chinese network), but which has yet to be completed between Savannakhet and Pakse. Next come the bridges over the Mekong, which ensure continuity with the Thai network. The Tha Deua bridge downstream from Vientiane, financed by Australia and inaugurated in April 1994, should soon make it possible to link Nongkai to Vientiane by railway, the first in Laos. There is also the Pakse bridge, financed by Japan and nearing completion. Technical studies for a third bridge, in Savannakhet, financed by the Asian Development Bank as part of the East–West Corridor highway project, are under way and the bank has commenced feasibility studies for a fourth bridge, in Huoixai or Pakbeng, in the northern economic development quadrangle. To facilitate domestic travel, the main airports are being modernised. Terminals and runways have been rebuilt in Vientiane and Luangphrabang, to be followed by Pakse and Savannakhet. However, the plan to open new international routes (particularly with Malaysia and Singapore) has not survived the Asian crisis.

Progress has been rapid in telecommunications. The first phase of a long-term plan, financed by Australia ($4 million) involved establishing a direct telephone link via satellite with Vientiane. In a second phase, at a cost of $41 million, lent by the World Bank and Japan, Vientiane was equipped with an additional 8,600 lines and the first link of a short-wave network between Luangphrabang and Pakse was set up. A third phase worth $45 million extended this network to all the provincial and district capitals on this axis. The mobile telephony market was opened to private operators with the Thai group Shinawatra, under a Build-Operate-Transfer (BOT) arrangement. A telecommunications network is thus emerging, with 18,100 telephone lines (one for every 261 persons), heavily concentrated in Vientiane. In 1996, the capital had 72% of existing lines; it accounted for 83% of local urban calls and 72% of international calls. The provinces accounted for 59% of inter-city calls and 82% of domestic telegrams.

*Atlas of Laos*

## Road, river and air transport networks

The density of the road network shows up two distinct areas that radiate out from Vientiane municipality: first the provinces of the Mekong Valley, then the peripheral provinces. However, the distribution of roads according to the type of surface shows the privileged position of the mountainous provinces of the North, disadvantaged until the recent work undertaken between Luangphrabang and Muong Xay, and of Savannakhet province, with Road 9. The choices made in the 1996-2000 plan explain these distributions. The western meridian axis of Road 13 services the five main towns of the Mekong Valley, the new nodes of the North (Muong Xay and Namtha) and the most populous plains of the Centre and the South. This is the backbone of the country and its modernisation is nearing completion. The modernisation of the eastern meridian axis (Road 1) is only at the study phase in this plan. It will begin with the Phonsavan–Khamkeuth section, at the junction between the northern and southern networks.

Of the transverse axes, priority is given to the Phoulao–Nameo section (Huaphanh), of strategic

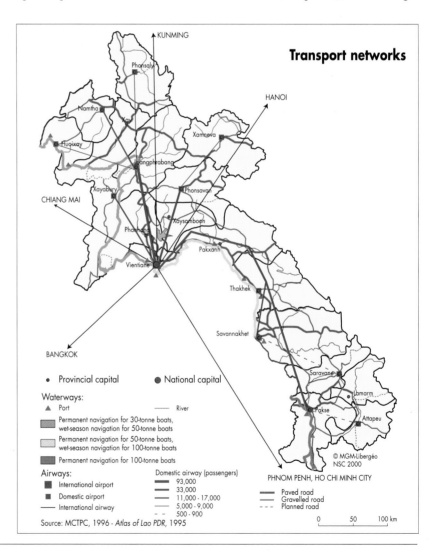

Source: MCTPC, 1996 - *Atlas of Lao PDR*, 1995

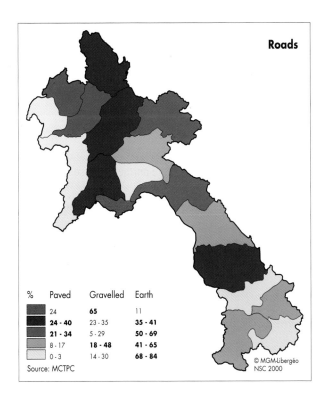

**Roads**

| % | Paved | Gravelled | Earth |
|---|-------|-----------|-------|
| | 24 | **65** | 11 |
| | **24 - 40** | 23 - 35 | **35 - 41** |
| | **21 - 34** | 5 - 29 | **50 - 69** |
| | 8 - 17 | **18 - 48** | 41 - 65 |
| | 0 - 3 | 14 - 30 | **68 - 84** |

Source: MCTPC

© MGM-Libergéo
NSC 2000

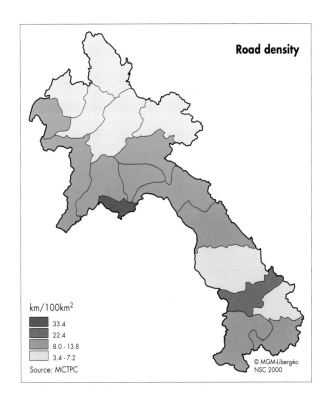

**Road density**

km/100km²

| | |
|---|---|
| | 33.4 |
| | 22.4 |
| | 8.0 - 13.8 |
| | 3.4 - 7.2 |

Source: MCTPC

© MGM-Libergéo
NSC 2000

importance (see page 19). It links Xamneua to Hanoi in the North-East, to Namtha in the west and to Phonsavan in the south. This North–East network is completed by the Phoukhoun (Road 13)–Phonsavan–Nam Kan link, extended towards Vinh. The reconstruction of the Huoixai–Namtha–Boten road in the northern economic development quadrangle is still only at the study phase, as is the alternative in the Nam Beng Valley. In the Centre, the road between the Mekong and the Keo Neua Pass was chosen over the more southerly route between Thakhek and the Kiou Mugia Pass, because it is closer to Vientiane. The road between Savannakhet and the Lao Bao Pass should be modernised as part of the East–West Corridor linking the Mekong to the South China Sea. Further south, the studies under way are investigating the most suitable transverse route to the plateaux of central Vietnam, via Pakse–Lamarm–Dakcheung or Ban Thangbeng (Road 13)–Attapeu–Ban Het. All these transverse roads have two functions: to link neighbouring provinces and to connect the Laotian network to the networks in neighbouring countries.

The Mekong is sectioned off by rapids into three navigable reaches, accessible year-round to vessels of 30-100 tonnes travelling downstream. The reach between Savannakhet and Pakse is impracticable because of the Khemmarat rapids. Separated into four sections, traffic diminishes from the centre towards the periphery. The most dense traffic flows are between Vientiane and Savannakhet, at the end of Road 9, which gives onto the port of Danang; followed by the link between the capital and Luangphrabang. In the North, traffic with Yunnan is limited because of the small tonnage of vessels; it is interrupted in the South by the Khone falls, which cut off access to Cambodia.

In 1996, the domestic air network radiated out from Vientiane, servicing all the provinces in the northern half of the country, except Muong Xay. In the South, where the Mekong Valley is at its broadest, only Savannakhet and Pakse were regularly serviced by air, and Saravane and Attapeu less frequently.

*Atlas of Laos*

# Vehicle fleet, river and road traffic

In one district of Vientiane municipality and the four main towns of the Mekong Valley, between 8% and 13% of the non-farm workforce are employed in the transport, post and telecommunications sector. This proportion is similar, for much smaller workforces, in two districts neighbouring Vientiane; in Huoixai, on the Laotian branch of the northern economic development quadrangle; and in stopover or border districts on road axes. This sector employs some 4.5% to 7.5% of the non-farm workforce in Vientiane municipality and southern Vientiane province, on the north–east axis, at the northern extremity of Road 13, on the road from Pakxanh to the Keo Neua Pass and on the Xe Done axis. In contrast, in the border districts governing access to Vietnam, such as Sepone on Road 9, fewer than 4% of the non-farm workforce are employed in this sector.

The distribution of motorcycles is in line with the population size of the provincial capitals, but their share in the vehicle fleet surpasses 75% in Thakhek, Savannakhet and Pakse, compared with less than 58% in Vientiane and Luangphrabang. Pick-ups are ahead of other types of private vehicle in all the provinces except on the Phonsavan–Xamneua axis, where they are in the same proportion as four-wheel drive vehicles. Pick-ups predominate mainly in Savannakhet and in the North-West, and are combined with cars in Vientiane municipality and downstream from it. As for utility vehicles, there are more lorries than *tuk-tuk* (motorised tricycles) in the provinces of the Mekong upstream from the capital and on the Vientiane–Xamneua axis and, to a lesser extent, in the mountainous peripheries of the South.

Rivers account for more than 75% of goods transport in Bokeo, where the road network is particularly deficient. The proportion is between 17% and 38% in Vientiane municipality and the upstream provinces of the Mekong. In Vientiane province and the mountainous provinces in the South and North, roads account for more than 75% of goods transport. The same differences are apparent for passenger transport, although less stark. Rivers account for less than 42% of the total and play no role at all in Vientiane municipality.

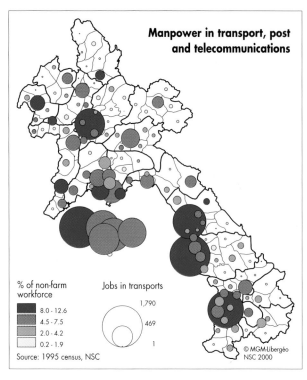

**Manpower in transport, post and telecommunications**

% of non-farm workforce
- 8.0 - 12.6
- 4.5 - 7.5
- 2.0 - 4.2
- 0.2 - 1.9

Jobs in transports
- 1,790
- 469
- 1

Source: 1995 census, NSC

© MGM-Libergéo
NSC 2000

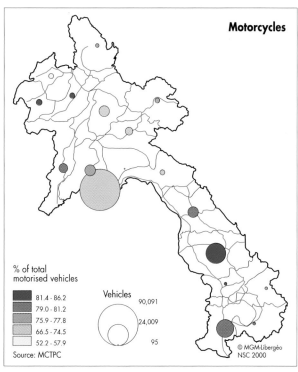

**Motorcycles**

% of total motorised vehicles
- 81.4 - 86.2
- 79.0 - 81.2
- 75.9 - 77.8
- 66.5 - 74.5
- 52.2 - 57.9

Vehicles
- 90,091
- 24,009
- 95

Source: MCTPC

© MGM-Libergéo
NSC 2000

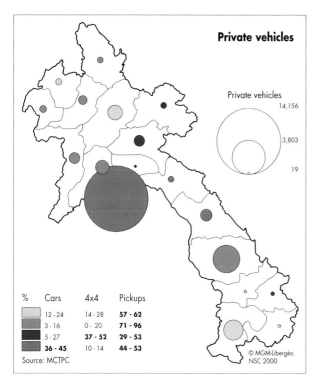

**Private vehicles**

Private vehicles
14,156
3,803
19

| % | Cars | 4x4 | Pickups |
|---|------|-----|---------|
| | 12 - 24 | 14 - 28 | **57 - 62** |
| | 3 - 16 | 0 - 20 | **71 - 96** |
| | 5 - 27 | **37 - 52** | 29 - 53 |
| | **36 - 45** | 10 - 14 | **44 - 53** |

Source: MCTPC

© MGM-Libergéo
NSC 2000

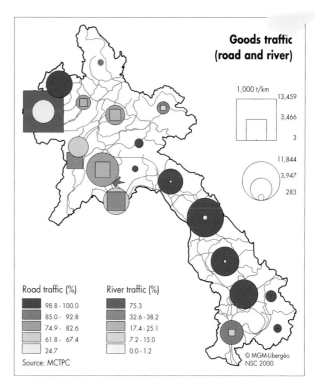

**Goods traffic
(road and river)**

1,000 t/km
13,459
3,466
3

11,844
3,947
283

Road traffic (%)
98.8 - 100.0
85.0 - 92.8
74.9 - 82.6
61.8 - 67.4
24.7

River traffic (%)
75.3
32.6 - 38.2
17.4 - 25.1
7.2 - 15.0
0.0 - 1.2

Source: MCTPC

© MGM-Libergéo
NSC 2000

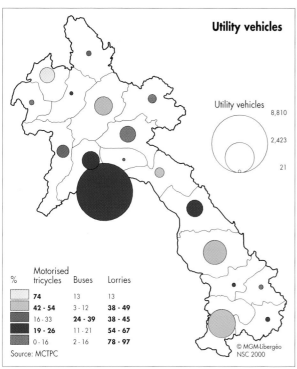

**Utility vehicles**

Utility vehicles
8,810
2,423
21

| % | Motorised tricycles | Buses | Lorries |
|---|---------------------|-------|---------|
| | **74** | 13 | 13 |
| | 42 - 54 | 3 - 12 | **38 - 49** |
| | 16 - 33 | **24 - 39** | **38 - 45** |
| | **19 - 26** | 11 - 21 | **54 - 67** |
| | 0 - 16 | 2 - 16 | **78 - 97** |

Source: MCTPC

© MGM-Libergéo
NSC 2000

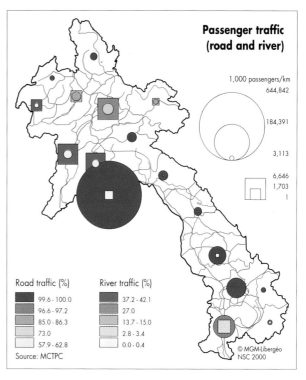

**Passenger traffic
(road and river)**

1,000 passengers/km
644,842
184,391
3,113

6,646
1,703
1

Road traffic (%)
99.6 - 100.0
96.6 - 97.2
85.0 - 86.3
73.0
57.9 - 62.8

River traffic (%)
37.2 - 42.1
27.0
13.7 - 15.0
2.8 - 3.4
0.0 - 0.4

Source: MCTPC

© MGM-Libergéo
NSC 2000

*Atlas of Laos*

# Air traffic

Watay Airport in Vientiane is the leading platform for domestic traffic, in terms of both passengers and freight. Luangphrabang is ahead of Pakse for both, because of its tourist function since the old royal capital was listed as World Heritage. For this reason, its airport was modernised at the same time as Vientiane's and became an international airport in 1999. The tourist attractions of the Plain of Jars and the Hmong villages, and the supply of fresh meat and mid-latitude fruit and vegetables grown on the Xiengkhuang Plateau to Vientiane explain why Phonsavan is ahead of Savannakhet. Namtha is also emerging as a centre for freight, an indicator of the success of consumer products imported from China.

The pattern of international air traffic highlights the preponderance of Bangkok Airport. In 1990, Bangkok's exchanges with Laos accounted for 55% of Watay's traffic in terms of passengers and 51% of freight. Singapore, a new destination created to prepare Lao PDR's integration into ASEAN, but which was subsequently closed as a result of the Asian crisis, was ahead of Kunming for tonnage transported per kilometre, because of its distance. Kunming's ranking is another indicator of the interest in Chinese consumer goods. Traffic with Phnom Penh and Yangon, although smaller, surpassed traffic with Hanoi, as most exchanges with Vietnam were by road. For passengers, Hanoi was just behind Singapore, because of the lack of a direct road link between Vientiane and Phonsavan, and because of the political, economic and cultural ties between Laos and Vietnam. Next came Kunming and Phnom Penh, which benefited from a modest tourist flow, which did not exist with Yangon.

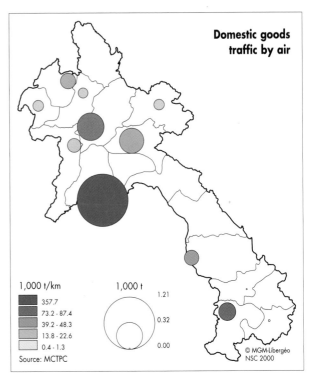

**Domestic goods traffic by air**

1,000 t/km

- 357.7
- 73.2 - 87.4
- 39.2 - 48.3
- 13.8 - 22.6
- 0.4 - 1.3

Source: MCTPC

1,000 t
- 1.21
- 0.32
- 0.00

© MGM-Libergéo
NSC 2000

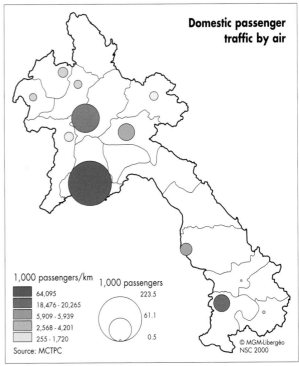

**Domestic passenger traffic by air**

1,000 passengers/km

- 64,095
- 18,476 - 20,265
- 5,909 - 5,939
- 2,568 - 4,201
- 255 - 1,720

Source: MCTPC

1,000 passengers
- 223.5
- 61.1
- 0.5

© MGM-Libergéo
NSC 2000

## International passenger traffic by air

1,000 passengers/km

- 86,487
- 47,523
- 16,999
- 6,403 - 11,114
- 518 - 3,929

1,000

- 138.0
- 39.1
- 0.6

Source: MCTPC
© MGM-Libergéo-NSC 2000

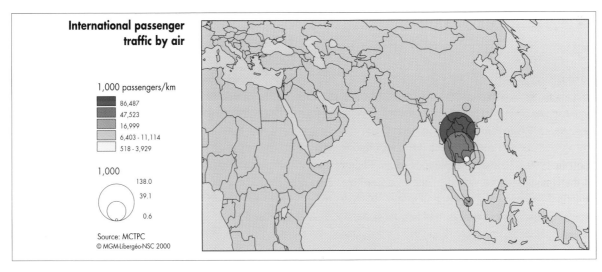

## International goods traffic by air

1,000 t/km

- 550.9
- 281.4
- 199.5
- 43.7
- 10.2 - 13.5
- 2.6

1,000 t

- 0.75
- 0.22
- 0.01

Source: MCTPC
© MGM-Libergéo-NSC 2000

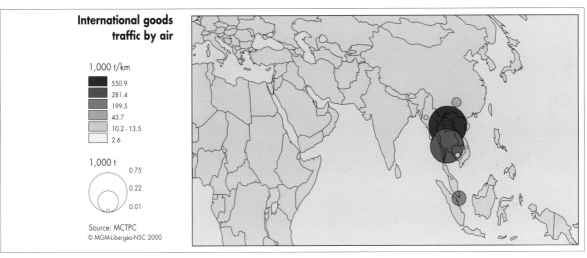

## Postal and telecommunications networks

The post is delivered by air to the provinces located a long distance from the capital. It is only delivered by boat to the districts bordering the Mekong upstream from Vientiane and between Luangphrabang and Muong Khua (Phongsaly) in speedboats along the Nam Ou. Postal deliveries by road extend beyond provincial borders in three regional centres of unequal size. The capital's area of distribution is not limited to the neighbouring provinces. It extends towards Thakhek downstream and southern Xayabury upstream of the Mekong. Luangphrabang services northern Xayabury and Phongsaly, which is also serviced by Muong Xay. Pakse distributes the post to the three mountainous provinces of the South. Sekong in the South and the western provinces of the North, from Xayabury to Phongsaly, do not have a network centred on the provincial capital, which accentuates their peripheral position.

The capital has the only international telecommunications centre, serviced by two satellites. A meridian network of short-wave stations connects Vientiane to the provincial capitals traversed by Road 13

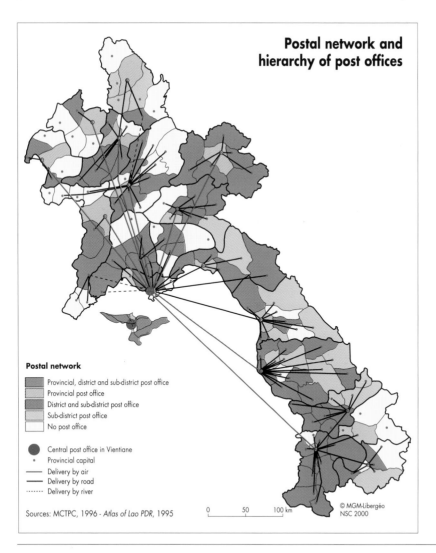

### Postal network and hierarchy of post offices

**Postal network**

- Provincial, district and sub-district post office
- Provincial post office
- District and sub-district post office
- Sub-district post office
- No post office

● Central post office in Vientiane
· Provincial capital
— Delivery by air
— Delivery by road
······ Delivery by river

Sources: MCTPC, 1996 - *Atlas of Lao PDR*, 1995

0    50    100 km

© MGM-Libergéo
NSC 2000

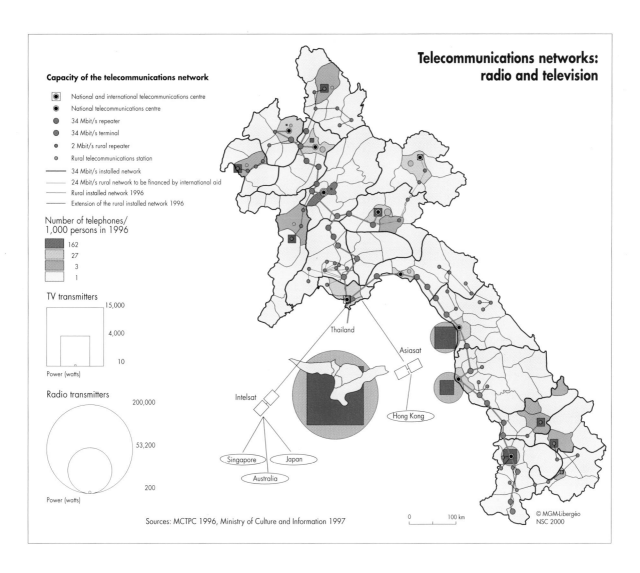

## Telecommunications networks: radio and television

**Capacity of the telecommunications network**

- ◉ National and international telecommunications centre
- ◉ National telecommunications centre
- ● 34 Mbit/s repeater
- ● 34 Mbit/s terminal
- • 2 Mbit/s rural repeater
- • Rural telecommunications station
- —— 34 Mbit/s installed network
- —— 24 Mbit/s rural network to be financed by international aid
- —— Rural installed network 1996
- —— Extension of the rural installed network 1996

**Number of telephones/ 1,000 persons in 1996**

- 162
- 27
- 3
- 1

**TV transmitters**

15,000

4,000

10

Power (watts)

**Radio transmitters**

200,000

53,200

200

Power (watts)

Thailand

Asiasat

Intelsat

Hong Kong

Singapore  Japan

Australia

Sources: MCTPC 1996, Ministry of Culture and Information 1997

0    100 km

© MGM-Libergéo
NSC 2000

---

from Namtha in the North to Khong in the South, favouring the more densely populated Mekong Valley. In addition to this axis, there are six branches. In the North, one branch, along the existing road, services Huoixai, in the northern economic development quadrangle; and another the districts in Phongsaly, thus offsetting the province's isolation. Two other branches in Luangphrabang link Xayabury and the two north-eastern provinces along the existing roads. A staggered fifth branch, that follows the old road from Hinboon to Khamkeuth, services the border districts that lead to the Keo Neua and Kiou Mugia Passes and the new

hydroelectric power plant sites. An open loop around the Bolovens Plateau connects the four provinces of the South. Here again, the axis along Road 9 in Savannakhet is neglected, as is most of Luangphrabang province.

## Postal and telephone traffic

In a country where the emerging telephone network is exclusively urban, domestic postal traffic shows a clear provincial hierarchy. Vientiane dominates three of the four other towns of the Mekong Valley, with Phonsavan a long way ahead of Thakhek, because of the large Hmong community in Vientiane. There is considerably more outbound than inbound post in two of the large towns—Vientiane and Pakse—and in two medium-sized towns in the North, Huoixai and Xamneua, which govern exchanges with Thailand and Vietnam. The dominance of Vientiane is more marked for international mail, ahead of Savannakhet and Luangphrabang. In a central group including the provinces neighbouring Vientiane, which centralises international exchanges, outbound post is a long way ahead of inbound post, with the tourist function explaining the leading position of Luangphrabang and the strong position of Phonsavan.

Urban local calls dominate the telephone traffic in Vientiane municipality and city, which has three-quarters of the available lines. Urban local calls are in equal proportion to intercity and international calls in the four other large towns of the Mekong Valley. Inter-city calls are predominant in the provincial capitals of the North, while lines are still being installed in the three mountainous provinces of the South. This disparity is corrected by domestic telegrams, with the peripheral provinces making up the bulk of the traffic with Vientiane municipality and Savannakhet, which has many districts not serviced by telephone.

Television transmitters, shown on the tele-communications map on the previous page, were first installed in the mainly lowland areas of Vientiane and the provinces of the Mekong Valley downstream from the capital. In a second phase, during the 1996-2000 plan, smaller transmitters are being installed in the provincial capitals of the plateaux of the South and North-East, to be followed by those of the North, partitioned by the mountains.

*Transport, post and telecommunications*

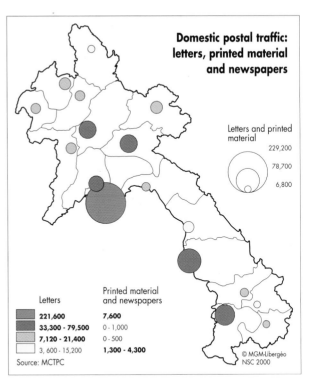

**Domestic postal traffic: letters, printed material and newspapers**

Letters and printed material

229,200
78,700
6,800

| Letters | Printed material and newspapers |
|---|---|
| 221,600 | 7,600 |
| 33,300 - 79,500 | 0 - 1,000 |
| 7,120 - 21,400 | 0 - 500 |
| 3,600 - 15,200 | 1,300 - 4,300 |

Source: MCTPC

© MGM-Libergéo
NSC 2000

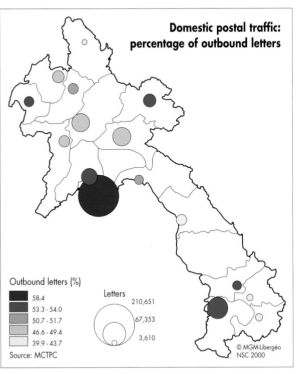

**Domestic postal traffic: percentage of outbound letters**

Outbound letters (%)

| | |
|---|---|
| 58.4 | |
| 53.3 - 54.0 | |
| 50.7 - 51.7 | |
| 46.6 - 49.4 | |
| 39.9 - 43.7 | |

Letters

210,651
67,353
3,610

Source: MCTPC

© MGM-Libergéo
NSC 2000

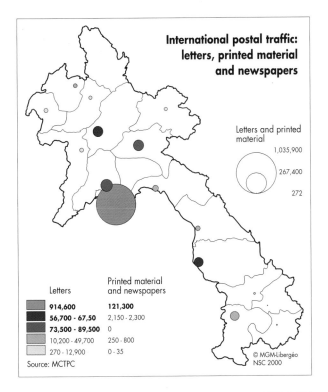

### International postal traffic: letters, printed material and newspapers

Letters and printed material

1,035,900
267,400
272

Letters
- 914,600
- 56,700 - 67,50
- 73,500 - 89,500
- 10,200 - 49,700
- 270 - 12,900

Printed material and newspapers
- 121,300
- 2,150 - 2,300 0
- 250 - 800
- 0 - 35

Source: MCTPC

© MGM-Libergéo
NSC 2000

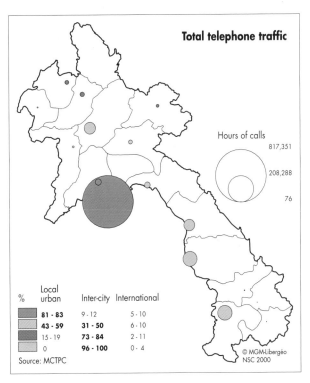

### Total telephone traffic

Hours of calls

817,351
208,288
76

| % | Local urban | Inter-city | International |
|---|---|---|---|
| | 81 - 83 | 9 - 12 | 5 - 10 |
| | 43 - 59 | 31 - 50 | 6 - 10 |
| | 15 - 19 | 73 - 84 | 2 - 11 |
| | 0 | 96 - 100 | 0 - 4 |

Source: MCTPC

© MGM-Libergéo
NSC 2000

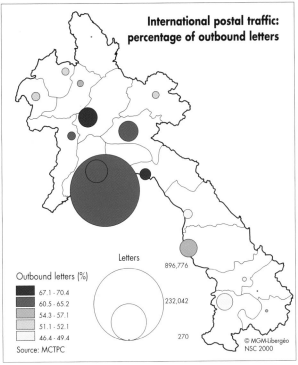

### International postal traffic: percentage of outbound letters

Outbound letters (%)
- 67.1 - 70.4
- 60.5 - 65.2
- 54.3 - 57.1
- 51.1 - 52.1
- 46.4 - 49.4

Letters

896,776
232,042
270

Source: MCTPC

© MGM-Libergéo
NSC 2000

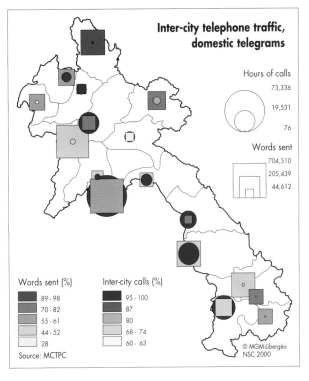

### Inter-city telephone traffic, domestic telegrams

Hours of calls

73,336
19,531
76

Words sent

704,510
205,439
44,612

Words sent (%)
- 89 - 98
- 70 - 82
- 55 - 61
- 44 - 52
- 28

Inter-city calls (%)
- 95 - 100
- 87
- 80
- 68 - 74
- 60 - 63

Source: MCTPC

© MGM-Libergéo
NSC 2000

*Atlas of Laos*

# Spatial structures of transport, post and telecommunications

The first map describes the spatial structures of the road network and the vehicle fleet. Class 1 follows Road 13, the backbone of the road network, with a combination of paved and earth roads, where utility vehicles predominate. The next three classes cover the western provinces of the North, plus Saravane and Attapeu. The heterogeneous road network there combines the three types of road surface in various ways. The second class is distinguished by the extremely low proportion of utility vehicles, and the third by that of private vehicles, with all the indicators around average in the fourth: in Xiengkhuang and Huaphanh provinces in the North-East and Sekong province in the South, which have a high proportion of earth roads, motorcycles prevail over other vehicles.

The second map shows transport flows. The first class comprises the provinces of the Centre linking the Mekong Valley to the Vietnamese border, and the provinces of the plateaux that extend them north and south, where road predominates for all traffic. In the second class, which is the extension of the first into the mountains in the North and into the plains in the South, road transport is less dominant and river traffic slightly more significant. The third class is distinguished by the importance of air traffic in Luangphrabang. In the fourth class, river traffic is predominant in the Mekong Valley upstream from Vientiane. Lastly, in the capital, air traffic attains its highest scores, combined with road for passenger transport and river for goods transport.

The last map shows postal and telephone traffic. Vientiane municipality, the first class, stands out for postal traffic and urban local calls and, to a lesser extent, international calls. The next two classes form a vast central area around the capital, plus the provinces of Savannakhet and Pakse, the second and third largest towns. They are distinguished from Vientiane by a difference of degree. Luangphrabang and Xiengkhuang provinces, which benefit from tourism, also belong to these classes. The last two classes, covering the mountains of North and South, have low postal traffic and are distinguished by the significance of inter-city telephone calls and telegrams.

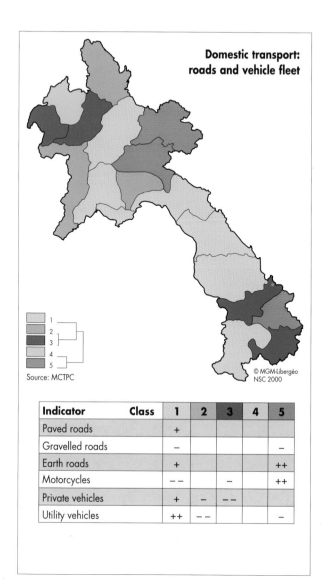

**Domestic transport: roads and vehicle fleet**

1
2
3
4
5

Source: MCTPC

© MGM-Libergéo
NSC 2000

| Indicator          Class | 1 | 2 | 3 | 4 | 5 |
|--------------------------|---|---|---|---|---|
| Paved roads | + | | | | |
| Gravelled roads | − | | | | − |
| Earth roads | + | | | | ++ |
| Motorcycles | − − | | − | | ++ |
| Private vehicles | + | − | − − | | |
| Utility vehicles | ++ | − − | | | − |

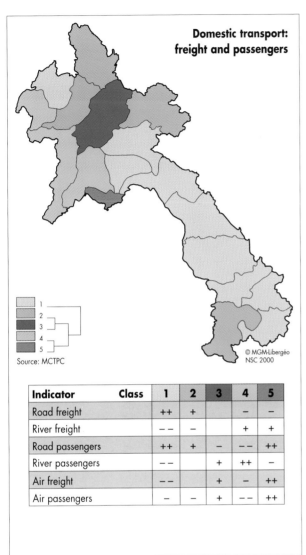

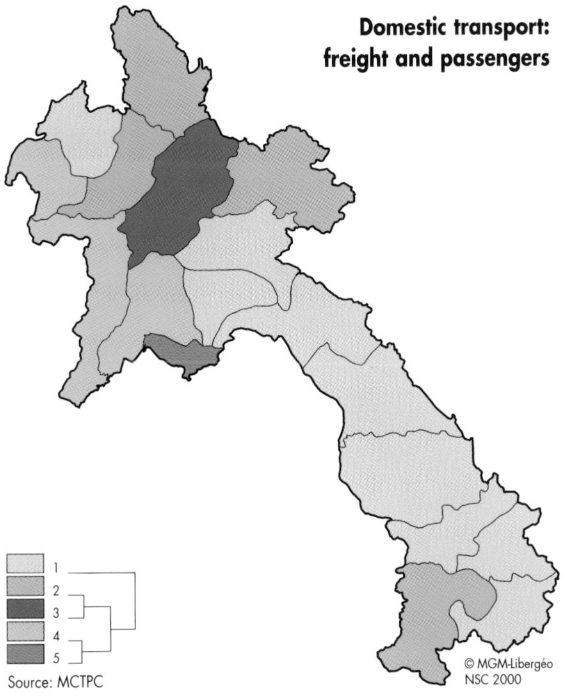
Domestic transport:
freight and passengers
1
2
3
4
5
Source: MCTPC
© MGM-Libergéo
NSC 2000

| Indicator Class | 1 | 2 | 3 | 4 | 5 |
|---|---|---|---|---|---|
| Road freight | ++ | + | | − | − |
| River freight | −− | − | | + | + |
| Road passengers | ++ | + | − | −− | ++ |
| River passengers | −− | | + | ++ | − |
| Air freight | −− | | + | − | ++ |
| Air passengers | − | − | + | −− | ++ |

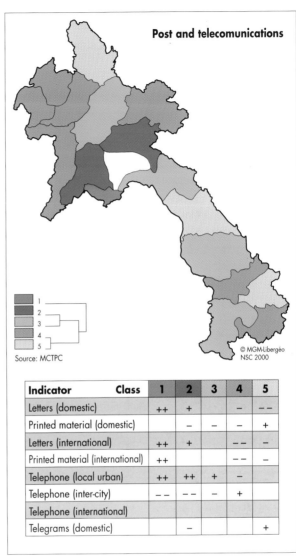

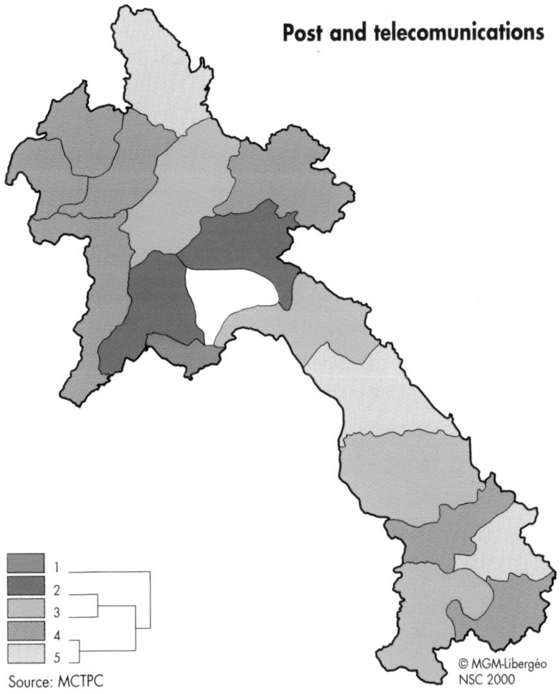
Post and telecomunications
1
2
3
4
5
Source: MCTPC
© MGM-Libergéo
NSC 2000

| Indicator Class | 1 | 2 | 3 | 4 | 5 |
|---|---|---|---|---|---|
| Letters (domestic) | ++ | + | | − | −− |
| Printed material (domestic) | | − | − | − | + |
| Letters (international) | ++ | + | | −− | − |
| Printed material (international) | ++ | | | −− | − |
| Telephone (local urban) | ++ | ++ | + | − | |
| Telephone (inter-city) | −− | −− | − | + | |
| Telephone (international) | | | | | |
| Telegrams (domestic) | | − | | | + |

# Chapter 8.
# Trade and tourism

The size of the market service sector is difficult to evaluate because market services are not generally distinguished from administrative services in the statistics. According to the National Bank (Bank of Lao PDR, 1997), this sector absorbed 11.5% of the foreign investment authorised over the period 1988-1996, which is considerably more than the transport, post and telecommunications sector (8.4%) treated in the previous chapter. This investment was mostly concentrated on hotels and tourism (9%). According to the 1995 census, the sector employs 31% of the non-farm workforce, somewhat less than the civil and military administration (39%). With around 24%, trade plays a dominant role.

Statistics showing the distribution of retail trade are not available. Household ownership of durable goods, derived from the expenditure and consumption survey conducted in 1997-1998 by the National Statistical Centre, provides an indirect indication of the distribution of retail trade, since people tend to buy goods in the town nearest their place of residence. Because of transport problems, domestic trade has been compartmentalised into three markets, although Laos is already a small country (population 4.7 million) with low per capita income ($381 in 1996), even if this has almost doubled since 1990 ($200), according to the National Bank.

The banking sector reforms implemented between 1991 and 1996 separated the central bank from the seven state-owned commercial banks: the Lao Foreign Trade Bank (BCEL), the Agricultural Promotion Bank and five regional banks that have branches in several provinces. The reforms also opened the sector to two joint banks and to seven foreign banks (six Thai banks and one Malaysian bank). The sector remains small, with deposits totalling 269 billion kip ($282.5 million) and loans 207 billion kip ($217.6 million) in 1996. The BCEL handles 45% of deposits and 30% of loans, the other state-owned or joint banks 35% and 22%, and the foreign banks 20% and 19% respectively.

Tourism has seen spectacular development, with an increase from 14,400 visitors in 1990 to 463,200 in 1997, the year in which tourism contributed $73.3 million, i.e. nearly 23% of foreign currency earnings from exports. International tourism contributed 55%, regional tourism from neighbouring countries 44% and tourism related to the extension of visas 1%. More than half (56.5%) of tourists are Thais; three-quarters are nationals from countries of the peninsula; and even 79% if the Chinese from Yunnan are included. ASEAN countries provide 76% of tourists and Asia as a whole 87%. International tourists enter mainly through Vientiane—via the airport and the bridge over the Mekong—followed by the most peripheral border checkpoints, Huoixai in the North (36% of local entries) and Songmek (Champassack) in the South (15%). The five other border checkpoints are open only to tourists from neighbouring countries. Despite the investments made, the development of tourism is limited by transport problems, and by the quality and capacity of accommodation, which counts only 7,120 beds—66% in hotels and 33% in guesthouses.

The 1,000 km river border along the Mekong with Thailand, separating population groups of the same Lao culture, and the 4,000 km of mostly mountainous land borders are difficult to monitor. The economy is therefore open by nature and trade with neighbouring countries is active because of the difficulty of domestic travel. Only a small proportion of this trade is recorded: official statistics largely underestimate the country's openness, but are a good indicator of trends. The share of foreign trade in GNP rose from 43% to 59% between 1991 and 1996, with exports accounting for 19% and imports 40%

| Sector (%) | Trade | Tourism | Banking | Services | Other | Total |
|---|---|---|---|---|---|---|
| Investment 1988-96[1] | 0.9 | 9.0 | 1.1 | 0.1 | 0.4 | 11.5 |
| Non-farm workforce[3] | 23.6 | 1.3 | 0.6 | 0.9 | 4.8 | 31.2 |

| Tourism[2] | 1996 | 1997 | Region of origin 1997 | Laos | Luangphrabang |
|---|---|---|---|---|---|
| Income ($m) | **43.6** | **73.3** | ASEAN | 76.3 | 7.8 |
| International | 58.6 | 54.7 | Rest of Asia | 10.9 | 17.0 |
| Regional | 36.6 | 44.2 | Europe | 8.3 | 59.1 |
| Visa extensions | 4.8 | 1.1 | North America | 3.9 | 15.3 |
|  |  |  | Other | 0.6 | 0.8 |
| Total | 100 | 100 |  | 100 | 100 |

| Exports [1] | 1991 | 1996 | Imports [1] | 1991 | 1996 |
|---|---|---|---|---|---|
| **Total ($m)** | **96.6** | **322.6** | **Total ($m)** | **215** | **690** |
| Timber and furniture | 39.2 | 28.0 | Consumer goods | 66.1 | 44.6 |
| Undressed timber | 3.1 | 10.6 | Capital goods, o/w | 20 | 40.2 |
| Garments | 15.7 | 19.9 | construction, electricity | 8.6 | 14.7 |
| Manufactured products | 13 | 8.6 | machinery, equipment | 4.0 | 10.3 |
| Electricity | 22.1 | 9.2 | other | 7.4 | 15.2 |
| Motorcycle assembly | – | 3.9 | Industrial inputs, o/w | 11.1 | 11.9 |
| Agricultural products | 3.8 | 5.5 | garments | 6.4 | 10.1 |
| Coffee | 31 | 7.7 | motorcycle assembly | 4.7 | 1.8 |
| Car re-export | – | 0.0 | Gold and silver | 2.3 | 2.7 |
| Gold re-export | – | 4.7 | Cars for re-export | – | 0.0 |
| Other | – | 1.9 | Electricity, other | 0.5 | 0.2 |
| Total | 100 | 100 |  | 100 | 100 |

Sources: 1. *Economic and Financial Sector Statistics*, Bank of Lao PDR, 1997. 2. *Laos Tourism Statistical Report* 1997, National Tourism Authority. 3. 1995 census, NSC.

in 1996. In the space of six years, exports were multiplied in absolute value by 3.3 ($96.6 million to $322.6 million), and imports by 3.2 ($215 million to $690.3 million). The pace of import growth caught up with that of export growth with the expansion of industrialisation, which requires the import of raw materials and spare parts. This trend is curbed by the cost of exporting goods that transit through Bangkok, which is 20-35% higher than that of goods whose final destination is the Thai capital. This also explains why the value of exports as a proportion of the value of imports rose only slightly from 45% to 47%.

There has been considerable diversification of exports. Between 1991 and 1996, the share of electricity shrank substantially, from 22% to 9%, and that of timber less sharply, from 42% to 39%, after the export of undressed timber from the reservoirs of future hydroelectric dams was reauthorised. Exports of manufactured products fell back to 29%, after peaking at 36% in 1993 (of which 20% were garments), while tripling in absolute value (from $28 million to $92

million). Agricultural products almost doubled their share (from 7% to 13%), while motorcycles dropped from 15% to 4% between 1993 and 1996, as the domestic market absorbed a larger share of output. Re-exported goods—cars to China until 1994, then gold—accounted for 5% of the total in 1996.

The structure of imports has been rebalanced and simplified. Between 1991 and 1996, the reduction of the share of consumer goods in imports from 66% to 45% was more than offset by a doubling of the share of capital goods, from 20% to 40%. This percentage breaks down as 15% for the hydroelectric dams under construction, 10% for other development projects, and most of the remaining 15% for imports financed by foreign aid. The contribution of industrial inputs grew slightly (12%) and imports of gold remained steady (3%). Cars for re-export have disappeared; imported electricity in the Centre diminished before disappearing altogether in 1998 after the operational start-up of the Nam Theun-Hinboon hydroelectric plant.

## Trading businesses and banks

Businesses that sell or repair cars and motorcycles are distributed fairly evenly in the districts of the capital and in the towns of the Mekong Valley from Thakhek to Pakse. Muong Xay, the main road node, is the only town in the North with this type of service. Import–export businesses, which are more numerous, follow the same basic pattern of distribution, with a few differences. Chanthabuly district in the capital and Savannakhet city, where Road 9 to Vietnam begins, are clearly ahead, while Pakse is further behind because import–export activities spread out into two neighbouring districts. Other important areas are the other districts of Vientiane municipality, central and peri-urban, the Bolovens Plateau for coffee and Kenethao for cotton, and, in the North, Huoixai in the northern economic development quadrangle and Muong Khua, on the road to Vietnam.

The network of state-owned commercial banks covers all the provinces except Xaysomboun. The branches in Vientiane handle 85% of deposits and 71% of loans. The dominance of the BCEL is more stark for deposits than for loans. Elsewhere, banking activity is generally proportional to the size of the provincial capitals, with one exception: Pakse is under-represented for deposits. The banks in the provinces neighbouring the capital and those in the mountainous peripheries of the South are the least active. The regionalisation of banking separates the North from the North-East and the Centre from the South. It also isolates Vientiane and its periphery, which have two banks, one of which is restricted exclusively to the municipality.

Foreign banks are authorised only in Vientiane. The most recent is the Lao-Viet Bank. The Malaysian Public Bank is marginal and the two joint banks are not performing better than the six Thai banks. Competition between the Thai banks limits their dominant position on the capital market.

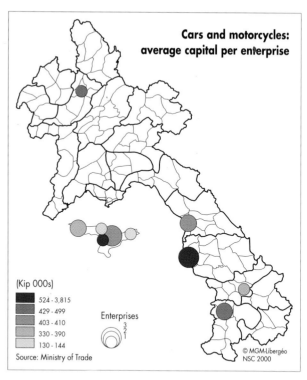

**Cars and motorcycles: average capital per enterprise**

(Kip 000s)
- 524 - 3,815
- 429 - 499
- 403 - 410
- 330 - 390
- 130 - 144

Enterprises

Source: Ministry of Trade

© MGM-Libergéo
NSC 2000

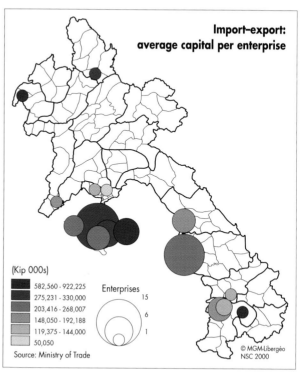

**Import–export: average capital per enterprise**

(Kip 000s)
- 582,560 - 922,225
- 275,231 - 330,000
- 203,416 - 268,007
- 148,050 - 192,188
- 119,375 - 144,000
- 50,050

Enterprises
- 15
- 6
- 1

Source: Ministry of Trade

© MGM-Libergéo
NSC 2000

*Trade and tourism*

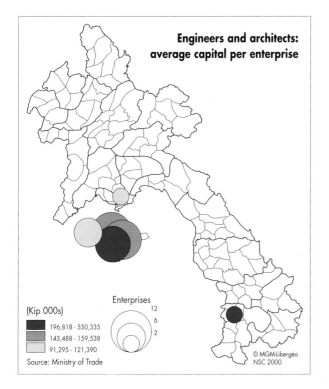

**Engineers and architects:
average capital per enterprise**

Enterprises

12
6
2

(Kip 000s)

- 196,818 - 550,335
- 143,488 - 159,538
- 91,295 - 121,390

Source: Ministry of Trade

© MGM-Libergéo
NSC 2000

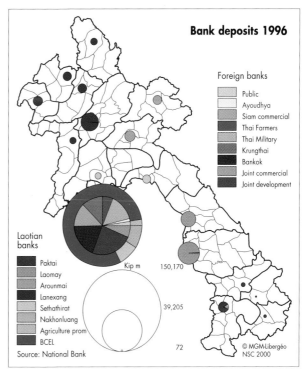

**Bank deposits 1996**

Foreign banks

- Public
- Ayoudhya
- Siam commercial
- Thai Farmers
- Thai Military
- Krungthai
- Bankok
- Joint commercial
- Joint development

Laotian
banks

- Paktai
- Laomay
- Arounmai
- Lanexang
- Sethathirat
- Nakhonluang
- Agriculture prom
- BCEL

Kip m

150,170

39,205

72

Source: National Bank

© MGM-Libergéo
NSC 2000

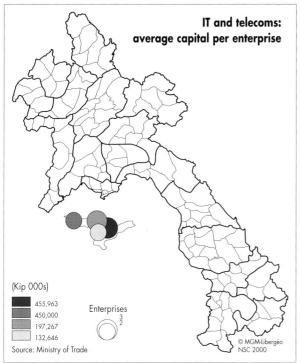

**IT and telecoms:
average capital per enterprise**

Enterprises

3
2

(Kip 000s)

- 455,963
- 450,000
- 197,267
- 132,646

Source: Ministry of Trade

© MGM-Libergéo
NSC 2000

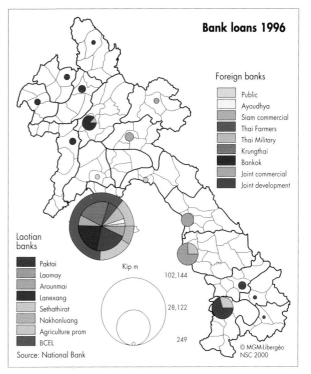

**Bank loans 1996**

Foreign banks

- Public
- Ayoudhya
- Siam commercial
- Thai Farmers
- Thai Military
- Krungthai
- Bankok
- Joint commercial
- Joint development

Laotian
banks

- Paktai
- Laomay
- Arounmai
- Lanexang
- Sethathirat
- Nakhonluang
- Agriculture prom
- BCEL

Kip m

102,144

28,122

249

Source: National Bank

© MGM-Libergéo
NSC 2000

*Atlas of Laos*

## Retail trade: household ownership of durable goods

Ownership of durable goods in 1997 is an indicator both of the standard of living of urban and rural households and of the availability of retail trading enterprises. Motorcycles, whose distribution as a proportion of the vehicle fleet is shown on page 110, are a good indicator of differentiation: 49% of urban households, while only 8% of rural households possess motorcycles. In Vientiane and its periphery, more than 13% of rural households have motorcycles, followed by households in Xiengkhuang and the Mekong Valley. Rural people in the mountainous peripheral provinces do not own motorcycles, even when there is a road junction, such as in Oudomxay. More than 30% of urban households in the Mekong Valley from Luangphrabang possess motorcycles, with the proportion exceeding 40% in the four largest towns and two-thirds in Vientiane. Here again, Phonsavan (Xiengkhuang) stands out from the mountains in the North, probably because of the financial assistance provided by the Hmong diaspora.

Ownership of refrigerators is an indicator both of electrification and of urban lifestyle; 48% of urban households own refrigerators, compared with only 4% of rural households. However, 40% of rural households in Vientiane municipality have refrigerators, and 10% of rural households in Vientiane and Khammouane provinces. In the five largest towns of the Mekong Valley, rates exceed 20%, attaining 72% in Vientiane.

Ownership of television sets is less selective: 72% of urban households and 22% of rural households have televisions. The two maps reflect the development of the network of transmitters, presented on page 115. The Mekong Valley, from Xayabury to Savannakhet, has the highest rates, with the rural households in Vientiane municipality and its periphery standing out from the other provinces. Very few rural households in the mountainous regions have television sets, even though some of the provincial capitals in these areas have low-power television transmitters.

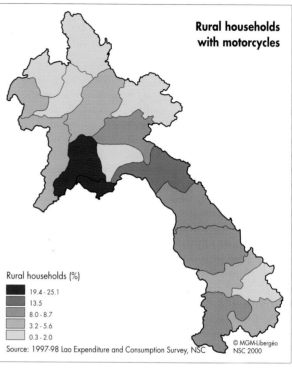

Rural households with motorcycles

Rural households (%)

- 19.4 - 25.1
- 13.5
- 8.0 - 8.7
- 3.2 - 5.6
- 0.3 - 2.0

Source: 1997-98 Lao Expenditure and Consumption Survey, NSC

© MGM-Libergéo
NSC 2000

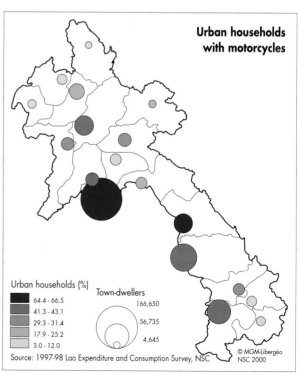

Urban households with motorcycles

Urban households (%)

- 64.4 - 66.5
- 41.3 - 43.1
- 29.3 - 31.4
- 17.9 - 25.2
- 3.0 - 12.0

Town-dwellers

166,650
56,735
4,645

Source: 1997-98 Lao Expenditure and Consumption Survey, NSC

© MGM-Libergéo
NSC 2000

*Trade and tourism*

**124**

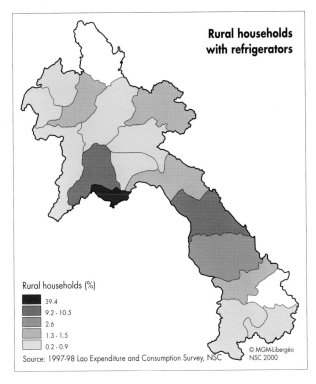

**Rural households
with refrigerators**

Rural households (%)
- 39.4
- 9.2 - 10.5
- 2.6
- 1.3 - 1.5
- 0.2 - 0.9

Source: 1997-98 Lao Expenditure and Consumption Survey, NSC

© MGM-Libergéo
NSC 2000

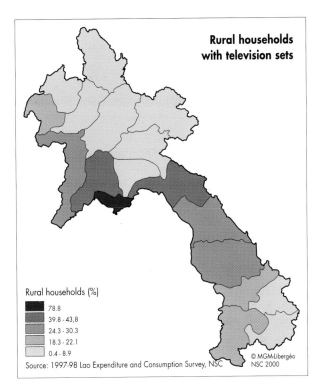

**Rural households
with television sets**

Rural households (%)
- 78.8
- 39.8 - 43,8
- 24.3 - 30.3
- 18.3 - 22.1
- 0.4 - 8.9

Source: 1997-98 Lao Expenditure and Consumption Survey, NSC

© MGM-Libergéo
NSC 2000

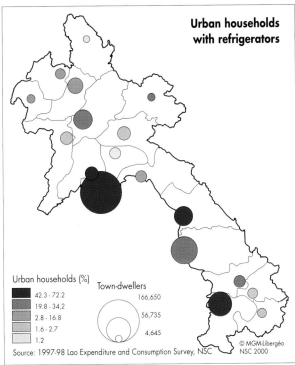

**Urban households
with refrigerators**

Urban households (%)
- 42.3 - 72.2
- 19.8 - 34.2
- 2.8 - 16.8
- 1.6 - 2.7
- 1.2

Town-dwellers
- 166,650
- 56,735
- 4,645

Source: 1997-98 Lao Expenditure and Consumption Survey, NSC

© MGM-Libergéo
NSC 2000

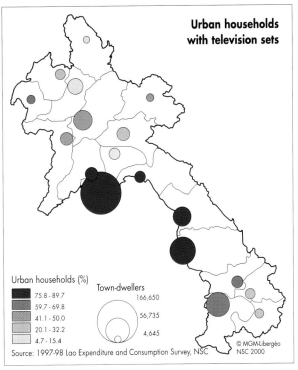

**Urban households
with television sets**

Urban households (%)
- 75.8 - 89.7
- 59.7 - 69.8
- 41.1 - 50.0
- 20.1 - 32.2
- 4.7 - 15.4

Town-dwellers
- 166,650
- 56,735
- 4,645

Source: 1997-98 Lao Expenditure and Consumption Survey, NSC

© MGM-Libergéo
NSC 2000

## Tourist flows

Vientiane and Savannakhet provinces receive the most visitors, respectively half and a quarter of all tourists, because Vientiane has the main bridge over the Mekong and, until 1999, had the only international airport, and Savannakhet has two immigration checkpoints on the borders with Thailand and Vietnam. Despite their attractions, described in the map of natural, historical and religious heritage on page 23, Luangphrabang (the old royal capital) and Champassack (with the ancient Khmer temple of Wat Phou, the Khone Falls and the Bolovens Plateau) receive only 5% of tourists, and Xiengkhuang (with the Plain of Jars and Hmong villages) a mere 2%.

The explanation for this is provided by the table in the introduction to this chapter and by the two maps comparing tourists by region of origin for Laos as a whole and for Luangphrabang. This explanation also applies to Champassack and Xiengkhuang. Almost 60% of visitors to the old royal capital now listed as World Heritage come from Europe. Combined with visitors from North America, the proportion rises to 75%, and to over 90% with other nationals from the Asia-Pacific region, half of whom are Japanese. ASEAN countries provide only 8% of visitors (with 6% coming from Thailand, where domestic tourism is highly developed), although they provide 76% of visitors to Laos as a whole. The majority of visitors from ASEAN countries are involved in cross-border tourism, limited to the province of point of entry and to short stays of a few days at the most, which does not leave time for inland travel.

Tourism accounts for 70% of entries by foreigners, with business and development cooperation accounting for 17% and 12% respectively. Departing Laotians use the same border crossing points in the same proportions as tourists, but these are strongly differentiated according to the purpose of travel. Departures from Vientiane are mainly family visits to the Lao diaspora via the bridge over the Mekong; there are also official missions via the airport. In Savannakhet and the other border provinces, travel for business prevails over cross-border tourism.

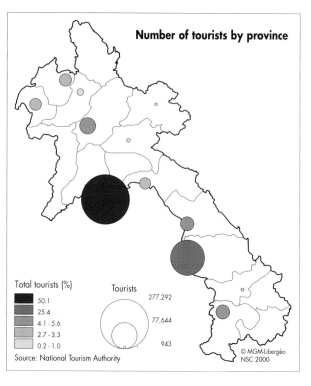

**Number of tourists by province**

Total tourists (%)
- 50.1
- 25.4
- 4.1 - 5.6
- 2.7 - 3.3
- 0.2 - 1.0

Tourists
- 277,292
- 77,644
- 943

Source: National Tourism Authority

© MGM-Libergéo
NSC 2000

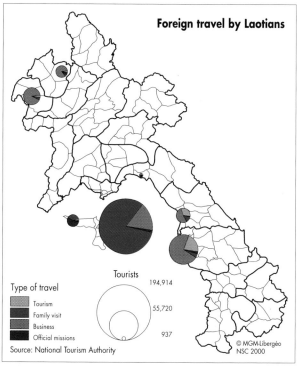

**Foreign travel by Laotians**

Type of travel
- Tourism
- Family visit
- Business
- Official missions

Tourists
- 194,914
- 55,720
- 937

Source: National Tourism Authority

© MGM-Libergéo
NSC 2000

*Trade and tourism*

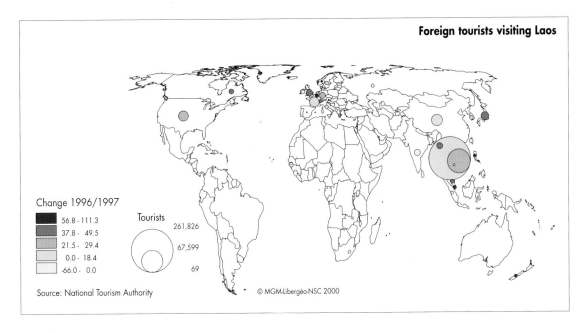

**Foreign tourists visiting Laos**

Change 1996/1997

- 56.8 - 111.3
- 37.8 - 49.5
- 21.5 - 29.4
- 0.0 - 18.4
- -66.0 - 0.0

Tourists

261,826

67,599

69

Source: National Tourism Authority

© MGM-Libergéo-NSC 2000

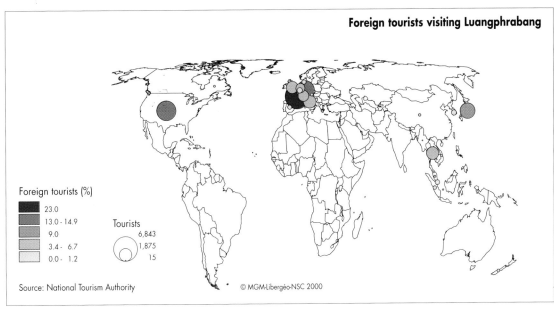

**Foreign tourists visiting Luangphrabang**

Foreign tourists (%)

- 23.0
- 13.0 - 14.9
- 9.0
- 3.4 - 6.7
- 0.0 - 1.2

Tourists

6,843

1,875

15

Source: National Tourism Authority

© MGM-Libergéo-NSC 2000

## Tourist infrastructure and manpower in market services

Tourist infrastructure is a major factor in the potential for the development of tourism. Two main types can be distinguished. The provinces that receive only cross-border tourism, from Huaphanh to Sekong, mainly have restaurants, and their accommodation capacity is low. Xiengkhuang belongs to this type, which explains the small number of visitors despite its tourist attractions. Accommodation capacity is more significant in the other type, which comprises the north-western part of the country, from Vientiane to Phongsaly, as well as Saravane and Champassack in the South. This type can be broken down further according to the predominance of hotels over guesthouses, which is shown in the second map. This map also highlights the meridian traffic axis of Road 13. Hotels predominate in Savannakhet and Khammouane, where cross-border tourism is combined with transit visitors. The proportion of hotels is still substantial in Pakse and Vientiane, where tourism is more diversified. Guesthouses are increasingly common further north, as traffic and tourist visits diminish.

At most, tourism employs only 3% of the non-farm workforce—in the two major tourist sites of Luangphrabang and Vientiane, and at the Vietnamese border in Sepone on Road 9—and 1-2% in the towns traversed by Road 13, in Xiengkhuang and at the Vietnamese border in Khamkeuth on Road 8. The proportion of the non-farm workforce employed in garages and car dealerships, and in services to business, is comparable to that of tourism. The distribution of manpower in garages and car dealerships recalls the map of the average capital of enterprises that sell or repair cars and motorcycles prsented on page 122. The distribution of manpower in services to business, can be compared to the map of loans by commercial banks, presented on page 123. The highest proportions of the non-farm workforce employed in trade (26-37%) are found in the four largest towns. High rates are also found along the road axes of the North and North-East, and the transverse roads in Borikhamxay and Savannakhet. Two regions stand out in particular: Vientiane Plain and the plain between the lower Xe Done and Pakse.

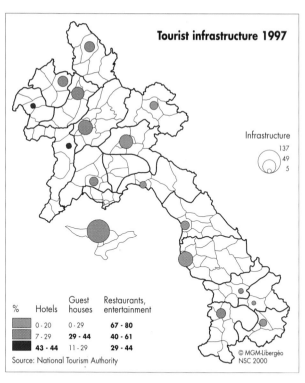

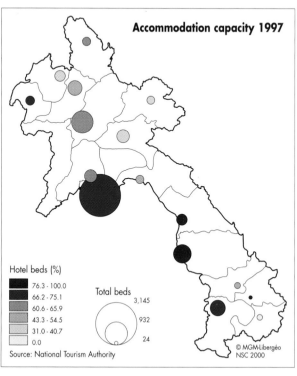

*Trade and tourism*

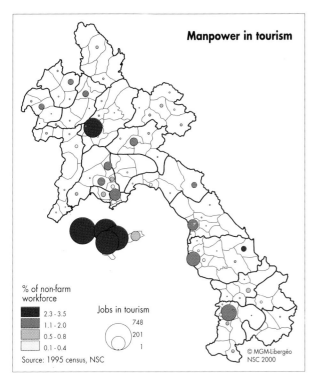

**Manpower in tourism**

% of non-farm workforce

- 2.3 - 3.5
- 1.1 - 2.0
- 0.5 - 0.8
- 0.1 - 0.4

Jobs in tourism

748
201
1

Source: 1995 census, NSC

© MGM-Libergéo
NSC 2000

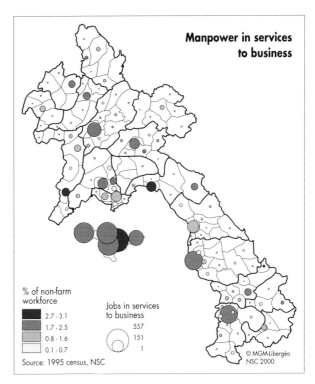

**Manpower in services to business**

% of non-farm workforce

- 2.7 - 3.1
- 1.7 - 2.5
- 0.8 - 1.6
- 0.1 - 0.7

Jobs in services to business

557
151
1

Source: 1995 census, NSC

© MGM-Libergéo
NSC 2000

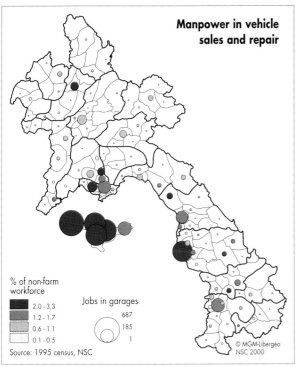

**Manpower in vehicle sales and repair**

% of non-farm workforce

- 2.0 - 3,3
- 1.2 - 1.7
- 0.6 - 1.1
- 0.1 - 0.5

Jobs in garages

687
185
1

Source: 1995 census, NSC

© MGM-Libergéo
NSC 2000

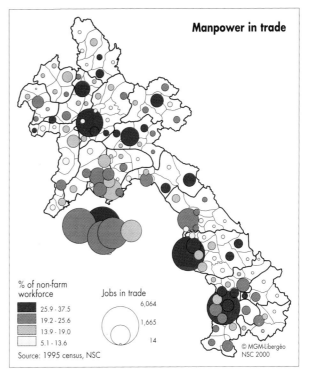

**Manpower in trade**

% of non-farm workforce

- 25.9 - 37.5
- 19.2 - 25.6
- 13.9 - 19.0
- 5.1 - 13.6

Jobs in trade

6,064
1,665
14

Source: 1995 census, NSC

© MGM-Libergéo
NSC 2000

*Atlas of Laos*

## Foreign trade

Laos has seen a complete turnaround of its foreign trade since the economic reforms introduced in 1986 and subsequently extended after the collapse of the Soviet Union in 1989. Over the period 1981-1984, 53.5% of imports and 31.2% of exports were with countries from the Socialist bloc, with the Soviet Union accounting for respectively 33.2% and 3.8% (Christian Taillard, 1989). Since the transition towards a market economy, 60% of trade in 1996 was with ASEAN countries, while Russia accounted for a mere 0.3%. This rapid switch was supported by assistance from western countries and international financial institutions, which took over from Soviet aid.

In 1996, Lao PDR's foreign trade was largely integrated into ASEAN, on which it is more dependent for exports (78%) than imports (52%), although it accounts for less than 1% of trade within this regional organisation. Thailand provides a higher proportion of Lao PDR's imports than Vietnam (45% compared with 30%), but Vietnam absorbs a much higher proportion of Laotian exports than Thailand (48% compared with 4%). Lao PDR's trade also extends to East Asia, which accounts for 9.4% of its foreign trade, totalling 13% of imports and only 1.5% of exports. Lao PDR's main suppliers are Japan (7.6% of imports) and the Chinese-speaking countries (5.4%, with 3.4% from the People's Republic of China). With the exception of Vietnam, Lao PDR has a severe trade deficit with the Asian countries, with imports accounting for over 80% of trade. Lao PDR enjoys a trade surplus with Europe, which accounts for only 3% of foreign trade, but which absorbs a higher proportion (7.4%) of Laotian exports than East Asia. France has an even balance of trade with Lao PDR. The United States absorbs only 2% of Laotian exports.

According to official data, foreign trade is concentrated in the capital (57%) and the two next-largest towns, Savannakhet and Pakse (26% and 11%), followed by the other provinces of the Mekong Valley downstream from Vientiane. The capital and Pakse have a trade deficit. Savannakhet has an even balance of trade and Vientiane province has a trade surplus.

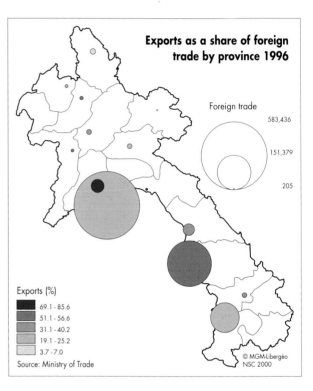

Exports as a share of foreign trade by province 1996

Foreign trade
583,436
151,379
205

Exports (%)
69.1 - 85.6
51.1 - 56.6
31.1 - 40.2
19.1 - 25.2
3.7 - 7.0

Source: Ministry of Trade

© MGM-Libergéo
NSC 2000

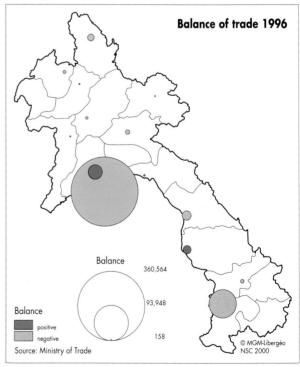

Balance of trade 1996

Balance
360,564
93,948
158

Balance
positive
negative

Source: Ministry of Trade

© MGM-Libergéo
NSC 2000

*Trade and tourism*

**130**

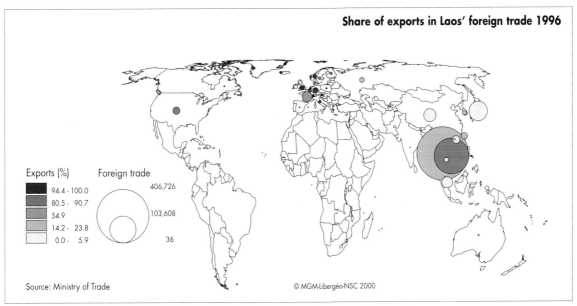

**Share of exports in Laos' foreign trade 1996**

Exports (%)

- 94.4 - 100.0
- 80.5 - 90.7
- 54.9
- 14.2 - 23.8
- 0.0 - 5.9

Foreign trade

- 406,726
- 103,608
- 36

Source: Ministry of Trade

© MGM-Libergéo-NSC 2000

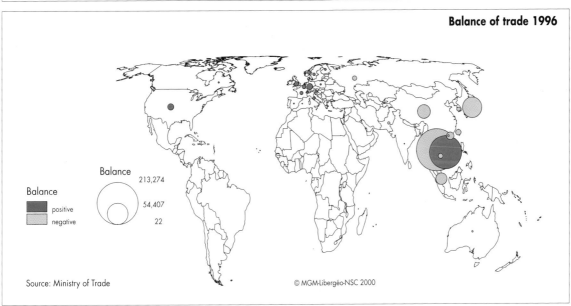

**Balance of trade 1996**

Balance

- 213,274
- 54,407
- 22

Balance

- positive
- negative

Source: Ministry of Trade

© MGM-Libergéo-NSC 2000

*Atlas of Laos*

## Spatial structures of trade and tourism

The structure of the workforce employed in market services is the most diversified in Vientiane, Luangphrabang and Pakse, the main tourist centres, and in Sepone on the main road to Vietnam. Trade and international tourism are at their peak in these areas. In the second class, the trade function prevails over cross-border tourism and services in the districts governing access to neighbouring countries or benefiting from international tourism (Xiengkhuang). The third class, characterised by services to businesses, comprises Pakxanh, a district of Vientiane, and Paklai, which is ahead of Xayabury in terms of trade with Thailand. The last two classes, with the lowest rates, consist of the peripheral, mountainous provinces of the North and South.

In terms of availability of market services, the first class comprises the main towns and has the highest rates for most of the variables, particularly banking and foreign trade. This class also includes towns that are less populous, but which have a border function, such as Huoixai (Bokeo) and Kenethao (Xayabury). In the second class, which includes Luangphrabang, medium-sized towns in intermediate locations and small peripheral towns, rates vary, with foreign trade remaining significant, but sales of cars and motorcycles at their lowest. In the third class, made up of the medium-sized towns of the North, rates decline except for banking, which is around average. Import–export businesses characterise the last two classes, positively in the fourth, especially with coffee from the Bolovens Plateau, and negatively in the last.

In the extreme classes for household ownership of durable goods—the well-equipped households in Vientiane municipality and the under-equipped households in the inland provinces of the North—there is no difference between urban and rural households. The second class has similar advantages to the first, but rural households clearly lag behind urban ones in Vientiane, Khammouane and Savannakhet provinces. The same disparity is found in the three last classes, with increasingly low levels, in Bokeo in the northern economic development quadrangle, in Saravane and Champassack in the South, followed by the central provinces of the North and the mountainous provinces of the South.

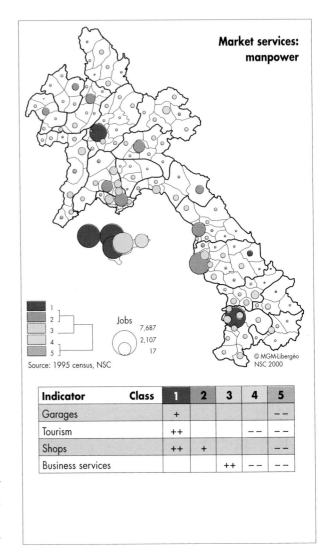

**Market services: manpower**

Jobs
7,687
2,107
17

Source: 1995 census, NSC

© MGM-Libergéo
NSC 2000

| Indicator | Class | 1 | 2 | 3 | 4 | 5 |
|---|---|---|---|---|---|---|
| Garages | | + | | | | – – |
| Tourism | | ++ | | | – – | – – |
| Shops | | ++ | + | | | – – |
| Business services | | | | ++ | – – | – – |

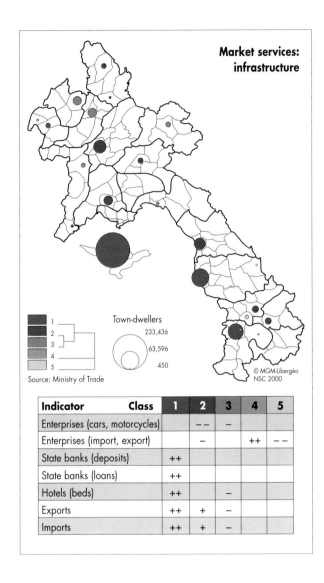

**Market services: infrastructure**

Town-dwellers
- 233,436
- 63,596
- 450

1
2
3
4
5

Source: Ministry of Trade

© MGM-Libergéo
NSC 2000

| Indicator Class | 1 | 2 | 3 | 4 | 5 |
|---|---|---|---|---|---|
| Enterprises (cars, motorcycles) | | – – | – | | |
| Enterprises (import, export) | | – | | ++ | – – |
| State banks (deposits) | ++ | | | | |
| State banks (loans) | ++ | | | | |
| Hotels (beds) | ++ | | – | | |
| Exports | ++ | + | – | | |
| Imports | ++ | + | – | | |

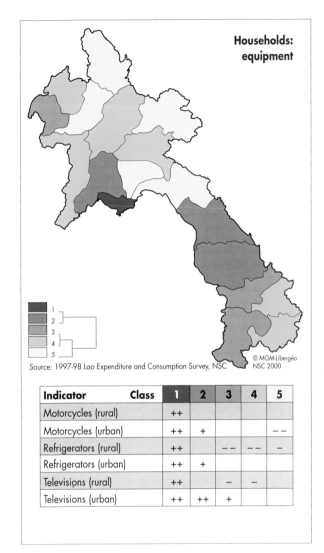

**Households: equipment**

1
2
3
4
5

Source: 1997-98 Lao Expenditure and Consumption Survey, NSC

© MGM-Libergéo
NSC 2000

| Indicator Class | 1 | 2 | 3 | 4 | 5 |
|---|---|---|---|---|---|
| Motorcycles (rural) | ++ | | | | |
| Motorcycles (urban) | ++ | + | | | – – |
| Refrigerators (rural) | ++ | | – – | – – | – |
| Refrigerators (urban) | ++ | + | | | |
| Televisions (rural) | ++ | | – | – | |
| Televisions (urban) | ++ | ++ | + | | |

# Chapter 9.
# Education, health and culture

Services to the population account for a slightly higher proportion of the tertiary sector than the market services presented in the previous chapter, with 39% and 37% respectively of the non-farm workforce. The administration, both civilian and military, is predominant with 21%, and education (13.5%) is a long way ahead of health (3.4%) and culture (0.7%). However, in terms of public investment, according to the report on the implementation of the 1991-1995 plan, the order is quite different: education received 6.6% of the 534.3 billion kip invested, health 3.5%, the administration nearly 3%, and information and culture 1.8%.

The education sector saw a massive increase in the number of pupils and teachers during the 20 years that followed the founding of Lao PDR. Numbers of pupils and teachers more than doubled in primary education, and were multiplied respectively by 4.5 and 6.6 in junior secondary education and by 17 and 25 in senior secondary education, which had dipped very low, mainly because a large number of teachers left the country in 1975. Despite this rapid expansion, primary school enrolment is 60-70% in the 6-10 age group, according to various sources cited by the World Bank and the International Monetary Fund (IMF). This rate is lower than that in Vietnam (78%) and most of the ASEAN countries.

Although the pace of increase in the number of pupils slowed during the 1991-1995 plan, particularly at primary and junior secondary level (25%), while the senior secondary level (14-16 year olds) maintained a high rate (38%), this rapid growth has posed numerous problems. First, a large number of teachers had to be trained. Despite the efforts made, 35% of primary teachers, 13% of junior secondary teachers and 16% of senior secondary teachers are under-qualified, according to the IMF (1994). This deficiency, combined with inadequate financial resources

(6.6% of public investment and 2.5% of GNP) and sustained population growth explain the low efficiency of education. Only 30% of primary and junior secondary pupils actually complete their course of study; the proportion is more than half in senior secondary school. More than a third of pupils are seriously behind in their primary or secondary education. The ethnic minorities, which account for 33% of the population, provide only 27% of primary pupils and only 5% of junior secondary pupils, although they have their own teacher training colleges. These indicators give an idea of the magnitude of what remains to be accomplished to improve both the coverage and the quality of teaching in the two priority levels of primary and junior secondary education.

Just over two-thirds of primary schools offer all five years of primary education; 85% of villages have their own school, but in 42% of these villages, especially in rural areas, only the first two years of primary schooling are offered. Primary education accounts for 78% of pupils and more than two-thirds of teachers, but receives only 43% of funding; in contrast, junior secondary education accounts for 12% of pupils, 19% of teachers and 21% of the budget. The lack of qualified trainers—all the more acute as trained teachers tend to leave the education sector for the civil service or the private sector—and the requirements of a market economy argue in favour of adapting resources to needs in a country where 85% of the economically active population is engaged in agriculture.

In number, pharmacies account for two-thirds of health infrastructure, and public hospitals and dispensaries only a quarter. The predominance of pharmacies, which can be attributed to the significance of self-medication, is confirmed by the share of health spending borne by families (57% of the total), according to the 1992-1993 expenditure and consumption survey, cited by the World Bank. To treat the sick, people turn to pharmacies in 58%

| Education 1995-6 [1] | Pupils/students | Teachers | Kip/pupil 93[2] | Pupils/class | Pupils/teacher | Teachers/10,000 persons [1] |
|---|---|---|---|---|---|---|
| Total | 970,648 | 39,006 | 5,810 | | | |
| Pre-school | 3.6% | 5.1% | 3.0% | 28 | 17.5 | 4.4 |
| Primary o/w | 78.1 | 63.6 | 43.0 | 31 | 31.0 | 54.2 |
|   early primary | 24.0 | 20.7 | | 28 | 29.0 | 17.6 |
|   complete primary | 54.1 | 42.9 | | 33 | 31.0 | 36.6 |
| Junior secondary | 12.4 | 18.8 | 21.0 | 34 | 16.0 | 16.0 |
| Senior secondary | 4.3 | 7.0 | 7.0 | 38 | 15.5 | 6.0 |
| Technical o/w | 0.6 | 2.0 | 3.0 | 23 | 7.0 | 1.7 |
|   junior | 0.1 | 0.6 | | 15 | 6.0 | |
|   senior | 0.5 | 1.4 | | 27 | 8.0 | |
| Higher education | 0.7 | 2.0 | 4.0 | 41 | 9.0 | 1.7 |
| Teacher training o/w | 0.3 | 1.5 | 9.0 | 23 | 5.0 | 1.2 |
|   junior secondary | 0.1 | 0.6 | | 18 | 3.0 | |
|   primary | 0.2 | 0.7 | | 26 | 7.0 | |
|   early primary | | 0.2 | | 28 | 4.0 | |
| Administration | | | 10.0 | | | |
| Total | 100 | 100 | 100 | | | |

Sources: 1. Ministry of Education; 2. Lao PDR Social Development Assessment, World Bank 1995.

| Health infrastructure [1] | % | No./10,000 persons | Manpower in health[2] | % | No./10,000 persons |
|---|---|---|---|---|---|
| Total, o/w | 2,455 | | Total, o/w | 10,671 | |
|   pharmacies | 68.2 | 3.7 | Postgraduate specialists | **1.3** | 0.3 |
|   dispensaries | 19.7 | 1.1 | Graduates, o/w | **13.9** | 3.5 |
|   clinics | 6.3 | 0.3 |   doctors | 10.4 | 2.4 |
|   hospitals | 5.8 | 0.3 |   pharmacists and chemists | 3.5 | 1.1 |
| **Total** | **100** | | Assistants, o/w | **29.5** | 6.8 |
| Hospital beds | 4,872 | 10.6 |   physician assistants | 15.9 | 3.7 |
| **Health funding** | **kip/capita [3]** | **1991-5 kip bn [4]** |   pharmacist/chemist assistants | 13.1 | 3.1 |
| Total, o/w | 6,706 | 18.78 | Other health workers, o/w | **49.4** | 11.5 |
|   families | 57 | |   nurses | 42.0 | 9.8 |
|   foreign assistance | 24 | 70.70 |   laboratory workers | 7.4 | 1.7 |
|   national budget | 19 | 29.30 | Administration | **5.9** | 1.3 |
| **Total** | **100** | **100** | **Total** | **100** | |

Sources: 1. National Statistical Centre; 2. Ministry of Health; 3. Lao PDR Social Development Assessment, World Bank 1995; 4. Implementation of the 1991-95 Socio-Economic Development Plan, SPC 1996.

of cases, to public health infrastructure in 12% of cases and to traditional healers in 17% of cases. In rural areas, the proportions are still 50%, 8% and 25% respectively, even though 66% of rural-dwellers have access to nurses and 43% to physician assistants.

The public health network is extensive but not very efficient and receives only 3.5% of public investment and 1.8% of GNP. As a result, the indicators for infant mortality (125 per 1,000 live births) and fertility (5.6 children per woman) are closer to patterns found in Africa than in Asia. The priority needs to be given to better distribution of skills—which are too concentrated in towns—and improved utilisation of spending, shared between families and the state. Cost recovery in exchange for quality service should make the public sector more competitive and properly remunerate the skills of health workers, 15% of whom have a university education and 30% an intermediate assistant level. Aligning wages with the cost of living should contribute to improving the productivity of health and education systems.

# Health infrastructure and manpower in health

There are strong contrasts in the distribution of hospital beds (11 per 10,000 persons on average). Beds are concentrated in the districts of the capital and the main towns of the Mekong Valley (with Savannakhet ranking some distance behind) and in the provincial capitals of the mountainous peripheries where development programmes have been undertaken: Huaphanh and Phongsaly in the North, Sekong and Attapeu in the South. The map of private clinics (0.3 per 10,000 persons) shows a similar distribution, with a stronger presence in the central part of the country and in the capitals of the northern provinces that occupy intermediate positions. Pharmacies (4 per 10,000 persons) are much better distributed along the Luangphrabang–Luangnamtha axis and spread out into the rural districts in Xiengkhuang, on Vientiane Plain and in the Mekong Valley south of Thakhek. They are also found in the border districts governing access to China and Vietnam.

Graduate pharmacists and chemists (1.1 per 10,000 persons on average) are much more concentrated in the capital than graduate and postgraduate doctors (2.4 per 10,000 persons), with a similar pattern for physician assistants and pharmacist assistants (3.1 and 3.7 per 10,000 persons respectively). Only the hospitals in Vientiane have modern diagnostic equipment, which increases the capital's domination. Furthermore, doctors are better represented in the capital and the neighbouring provinces, and to a lesser extent in the Mekong Valley downstream, while physician assistants predominate in the peripheries of the South and in Luangphrabang in the North.

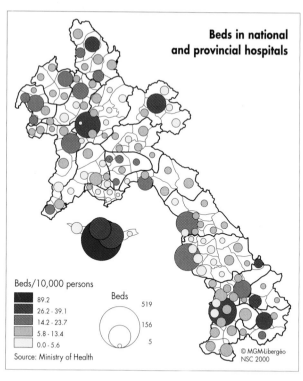

**Beds in national and provincial hospitals**

Beds/10,000 persons
- 89.2
- 26.2 - 39.1
- 14.2 - 23.7
- 5.8 - 13.4
- 0.0 - 5.6

Beds
- 519
- 156
- 5

Source: Ministry of Health

© MGM-Libergéo
NSC 2000

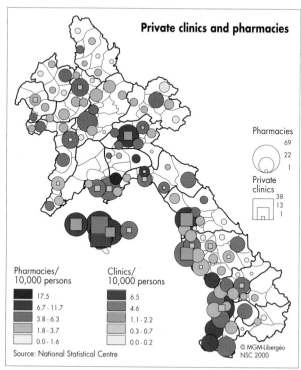

**Private clinics and pharmacies**

Pharmacies
- 69
- 22
- 1

Private clinics
- 38
- 13
- 1

Pharmacies/ 10,000 persons
- 17.5
- 6.7 - 11.7
- 3.8 - 6.3
- 1.8 - 3.7
- 0.0 - 1.6

Clinics/ 10,000 persons
- 6.5
- 4.6
- 1.1 - 2.2
- 0.3 - 0.7
- 0.0 - 0.2

Source: National Statistical Centre

© MGM-Libergéo
NSC 2000

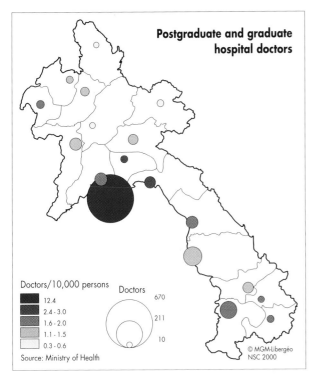

**Postgraduate and graduate hospital doctors**

Doctors/10,000 persons
- 12.4
- 2.4 - 3.0
- 1.6 - 2.0
- 1.1 - 1.5
- 0.3 - 0.6

Doctors
- 670
- 211
- 10

Source: Ministry of Health

© MGM-Libergéo
NSC 2000

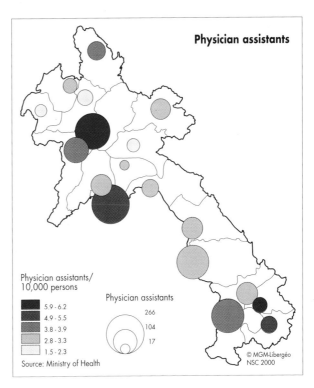

**Physician assistants**

Physician assistants/
10,000 persons
- 5.9 - 6.2
- 4.9 - 5.5
- 3.8 - 3.9
- 2.8 - 3.3
- 1.5 - 2.3

Physician assistants
- 266
- 104
- 17

Source: Ministry of Health

© MGM-Libergéo
NSC 2000

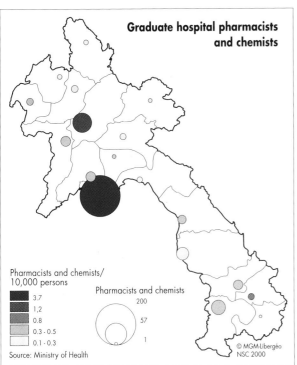

**Graduate hospital pharmacists and chemists**

Pharmacists and chemists/
10,000 persons
- 3.7
- 1,2
- 0.8
- 0.3 - 0.5
- 0.1 - 0.3

Pharmacists and chemists
- 200
- 57
- 1

Source: Ministry of Health

© MGM-Libergéo
NSC 2000

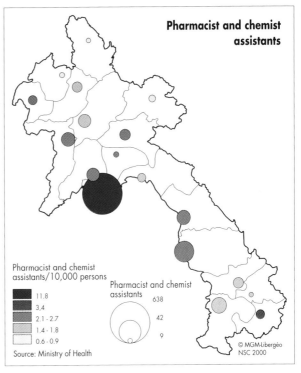

**Pharmacist and chemist assistants**

Pharmacist and chemist
assistants/10,000 persons
- 11.8
- 3,4
- 2.1 - 2.7
- 1.4 - 1.8
- 0.6 - 0.9

Pharmacist and chemist
assistants
- 638
- 42
- 9

Source: Ministry of Health

© MGM-Libergéo
NSC 2000

*Atlas of Laos*

## Manpower in health and education, pre-school and primary education

There is a clear contrast between pharmacist assistants and laboratory workers (1.7 per 10,000 persons on average), highly concentrated in the capital, and nurses (9.8 per 10,000 persons), who are most numerous in Luang-phrabang, in the northern economic development quadrangle and in Khammouane, which occupies an intermediate position between Vientiane and Savannakhet. The distribution of manpower in health, taken from the 1995 population census, confirms the significance of the five largest towns in absolute value, although not relative value, because manpower in industry and market services is higher. The health sector accounts for over 4% of non-farm jobs in the capitals of the peripheral provinces of the North and in the districts of two intermediate provinces between the towns of the Mekong Valley in the South: Khammouane and Saravane.

The education sector employs a much larger workforce (13.5% of non-farm jobs) than the health sector (3.4%) and it is much better distributed. It highlights the meridian urban axis, particularly south of Khammouane, where it extends to the rural riparian districts, and where education accounts for between a quarter and a half of non-farm jobs. This proportion recurs along a diagonal running from southern Xayabury to Huaphanh, via Luangphrabang and Xiengkhuang.

Primary school teachers (54 per 10,000 persons on average) account for two-thirds of all teachers. Therefore the corresponding map shows a similar pattern to the map of manpower in education in absolute value, but differs in relative value. The five main towns and the districts in a broad region around Vientiane have the highest proportions of primary teachers. The first three classes clearly follow the distribution of the Tai-Kadai, with a slight extension in Xiengkhuang province. Pre-school education, much more modest (5% of teachers, 4.4 per 10,000 persons), is mainly present in Vientiane, in the two districts on the north of the plain, and in Thakhek and Savannakhet, while the North is particularly disadvantaged.

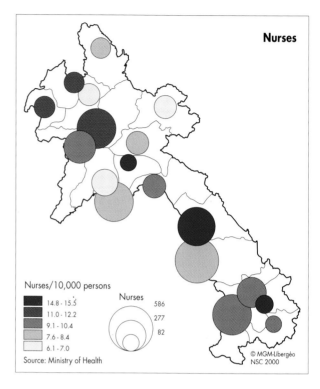

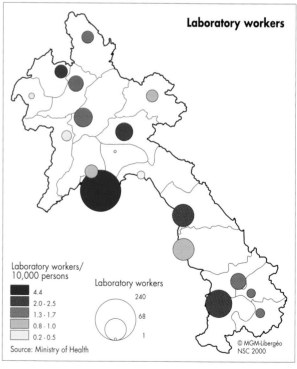

*Education, health and culture*

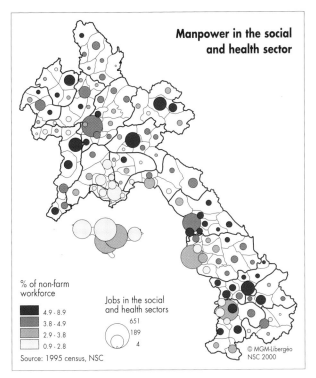

**Manpower in the social and health sector**

% of non-farm workforce

- 4.9 - 8.9
- 3.8 - 4.9
- 2.9 - 3.8
- 0.9 - 2.8

Jobs in the social and health sectors

- 651
- 189
- 4

Source: 1995 census, NSC

© MGM-Libergéo
NSC 2000

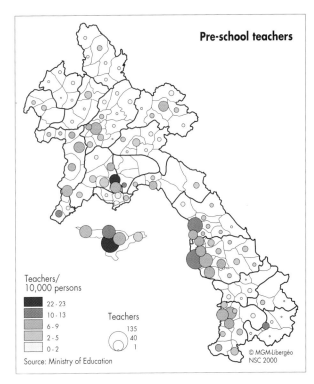

**Pre-school teachers**

Teachers/ 10,000 persons

- 22 - 23
- 10 - 13
- 6 - 9
- 2 - 5
- 0 - 2

Teachers

- 135
- 40
- 1

Source: Ministry of Education

© MGM-Libergéo
NSC 2000

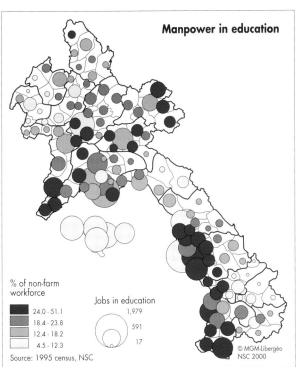

**Manpower in education**

% of non-farm workforce

- 24.0 - 51.1
- 18.4 - 23.8
- 12.4 - 18.2
- 4.5 - 12.3

Jobs in education

- 1,979
- 591
- 17

Source: 1995 census, NSC

© MGM-Libergéo
NSC 2000

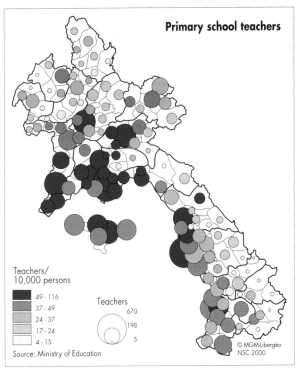

**Primary school teachers**

Teachers/ 10,000 persons

- 49 - 116
- 37 - 49
- 24 - 37
- 17 - 24
- 4 - 15

Teachers

- 670
- 198
- 5

Source: Ministry of Education

© MGM-Libergéo
NSC 2000

*Atlas of Laos*

# Secondary and technical education, higher education and teacher training

Junior and senior secondary teachers (16 and 6 per 10,000 persons respectively on average) show a similar distribution, on a smaller scale, to that of primary teachers. The density of junior secondary teachers declines mainly in the North, particularly in northern Xayabury and in Huaphanh. Rates of senior secondary teachers in the strong points along the Mekong Valley—Vientiane, Savannakhet and Pakse—decline in a southward direction.

Technical education accounts for only 2% of teachers, compared with 26% for conventional secondary education. There are only 1.7 technical teachers per 10,000 persons on average, and these are concentrated in the five main towns of the Mekong Valley. The density of junior technical teachers decreases from north to south. The density of senior technical teachers is the highest in Vientiane municipality and in Pakxanh. Luangphrabang is more advantaged than the towns of the South, because it is the only centre in the North, while the South has two: Savannakhet and Pakse. Technical education is also strongly compartmentalised, because the technical ministries have their own colleges, distinct from those run by the Ministry of Education.

Higher education is exclusive to Vientiane municipality. The peri-urban district of Xaythany, with the science and social science faculties of the National University, is ahead of the urban districts, where the faculty of medicine and the National Polytechnic Institute are located. Senior secondary teachers are trained at the National University. There are four training colleges for junior secondary teachers, located in the four main towns of the Mekong Valley. The density of teachers there is proportional to the population, with the exception of Vientiane, which comes last. Training colleges for primary teachers are concentrated mainly in the provinces of the Mekong Valley. There are four colleges—two in the North and two in the South—to train elementary primary teachers for the main ethnic minorities.

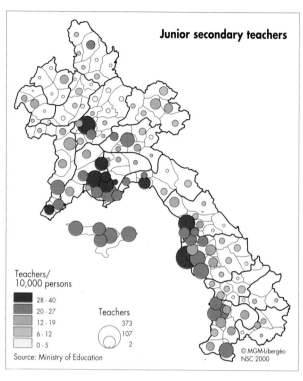

Junior secondary teachers

Teachers/ 10,000 persons

- 28 - 40
- 20 - 27
- 12 - 19
- 6 - 12
- 0 - 5

Teachers
373
107
2

Source: Ministry of Education

© MGM-Libergéo NSC 2000

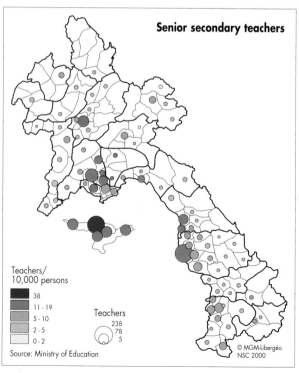

Senior secondary teachers

Teachers/ 10,000 persons

- 38
- 11 - 19
- 5 - 10
- 2 - 5
- 0 - 2

Teachers
238
78
5

Source: Ministry of Education

© MGM-Libergéo NSC 2000

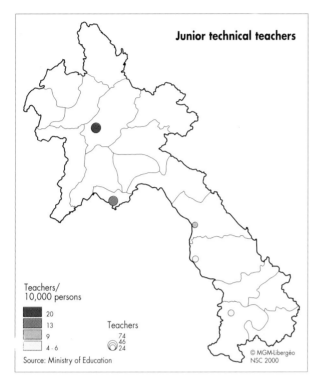

# Junior technical teachers

Teachers/
10,000 persons

- 20
- 13
- 9
- 4 - 6

Teachers
74
46
24

Source: Ministry of Education

© MGM-Libergéo
NSC 2000

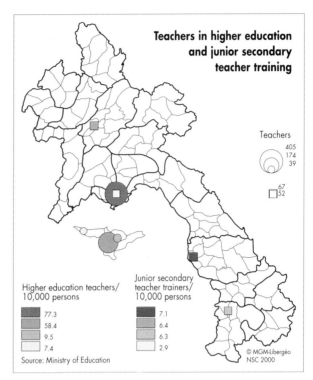

# Teachers in higher education and junior secondary teacher training

Teachers
405
174
39

67
52

Higher education teachers/
10,000 persons

- 77.3
- 58.4
- 9.5
- 7.4

Junior secondary
teacher trainers/
10,000 persons

- 7.1
- 6.4
- 6.3
- 2.9

Source: Ministry of Education

© MGM-Libergéo
NSC 2000

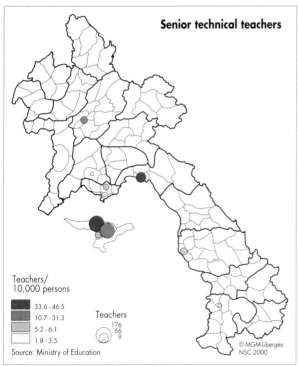

# Senior technical teachers

Teachers/
10,000 persons

- 33.6 - 46.5
- 10.7 - 31.3
- 5.2 - 6.1
- 1.8 - 3.5

Teachers
176
66
9

Source: Ministry of Education

© MGM-Libergéo
NSC 2000

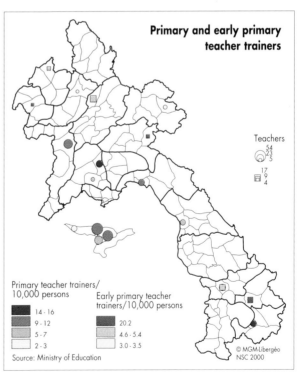

# Primary and early primary teacher trainers

Teachers
54
23
5

17
9
4

Primary teacher trainers/
10,000 persons

- 14 - 16
- 9 - 12
- 5 - 7
- 2 - 3

Early primary teacher
trainers/10,000 persons

- 20.2
- 4.6 - 5.4
- 3.0 - 3.5

Source: Ministry of Education

© MGM-Libergéo
NSC 2000

# Culture, manpower in culture and public administration

There are 6,900 Buddhist monks in Laos (15 per 10,000 persons on average), which is slightly fewer than junior secondary teachers (8,000, i.e. 18 per 10,000 persons), and 11,100 novice monks (23 per 10,000 persons). Since the 1995 census does not give their distribution, provincial data from the Ministry of Culture are used here. The provinces of the Centre, from the Mekong Valley to the Annamese Cordillera, where the ethnic minorities represent a significant share of the population, show a lower density of monks and novice monks (20 to 39 per 10,000 persons; national average 38 per 10,000 persons) than the other riparian provinces, with a majority Tai-Kadai population. Density is over 60 per 10,000 persons in Vientiane municipality and Champassack, but the average number of Buddhist pagodas is higher in Savannakhet, Xayabury and Luangnamtha.

The print media are another indicator of cultural dissemination, in addition to the network of radio and television stations presented on page 115. The distribution of the Party daily *Paxasonj* shows a clear distinction between the Mekong Valley, with a dominant Lao population, and the mountainous inland provinces. The distribution of the literary journal *Vannasinh* is higher in the North, and in Champassack.

The culture, sport and entertainment sector never accounts for more than 2% of the non-farm workforce. The distribution of manpower in this sector, in absolute value, is similar, on a smaller scale, to that of manpower in health (see page 139). In relative value, however, the provinces of the North in an intermediate position are in the lead, alongside the centre of Vientiane city. The workforce in the administration, both civilian and military, accounts for 55% of public-sector workers. Reflecting a similar pattern to health and education, the administration accounts for over 35% of non-farm jobs in the peripheral mountainous districts, and fewer than 20% in the Mekong Valley, in Vientiane and downstream, and in the towns of Luangphrabang and Phonsavan.

*Education, health and culture*

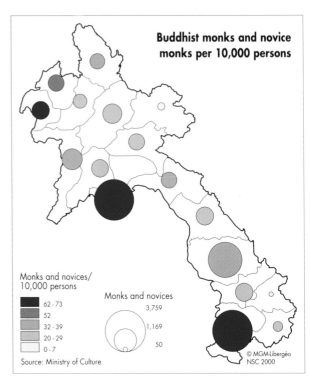

**Buddhist monks and novice monks per 10,000 persons**

Monks and novices/
10,000 persons

- 62 - 73
- 52
- 32 - 39
- 20 - 29
- 0 - 7

Monks and novices
3,759
1,169
50

Source: Ministry of Culture

© MGM-Libergéo
NSC 2000

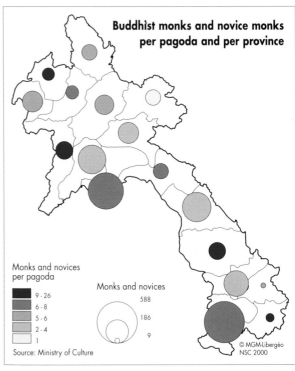

**Buddhist monks and novice monks per pagoda and per province**

Monks and novices
per pagoda

- 9 - 26
- 6 - 8
- 5 - 6
- 2 - 4
- 1

Monks and novices
588
186
9

Source: Ministry of Culture

© MGM-Libergéo
NSC 2000

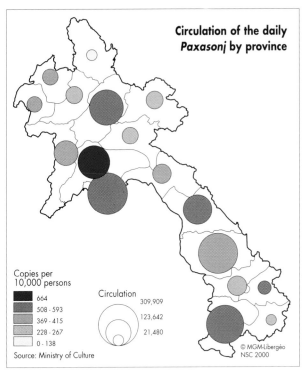

**Circulation of the daily *Paxasonj* by province**

Copies per
10,000 persons

- 664
- 508 - 593
- 369 - 415
- 228 - 267
- 0 - 138

Circulation
- 309,909
- 123,642
- 21,480

© MGM-Libergéo
NSC 2000

Source: Ministry of Culture

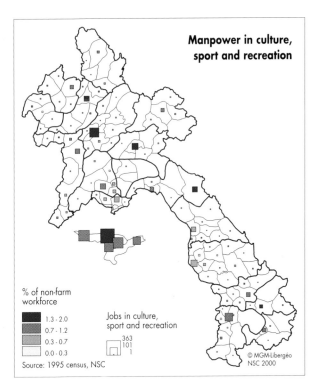

**Manpower in culture, sport and recreation**

% of non-farm
workforce

- 1.3 - 2.0
- 0.7 - 1.2
- 0.3 - 0.7
- 0.0 - 0.3

Jobs in culture,
sport and recreation
- 363
- 101
- 1

© MGM-Libergéo
NSC 2000

Source: 1995 census, NSC

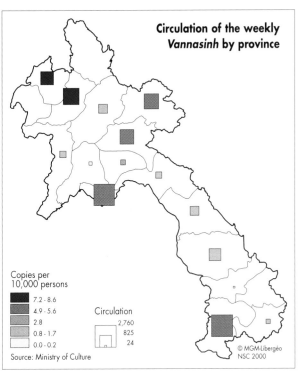

**Circulation of the weekly *Vannasinh* by province**

Copies per
10,000 persons

- 7.2 - 8.6
- 4.9 - 5.6
- 2.8
- 0.8 - 1.7
- 0.0 - 0.2

Circulation
- 2,760
- 825
- 24

© MGM-Libergéo
NSC 2000

Source: Ministry of Culture

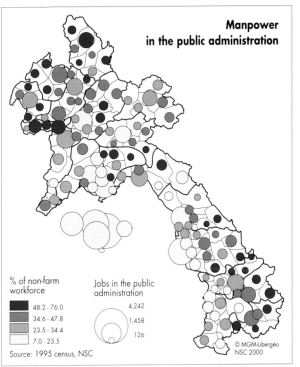

**Manpower in the public administration**

% of non-farm
workforce

- 48.2 - 76.0
- 34.6 - 47.8
- 23.5 - 34.4
- 7.0 - 23.5

Jobs in the public
administration
- 4,242
- 1,458
- 126

© MGM-Libergéo
NSC 2000

Source: 1995 census, NSC

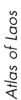

*Atlas of Laos*

## Spatial structures of health and education

The first two classes for health infrastructure contain only one district each. Sisattanak in Vientiane, with several hospitals, represents the first. Longsan (Xaysomboun) represents the second, because of the large number of pharmacies accessible by boat via the Nam Ngum reservoir. The third class, which includes the other districts of the capital and the three large towns downstream, is distinguished by pharmacies, while clinics are around average. Clinics are barely represented in the fourth class, which is by far the largest. In the whole of the North and the mountainous periphery of the South, there is no difference between the provincial capitals and the rural districts. The last two classes, in peri-urban areas (in Vientiane and Pakse) and along the Mekong upstream from Luangphrabang, have low rates of infrastructure.

Vientiane municipality (class 1) has the best qualified health workforce. In most of the Mekong Valley (class 2), nurses and, to a lesser extent, laboratory workers, are more numerous than the two other higher levels of qualification, which are close to the national average. Classes 3 and 4 are clearly more disadvantaged, particularly in terms of graduate pharmacists, and the provinces of Vientiane, Huaphanh and Savannakhet are ahead of the peripheries of the North. The rates of physician assistants and nurses are high (class 5) in Luangphrabang province, the regional hospital centre of the North, and in Sekong and Attapeu provinces, which benefit from numerous development projects.

Vientiane city and the peri-urban district of Xaythany with the National University, plus Savannakhet, Pakse and Sekong, offer the best coverage of teachers across the different levels of education. The districts in the next two classes have average to high rates. The second class, in the northern half, follows the axes linking the capital to Luangphrabang and Xamneua, plus southern Xayabury and Thakhek. The third class, on the periphery of the three main towns of the Mekong Valley, is distinguished by high rates of primary and university teachers. Moving from the fourth to the last class, the decline in the number of primary and junior secondary teachers sharpens in the mountainous districts with an ethnic minority population, especially in the North.

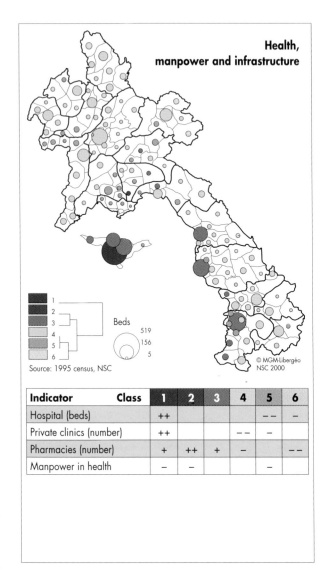

**Health, manpower and infrastructure**

1
2
3
4
5
6

Beds
519
156
5

Source: 1995 census, NSC

© MGM-Libergéo
NSC 2000

| Indicator          Class | 1 | 2 | 3 | 4 | 5 | 6 |
|---|---|---|---|---|---|---|
| Hospital (beds) | ++ | | | | − − | − |
| Private clinics (number) | ++ | | | − − | − | |
| Pharmacies (number) | + | ++ | + | − | | − − |
| Manpower in health | − | − | | | − | |

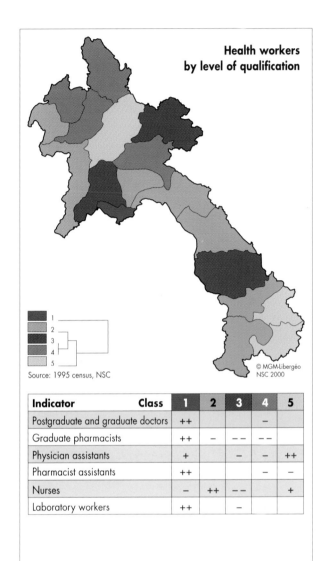

### Health workers by level of qualification

Legend:
1
2
3
4
5

Source: 1995 census, NSC

© MGM-Libergéo
NSC 2000

| Indicator                          Class | 1  | 2  | 3  | 4  | 5  |
|------------------------------------------|----|----|----|----|----|
| Postgraduate and graduate doctors        | ++ |    |    | –  |    |
| Graduate pharmacists                      | ++ | –  | – –| – –|    |
| Physician assistants                      | +  |    | –  | –  | ++ |
| Pharmacist assistants                     | ++ |    |    | –  | –  |
| Nurses                                    | –  | ++ | – –|    | +  |
| Laboratory workers                        | ++ |    | –  |    |    |

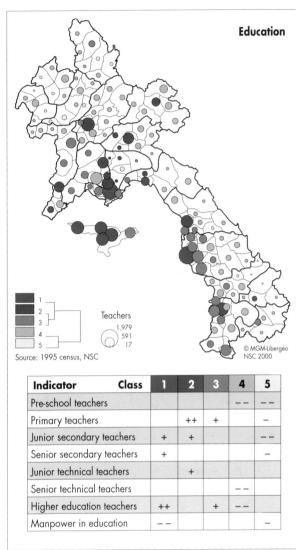

### Education

Legend:
1
2
3
4
5

Teachers
1,979
591
17

Source: 1995 census, NSC

© MGM-Libergéo
NSC 2000

| Indicator                   Class | 1  | 2  | 3  | 4  | 5  |
|-----------------------------------|----|----|----|----|----|
| Pre-school teachers               |    |    |    | – –| – –|
| Primary teachers                  |    | ++ | +  |    | –  |
| Junior secondary teachers         | +  | +  |    |    | – –|
| Senior secondary teachers         | +  |    |    |    | –  |
| Junior technical teachers         |    | +  |    |    |    |
| Senior technical teachers         |    |    |    | – –|    |
| Higher education teachers         | ++ |    | +  | – –|    |
| Manpower in education             | – –|    |    |    | –  |

# Chapter 10.
# Spatial organisation

The conclusion of this atlas combines two approaches to capture the spatial organisation of Lao PDR. First, a ranking index is applied to the districts that appear in the seven synthetic maps constructed with data from 1995 and 1996 in the sectoral chapters. This index is then used to identify eight spatial entities that make up the national territory. Secondly, scales of time and space beyond this spatial and temporal framework are introduced to organise these spatial entities into three regions, with the aid of modelling based on the main territorial structures revealed in the atlas.

## The territorial entities according to the district classification

As with the construction of the synthetic maps according to an ascending hierarchical classification in the sectoral chapters, the classification of the 133 districts that appear in these maps was directed by Franck Auriac. Only the synthetic maps on the scale of the districts and corresponding to the whole population were used. There are seven altogether, which appear at the end of four of the chapters in the atlas and treat the following variables: housing (settlement), manpower in industry (level of education, activity and employment), manpower in market services (trade and tourism), and health and education infrastructure (education, health and culture).

A ranking index was calculated for each district, by adding its ranks in each of the seven synthetic maps. For the map of market services, the districts that do not have this type of business were given a rank of 6, while each of the four districts of Vientiane municipality was given its rank in the map of the urban hierarchy opposite. According to this index, the districts are mapped on a scale ranging from the four most urban districts of

Vientiane city (with the lowest index values) to the isolated peripheral districts (with the highest index values). The territorial discontinuities between neighbouring districts can thus be measured by the differences between their values in the index, which makes it possible to identify the main territorial entities that make up Lao PDR.

The first map shows the structures highlighted throughout the atlas: the contrast between the Mekong Valley and the mountainous inland and border regions in the southern half of the country; the region of Vientiane which extends beyond the plain onto its mountainous edges, the diagonal linking northern Vientiane province to Xiengkhuang and Huaphanh provinces; the divide between the former special zone of Xienghone-Hongsa in northern Xayabury and the southern part of the province; and the homogeneous, low-ranking central block of Luangphrabang province contrasting with the relative differentiation of the provinces that border it to the north and west.

The classification of the most urbanised districts in the first map is still rough, with only three levels. Therefore, a map of the urban hierarchy was constructed, with the size of the population represented by circles and the ranking index by a range of colours. The hierarchisation of the urban network, one of the major factors in territorial management and regional planning, is broken down into five classes. The first three comprise the main towns of the Mekong Valley and the last two the capitals of the peripheral provinces and districts on Vientiane Plain.

The first class, both by population size (55,000 to 65,000 according to the 1995 census) and by ranking index (between 10 and 13.5), is composed of the three districts of Vientiane bordering the Mekong, with the main structural element of the city being the arc formed by the river bank. The second class comprises the second and third-largest

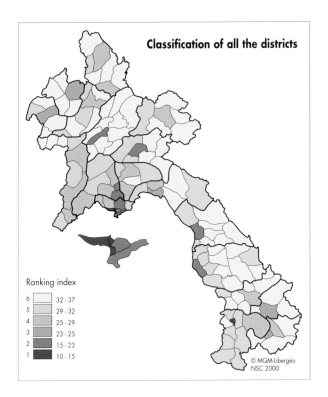

**Classification of all the districts**

Ranking index

| | |
|---|---|
| 6 | 32 - 37 |
| 5 | 29 - 32 |
| 4 | 25 - 29 |
| 3 | 23 - 25 |
| 2 | 15 - 23 |
| 1 | 10 - 15 |

© MGM-Libergéo
NSC 2000

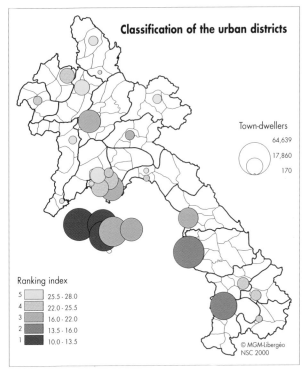

**Classification of the urban districts**

Town-dwellers
64,639
17,860
170

Ranking index

| | |
|---|---|
| 5 | 25.5 - 28.0 |
| 4 | 22.0 - 25.5 |
| 3 | 16.0 - 22.0 |
| 2 | 13.5 - 16.0 |
| 1 | 10.0 - 13.5 |

© MGM-Libergéo
NSC 2000

towns, Savannakhet and Pakse (with respective populations of 62,200 and 47,600). The third class, with indices between 16 and 22, consists of the fourth urban district of the capital (Xaysetha, population 55,000) and two peri-urban districts, Xaythany to the north and Hadxaifong to the east (which count 38,000 and 33,000 town-dwellers respectively). Xaythany governs the road to the South and Hadxaifong the road that leads downstream to the bridge over the Mekong. This class also includes the two other towns on the bank of the Mekong, Luangphrabang and Thakhek (with respective populations of 31,800 and 25,800), as well as Phonsavan (Xiengkhuang), which is the only inland town with a comparable level of urbanisation to those of the Mekong Valley. The Housing and Urban Planning Department's estimate of the population of Phonsavan (16,800) is more in line with its ranking here than the 5,600 town-dwellers indicated in the census.

The fourth and fifth classes, with indices ranging from 22 to 28, cover provincial capitals with populations of less than 15,000, usually in peripheral locations, with the exception of the districts on Vientiane Plain. These

classes are distinguished first by their border functions, such as in Namtha and Huoixai in the northern economic development quadrangle or by a concentration of development projects, such as in Lamarm in the South. Their main feature is relationships of proximity: Xayabury with Luangphrabang; the northern triangle (Namtha, Muong Xay and Muong Khua); and the arc bordering the north and east of the Bolovens Plateau (Saravane, Lamarm and Attapeu). Urban areas are emerging where the close proximity of towns compensates for their relatively small size. These new areas have their own dynamic, which contrasts with the isolation of the most remote provincial capitals where urbanisation is slower, such as Phongsaly compared with Muong Xay and Namtha, or Xamneua compared with Phonsavan. Beyond this, there are only capitals of rural or peri-urban districts with a very low level of urbanisation, typically market centres in the countryside or urban villages.

*Atlas of Laos*

# Identifying eight territorial entities

On the basis of this urban hierarchy, together with the provincial divisions (the main units of territorial management) and the road network, eight territorial entities can be identified referring to elementary models of spatial organisation, presented here from south to north, from the simplest and most common to the more complex and less clearly identifiable.

A model of parallel belts is by far the most common, corresponding to five of the eight territorial entities identified, which is not surprising in a country with a meridian structure that stretches over 1,835 km with a contrast between the Mekong Valley and the mountainous and border interior. In the four provinces of the South, the model has three belts, because of an emerging intermediate area, comprising the Bolovens Plateau and the arc of the three towns that border it to the north and east. The four other entities described by this model have only two belts. In Savannakhet and Khammouane provinces and in eastern Borikhamxay province, the two belts emphasise the opposition between the valley and the mountainous interior. In the meridian section of the Mekong that separates southern Xayabury province from western Vientiane province, the two belts distinguish between the two banks of the river, with more lowlands on the right bank. Lastly, in the provinces of the North-East, two belts separate the western districts, where the Tai-Kadai prevail over the Hmong, from the eastern districts, where the settlement pattern is reversed.

A model of three concentric circles characterises the area in Vientiane's direct sphere of influence. This model is partly inherited from Thai political systems, in which control and obligations diminished and ties became looser between the kingdom and the principalities as their distance from the centre increased (C. Taillard, 1989). This pattern also reflects the conventional model of metropolisation around national capitals: the three urban districts bordering the Mekong form the core; the second circle consists of the centrally located plain districts of Vientiane municipality and Vientiane province; the third circle extends onto the mountainous borders of the plain and into the Mekong Valley downstream from the capital as far as Pakxanh.

A third, more complex model describes the central block of the North, in an intermediate area between the eastern and western parts, organised around the meridian axes of Road 13, the Nam Ou Valley and the Nam Beng Valley, which cannot be hierarchised from the map at this stage of analysis. This is also the case for the two peripheries of the North-West (Bokeo and Luangnamtha) and the North (Phongsaly), which are distinguished by their double remoteness: from the central block of the North and from the national capital.

However, this analysis does not give any indications as to how to group the eight territorial entities identified into a limited number of regions. This is the aim of the five maps presented on the following pages, which add other spatial structures identified in the various chapters of the atlas. These show the correlation between ethnolinguistic and agro-ecological areas, the legacy of transverse and meridian partitions, the return of transnational networks in the Indochinese Peninsula (highlighted by the northern economic development quadrangle in the North-West and the north-eastern diagonal), the network of physical networks and settlement patterns.

The first problem consists in attaching the intermediate provinces—such as eastern Borikhamxay or the special zone of Xayasomboun—to one of the entities they separate. The second problem concerns the provinces split between two entities, such as Borikhamxay (the western part is linked to Vientiane, while the eastern part forms an intermediate transition with the South), and Xayabury (the former special zone of Xienghone–Hongsa belongs to the mountainous North, while the southern part is located at the junction with the region of Vientiane). The third problem is the originality of the north-east diagonal, which, although part of the northern highlands, is distinguished by a higher proportion of Tai-Kadai and by a strong state administration linked to the proximity of Xamneua, the former capital of the zone controlled by the Pathet Lao until reunification. The fourth and last problem concerns the relationship between the central block of the North and its north-eastern and northern peripheries. The five maps that follow attempt to resolve these four problems and to construct an appropriate regional model.

# The eight territorial entities

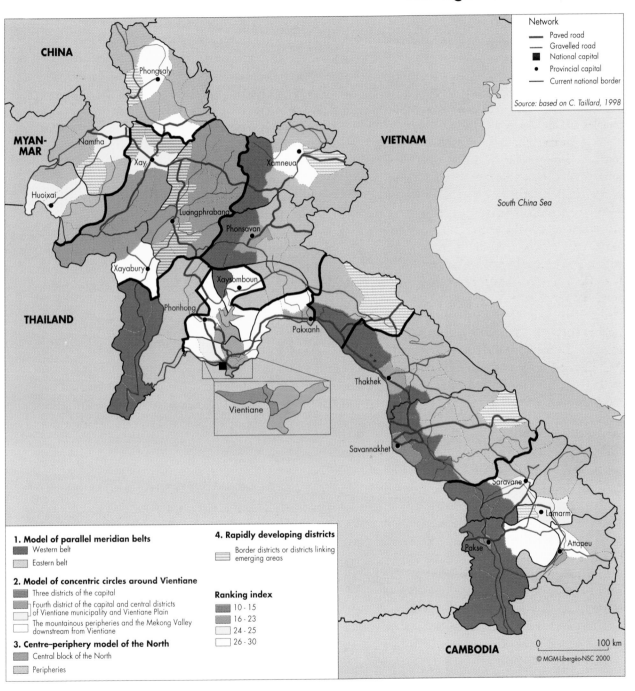

Network
- —— Paved road
- —— Gravelled road
- ■ National capital
- • Provincial capital
- —— Current national border

Source: based on C. Taillard, 1998

CHINA

MYAN-
MAR

Phongsaly

Namtha

Xay

Huoixai

Luangphrabang

Phonsavan

Xamneua

VIETNAM

South China Sea

Xayabury

Xaysomboun

THAILAND

Phonhong

Pakxanh

Vientiane

Thakhek

Savannakhet

Saravane

Lamarm

Pakse

Attapeu

CAMBODIA

**1. Model of parallel meridian belts**
- ▨ Western belt
- ▨ Eastern belt

**2. Model of concentric circles around Vientiane**
- ▨ Three districts of the capital
- ▨ Fourth district of the capital and central districts of Vientiane municipality and Vientiane Plain
- ▨ The mountainous peripheries and the Mekong Valley downstream from Vientiane

**3. Centre–periphery model of the North**
- ▨ Central block of the North
- ▨ Peripheries

**4. Rapidly developing districts**
- ▨ Border districts or districts linking emerging areas

**Ranking index**
- ▨ 10 - 15
- ▨ 16 - 23
- ▨ 24 - 25
- □ 26 - 30

0    100 km

© MGM-Libergéo-NSC 2000

*Atlas of Laos*

# Cultural and natural areas

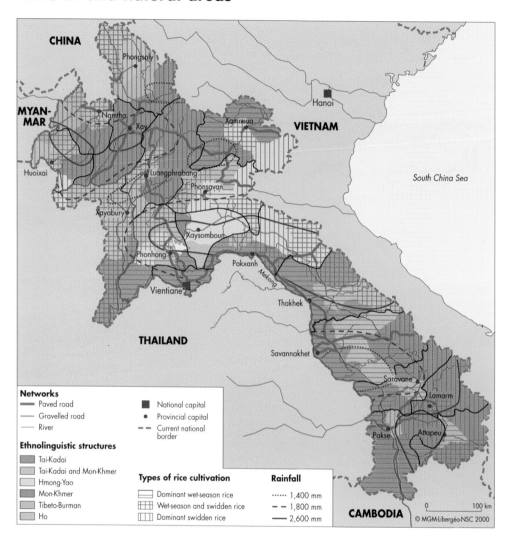

**Networks**
- Paved road
- Gravelled road
- River
- ■ National capital
- ● Provincial capital
- – – Current national border

**Ethnolinguistic structures**
- Tai-Kadai
- Tai-Kadai and Mon-Khmer
- Hmong-Yao
- Mon-Khmer
- Tibeto-Burman
- Ho

**Types of rice cultivation**
- Dominant wet-season rice
- Wet-season and swidden rice
- Dominant swidden rice

**Rainfall**
- ·········· 1,400 mm
- – – 1,800 mm
- —— 2,600 mm

0    100 km

© MGM-Libergéo-NSC 2000

*Spatial organisation*

There is a correlation between the distribution of ethno-linguistic and agro-ecological structures, with wet-season rice dominant in the Mekong Valley populated by the Tai-Kadai, and swidden rice (ray) dominant in the highlands of the North and South populated by Austro-Asiatics. Relief explains certain overlaps, such as wet-season rice in the Austro-Asiatic area of settlement on Savannakhet Plain.

This map suggests a way to organise the territorial entities in the northern part of the country. The entire province of Xayabury, with a combination of wet-season rice and swidden rice and a Tai-Kadai population, is clearly distinct from the central block of the North and bears more resemblance to Vientiane province. This same combination, with the addition of Hmong people, characterises the two provinces of the North-East, which are completely differentiated from the central block of the North and are also attached to Vientiane province. The same agro-ecological combination linked with Tibeto-Burmans and Ho also distinguishes the peripheries to the north and north-west of this central block.

**150**

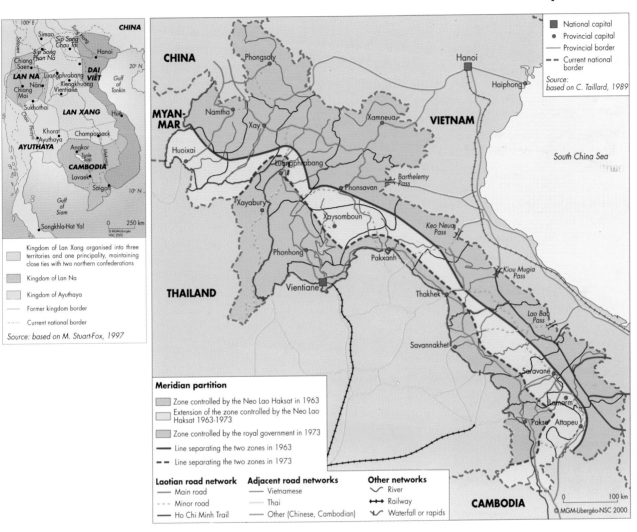

Kingdom of Lan Xang organised into three territories and one principality, maintaining close ties with two northern confederations

Kingdom of Lan Na

Kingdom of Ayuthaya

Former kingdom border

Current national border

*Source: based on M. Stuart-Fox, 1997*

**Meridian partition**

Zone controlled by the Neo Lao Haksat in 1963

Extension of the zone controlled by the Neo Lao Haksat 1963-1973

Zone controlled by the royal government in 1973

Line separating the two zones in 1963

Line separating the two zones in 1973

| **Laotian road network** | **Adjacent road networks** | **Other networks** |
|---|---|---|
| Main road | Vietnamese | River |
| Minor road | Thai | Railway |
| Ho Chi Minh Trail | Other (Chinese, Cambodian) | Waterfall or rapids |

National capital

Provincial capital

Provincial border

Current national border

*Source: based on C. Taillard, 1989*

Because of its meridian structure and even before the loss of the territories on the right bank of the Mekong to Thailand, Lan Xang never had centralised management. In the 17th and 18th centuries the kingdom was composed of three entities: the royal territory at Vientiane, surrounded by two others—Luangphrabang in the north and Champassack in the south. It maintained close relations with the Phuan kingdom of Xiengkhuang in the North-East, and with the two confederations of principalities in the north (Sip Song Phan Na to the west and Sip Song Chau Tai to the east). This organisation into three territories distributed along the Mekong dated from its founding in the 14th century; the capital and royal territory were moved from Luangphrabang to Vientiane in 1553. This legacy is still evident today, but the three entities need to be redefined.

The meridian partition between the zones controlled by the Pathet Lao, which was extended at the expense of that controlled by the royal government between 1963 and 1973, gave a new territorial form to the contrast between the Mekong Valley and the mountainous interior. This constitutive element of the Laotian territory explains the predominance of an organisation in parallel belts.

*Atlas of Laos*

# The return of transnational networks in the Indochinese Peninsula

In the 1980s, the position of Laos in the Indochinese Peninsula saw a complete turnaround (C. Taillard, 1998). From a fringe area during the colonial period (separating the "useful" part of Indochina—Vietnam—from Thailand), then a landlocked country after independence (when it no longer benefited from links connecting it to maritime flows), Laos became a "crossroads" linking the countries of continental South-East Asia, including Yunnan province. It has thus returned to the position it occupied during the pre-colonial period, when caravan trails of pack oxen criss-crossed the peninsula, linking Yunnan on the southern silk road to the Irrawadi and Menam deltas.

The kingdom of Lan Xang, like that of Lan Na in northern Thailand, was located on the western meridian axis of these caravan trails. It had two heads, Kunming and Dali further north, Moulmein and Bangkok in the south, relayed respectively by two nodes located on key river junctions, Simao-Jang Cheng and Tak-Ayuthaya. Linked to this meridian network was an adjacent eastern network, connecting the Red River delta and Annam to the principalities of the Mekong Valley, where it joined up again with the meridian network. The principalities of Lan Xang were supplied by these networks and the kingdom derived most of its revenue from taxes levied on the international traffic generated by the caravan trails.

Today, in an extraordinary reversal of the situation, Laos is rediscovering, in a new political context, its intermediate position at the crossroads of the peninsula, benefiting from the shift from a logic of confrontation between different political systems (colonial versus Siamese, then socialist versus capitalist) to a logic of cooperation since all the countries of the peninsula joined ASEAN. Anticipating and supporting this dynamic, the Asian Development Bank (ADB) has proposed the construction of major transportation axes to structure the peninsula, dubbed "Greater Mekong Subregion" (ADB, 1994). Far from being new, the proposed axes follow the ancient routes of the caravan trails, particularly those that cross Laos.

The Trans-Asian Highway from Singapore to Beijing in its entirety is more of a technocratic vision than an economic reality. However, on the scale of the peninsula, trade is intensifying between the two Chinese provinces of Yunnan and Sichuan, and between Myanmar and Thailand. These two provinces have a population of 205 million in 2000, a size similar to the combined population of the countries of the peninsula (213 million). Although in the past few years China has invested in the eastern meridian axis crossing Myanmar, it is not overlooking the fact that Sino-Thai entrepreneurs are the leading ASEAN investors in China and that Thailand is their main trading rival. China is therefore paying close attention to the economic development quadrangle in the north of the peninsula.

The eastern branch of this quadrangle, which links Thailand to Yunnan via Huoixai and Namtha, is the first axis that crosses Laos. However, the agreements reached between the government in Yangon and minority ethnic states have restored credibility to the alternative eastern branch through Kentung. If Laos is to retain the advantage over the rival axis in Myanmar, it needs rapidly to reconstruct the road and provide economic services that will attract a continuous traffic flow.

The next project is the East–West corridor between the Mekong and the South China Sea, which will link Khon Kaen to Danang via Savannakhet, where the ADB is studying the construction of a bridge. With the completion of another bridge over the Mekong in Pakse, financed by Japan, there will soon be an alternative route between Bangkok and central Vietnam if Laos decides to rebuild the old road linking the Bolovens and Kontum Plateaux.

However, the most important, and long overlooked, link for Laos is located in the Centre: the diagonal that will put Vientiane back on the axis between Bangkok and Hanoi. Vientiane is the only ASEAN capital not to be located on an international axis. The economic reforms undertaken in Vietnam since 1986 should allow Hanoi to catch up some of its lag on the rival metropolis in the South, Ho Chi Minh City. The congested ports of Haiphong and Bangkok should also boost overland trade.

# From the caravan trails to the new transportation axes of the peninsula

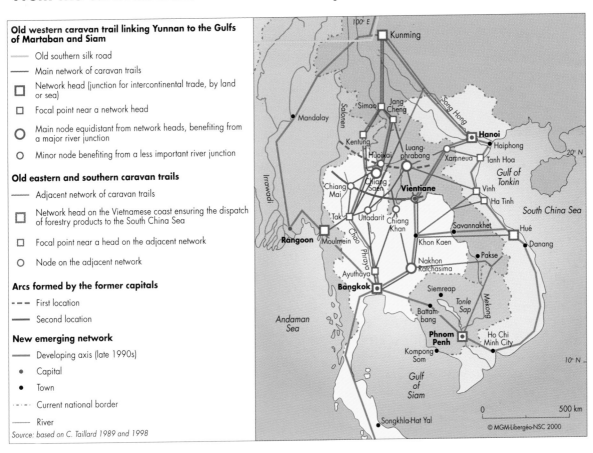

**Old western caravan trail linking Yunnan to the Gulfs of Martaban and Siam**

— Old southern silk road

— Main network of caravan trails

☐ Network head (junction for intercontinental trade, by land or sea)

☐ Focal point near a network head

○ Main node equidistant from network heads, benefiting from a major river junction

○ Minor node benefiting from a less important river junction

**Old eastern and southern caravan trails**

— Adjacent network of caravan trails

☐ Network head on the Vietnamese coast ensuring the dispatch of forestry products to the South China Sea

☐ Focal point near a head on the adjacent network

○ Node on the adjacent network

**Arcs formed by the former capitals**

- - - First location

— Second location

**New emerging network**

— Developing axis (late 1990s)

• Capital

• Town

·-·-· Current national border

— River

Source: based on C. Taillard 1989 and 1998

© MGM-Libergéo-NSC 2000

Moreover, this diagonal links Vientiane to the two provinces of the North-East and services the Xiengkhuang Plateau, one of the last agricultural "frontiers" of the peninsula together with the Bolovens Plateau. During the colonial period, this area was used to grow tea seedlings for export to India and to breed oxen for the caravan trails. In addition to the development of hydroelectric resources on the periphery of the plateau is the prospect of an open-cast mine to reach a high iron-content deposit.

# The network of networks

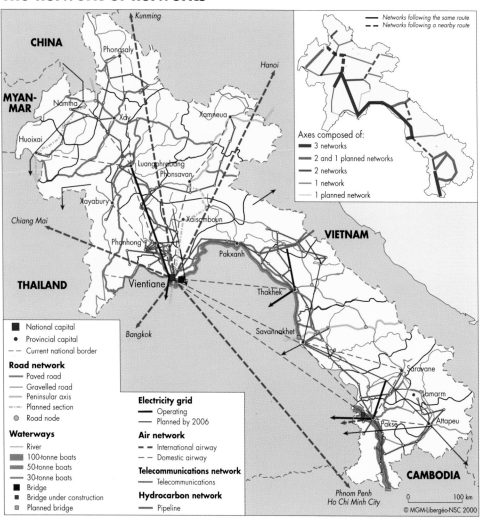

Networks following the same route
Networks following a nearby route

**Axes composed of:**
- 3 networks
- 2 and 1 planned networks
- 2 networks
- 1 network
- 1 planned network

**Legend:**

- National capital
- Provincial capital
- Current national border

**Road network**
- Paved road
- Gravelled road
- Peninsular axis
- Planned section
- Road node

**Waterways**
- River
- 100-tonne boats
- 50-tonne boats
- 30-tonne boats
- Bridge
- Bridge under construction
- Planned bridge

**Electricity grid**
- Operating
- Planned by 2006

**Air network**
- International airway
- Domestic airway

**Telecommunications network**
- Telecommunications

**Hydrocarbon network**
- Pipeline

0        100 km

© MGM-Libergéo-NSC 2000

*Spatial organisation*

The caravan trails described (meridian, transverse and diagonal) will regain the economic, political and cultural functions they enjoyed in the past and which colonisation temporarily interrupted. Paradoxically, it is the Mekong–South China Sea link, materialised by the only well-maintained road, which organises the territory of Laos the least, because of the corridor effect crossing a single Laotian province, while the Pakxanh–Vietnam road via Khamkheut crosses two provinces. In contrast, structuring effects are already appearing around the other two axes, although the road links are poor. In the northern economic development quadrangle where the road has not yet been rebuilt, the road axis is enhanced by a telecommunications network, and will soon be equipped with a high-voltage power line to transmit electricity from the dams in Yunnan to Thailand. On the north-east diagonal, the construction of a direct road link between Phonsavan and Vientiane via Xaysomboun is included in the plan, but the social reality of the axis already exists, and telecommunications relays follow it part of the way. The most multi-functional axis is still the meridian road along the Mekong, which often joins three networks.

# Settlement patterns and accessibility

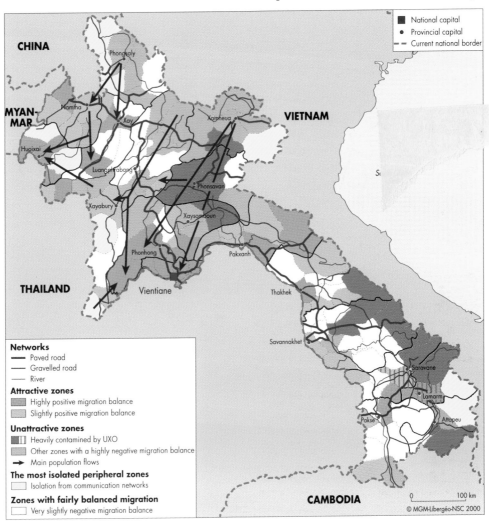

This map shows four attractive zones. The first two, in the southern half of the country, are not accompanied by inter-provincial migration. The Xe Done Valley and the Pakse, Saravane and Lamarm road, have profited from the Xe Xet dam and the integrated development programmes in Sekong province. This dynamic will extend to the eastern and southern parts of the Bolovens Plateau with the completion of the Houay Ho hydroelectric power plant and the start-up of construction on the Xe Kaman hydroelectric power plant. Next come the districts of Pakkading and Khamkeuth on the road from Pakxanh to the Keo Neua Pass, the shortest link between Vientiane and Vietnam, which connects the North-East and the South to the Vientiane region. Road 9 between Savannakhet and the Lao Bao Pass, an international transverse link, is not yet accompanied by any population movement. In contrast, population flows from Xamneua and Xiengkhuang provinces towards the region of Vientiane are strengthening the north-eastern diagonal. Similarly, the flows from Phongsaly and Oudomxay provinces support the emerging dynamic of the northern economic development quadrangle.

*Atlas of Laos*

# A model of the spatial dynamics of Lao PDR

The spatial structures described in the previous five maps make it possible to organise these eight territorial entities into three regions, returning to the regional organisation inherited from the kingdom of Lan Xang, but redefined in the current context, taking into account the existing provincial divisions—the main units of territorial management—and international links.

The region of Vientiane combines two of the models described in the map of the eight territorial entities on page 149: three concentric circles and core–periphery. Around the core of the capital, the central districts of Vientiane municipality and province form the second circle, and the third encroaches on the mountainous borders of the plain and continues along the Mekong Valley as far as Pakxanh (Borikhamxay). Beyond this central nucleus, there are three peripheries, structured in parallel belts, which represent national or international links. The first belt, the north-eastern diagonal, links Xiengkhuang and Huaphanh provinces to the capital and places Vientiane on the Bangkok–Hanoi axis. The construction of a direct road link between Phonsavan and Vientiane, passing through Xaysomboun, will turn this diagonal into a main transportation axis on the scale of the peninsula and make it possible to develop the resources of the Xiengkhuang Plateau, which remain under-utilised. The second periphery, eastern Borikhamxay province, connects the region of Vientiane to the South, and to the region of Vinh in Vietnam, with Road 8 playing an increasingly integrating role. The third periphery, on both sides of the Mekong in its meridian section to the west of the capital and spanning Xayabury and Vientiane provinces, borders the central block of the North. The extension of the road along the Mekong upstream from Vientiane as far as Paklai should confirm the attraction of the region of Vientiane over southern Xayabury province.

Six provinces form the southern region. With a meridian structure, this region is organised in parallel belts that separate the Mekong Valley from the mountainous and border interior. Based on their distance from Vientiane, two sub-regions can be delineated,

governed respectively by Savannakhet and Pakse. The northern part of the South (Khammouane and Savannakhet provinces) is off-centre from the Mekong and Road 13, the location of the two provincial capitals, which do not have any secondary urban nodes inland. Only Sepone district, on Road 9, occasionally stands out, because of cross-border trade. The corridor effect is strongest here and explains why the international Mekong–South China Sea axis does not have a structuring effect on a national scale. In contrast, this axis gives Khon Kaen in Thailand the last highway it needed to bolster its function as the regional capital of the North-East, and Hué-Danang the continental base required to strengthen Central Vietnam, threatened by the double metro-polisation around Hanoi and Ho Chi Minh City (Vu Tu Lap, Christian Taillard, 1993). In the southern part of the South of Laos (Saravane, Champassack, Sekong and Attapeu provinces), the dissymmetry and the corridor effect are mitigated by the Bolovens Plateau and the Xe Done and Xe Kong Valleys. Although Pakse, the capital of this sub-region, is also located on the Mekong, it is balanced by the urban arc bordering the Bolovens Plateau, from Saravane to Attapeu. This is an emerging development area spanning three provinces, with an organisation in three parallel belts. This pattern will be reinforced by the bridge over the Mekong at Pakse and by the opening of a road link to the Bolovens Plateau and to Kontum Plateau in Vietnam, which has yet to be designed.

The North region has a reticulated, multipolar organisation, covering spatial units differentiated by dominant relief directions and human settlements. It is organised around a central block (Luangphrabang and Oudomxay), structured by the meridian axis of Road 13 and two nodes, off-centre from their provinces and located at the junction with transverse traffic axes. These nodes form emerging development areas. Luangphrabang, the southern node, connects the meridian road axis of Road 13 and meridian river axis of the Nam Ou, extended by the Mekong to the south, with the east–west axis of the upstream course of the Mekong towards northern Thailand. A development area is appearing between the old royal capital and the town of Xayabury; in the longer term it could encompass the districts in the north of this

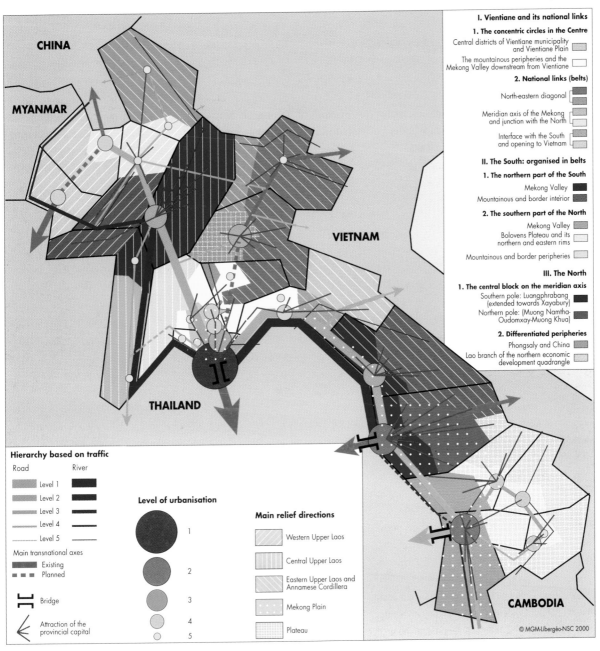

Legend:

**I. Vientiane and its national links**

**1. The concentric circles in the Centre**

Central districts of Vientiane municipality and Vientiane Plain

The mountainous peripheries and the Mekong Valley downstream from Vientiane

**2. National links (belts)**

North-eastern diagonal

Meridian axis of the Mekong and junction with the North

Interface with the South and opening to Vietnam

**II. The South: organised in belts**

**1. The northern part of the South**

Mekong Valley

Mountainous and border interior

**2. The southern part of the North**

Mekong Valley

Bolovens Plateau and its northern and eastern rims

Mountainous and border peripheries

**III. The North**

**1. The central block on the meridian axis**

Southern pole: Luangphrabang (extended towards Xayabury)

Northern pole: (Muong Namtha-Oudomxay-Muong Khua)

**2. Differentiated peripheries**

Phongsaly and China

Lao branch of the northern economic development quadrangle

**Hierarchy based on traffic**

Road      River
Level 1
Level 2
Level 3
Level 4
Level 5

Main transnational axes
Existing
Planned

Bridge

Attraction of the provincial capital

**Level of urbanisation**
1
2
3
4
5

**Main relief directions**
Western Upper Laos
Central Upper Laos
Eastern Upper Laos and Annamese Cordillera
Mekong Plain
Plateau

CHINA

MYANMAR

VIETNAM

THAILAND

CAMBODIA

© MGM-Libergéo-NSC 2000

*Atlas of Laos*

province and those of Oudomxay province bordering the Mekong. Muong Xay, the northern node, is a stopover on the meridian axis that leads to Namtha and China, and to Muong Khua and Vietnam. These three towns form an emerging developing area, spanning three provinces. Muong Xay is also located on the former strategic transverse axis leading to Xamneua, which is less important today. International relations and settlement patterns differentiate the two peripheries of this central Austro-Asiatic block. The dynamic of the northern economic development quadrangle appears in many maps, particularly the map of population flows; it should be supported by the reconstruction of the Huoixai–Namtha axis and the provision of economic services along it, so that it can compete with the road through Kentung in Myanmar. The northern periphery (most of Phongsaly), long neglected, is now benefiting from numerous development projects to compensate for its remoteness.

## Regional planning perspectives

The interruption of the caravan trails during the colonial and post-colonial periods now seems like an accident in the history of the Indochinese Peninsula. A turnaround occurred at the beginning of the 1990s, when the peninsula began to revive the organisation of networks that existed in the pre-colonial period. Laos, and regions such as Chiang Mai in northern Thailand and Mandalay in central Myanmar, will once again become intermediate spaces on meridian and transverse axes planned on the scale of continental Asia. These road axes, which the Asian Development Bank plans to modernise, will criss-cross the peninsula and link the metropolises of Yunnan and Sichuan in China with those of the southern deltas, and, in the longer term, with the peninsula's eastern and western sea-front towns. By reforging ties from the pre-colonial past, these axes will benefit from the flows generated by the process of regional integration.

The Lao People's Democratic Republic needs to prepare for this evolution towards a peninsula reorganised into networks, through a regional planning policy that fosters international links, while ensuring that its regions are fully integrated into the national territory. These two objectives, which may appear contradictory for a country with a meridian structure, are nevertheless the precondition for its successful integration into the new peninsular organisation. The example of the kingdom of Lan Xang at its height in the 16th century shows that this goal is not beyond reach, so long as regional implications are taken into account. There is a need to reflect on a new configuration for the buffer state at the heart of the peninsula: no longer as one that separates potential enemies to preserve peace, but as one that links partners and combines meridian and transverse flows.

The model presented in the conclusion to this atlas can contribute to such a reflection. It organises the eight territorial entities identified into three regions, recalling the historical divisions of this meridian state, but redefining them. These three regions differ from the regions in the statistical yearbooks, shown in the first map of the atlas on page 15. Huaphanh province, attached to the region of Vientiane, as well as Xiengkhuang province, is dissociated from the North, which no longer comprises the southern part of Xayabury. The South region, which some reports extend to Savannakhet province, is broadened here to include Khammouane province, but is divided into two sub-regions.

The regional organisation derived from this model reduces the population disparities between the regions; the size of the region of Vientiane falls from 2.2 million to 1.6 million, that of the North from 1.5 million to 1.1 million, while that of the South rises from 0.9 million to 1.9 million (comprising two sub-regions of 0.9 million each), making up a total population of 4.6 million according to the 1995 census. This regional organisation emphasises the spatial structures existing just prior to the onset of the Asian financial crisis in July 1997, which has since curbed trends. It is not a plan for regional development. It stresses the territorial constraints that such a plan should take into account to enable Laos to benefit once again from its location at the junction between the powers of the peninsula, once the current crisis has been surmounted.

# Bibliography

Asian Development Bank (1994). *Economic Cooperation in the Greater Mekong Subregion: Toward Implementation.* Manila, 406 pp.

Asian Development Bank (1996). *Key Indicators of Developing Asian and Pacific Countries.* Manila, Vol. XXVII, 435 pp.

Bank of Lao PDR (1997). *Economic and Financial Sector Statistics.* Vientiane, 30 pp.

Bourdet, Y. (1998). "The Dynamics of Regional Disparities in Laos". *Asian Survey*, no. 7, July, pp. 629-652.

Bourdet, Y. (2000). *The Economics of Transition in Laos from Socialism to Asian Integration.* Cheltenham, North Hampton: Edward Elgar, 173 pp.

Brunet, R. (1987). *La Carte mode d'emploi.* Paris-Montpellier: Fayard-RECLUS, 270 pp.

Chen E. and Kwan, C.H. (1997). *Asia's Borderless Economy: The Emergence of Sub-regional Zones.* St Leonard: Allen and Unwin, 204 pp.

Gendreau F., Fauveau V., and Dang Thu (1997). *Démographie de la péninsule Indochinoise.* Paris: ESTEM and AUPELF-UREF, coll. "Savoir plus Universités", 132 pp.

GERPA (1996). *Mékong 6 à l'horizon 2020: une vision prospective de l'évolution des six pays du Mékong au regard du développement et de l'aménagement du territoire.* Paris: Ministry of Foreign Affairs, 115 pp.

Goudineau, Y. ed. (1997). *Resettlement and Social Characteristics of New Villages: Basic Needs for Resettled Communities in the Lao PDR.* Vientiane: UNDP-ORSTOM, Vol. 1, 186 pp.; Vol. 2, 204 pp.

International Monetary Fund (1994). *Economic Development in Lao PDR: Horizon 2000.* Vientiane: Chi Do Pham, 322 pp.

Lahmeyer International, Worley International (1997). *Prospects for Lao Power Export.* Vientiane: Nam Theun 2, Study of Alternatives, 15 pp.

Ministry of Agriculture and Forestry (1992). *Forest Cover and Land Use in Lao PDR.* Vientiane: NOFIP, report no. 5, 78 pp.

Ministry of Agriculture and Forestry (1996). *20 Years of Agricultural Statistics 1976-1995.* Vientiane, 87 pp.

Mya Than and J.L.H. Tan eds. (1997). *Laos' Dilemmas and Options: The Challenge of Economic Transition in the 1990s.* Singapore: ISEAS, 319 pp.

Myo Thant, Ming Tan, and Hiroshi Kakazu, eds. (1994). *Growth Triangles in Asia.* Oxford: Oxford Press-ADB, 306 pp.

National Geographic Department (1995). *Atlas of the Lao PDR.* Vientiane, 24 pp.

National Laos Tourism Authority (1998). *Laos Tourism Statistical Report 1997.* Vientiane, 17 pp.

National Statistical Centre (1995). *Expenditure and Consumption Survey and Social Indicator Survey 1992-1993.* Vientiane, 116 pp.

National Statistical Centre (1996). *Basic Statistics about the Socio-Economic Development in the Lao PDR 1995, 1996.* Vientiane: State Planning Committee, 122 pp.

National Statistical Centre (1997). *Results from the Population Census 1995.* Vientiane: State Planning Committee, 94 pp.

National Statistical Centre (1999). *The Households of Lao PDR: Social and Economic Indicators, Facts from Lao Expenditure and Consumption Survey 1997-1998.* Vientiane: State Planning Committee, 38 pp.

State Planning Committee (1996). *Implementation of the 1991-1995 Socio-Economic Plan and Presentation of the 1996-2000 Socio-Economic Development Plan.* Vientiane, 34 pp.

Stuart-Fox, M. (1997). *A History of Laos.* Cambridge: Cambridge University Press, 253 pp.

Taillard, C. (1989). *Le Laos, stratégies d'un état-tampon.* Montpellier: RECLUS, coll. "Territoires", 200 pp.

Taillard, C. (1995). "Le Laos, enclave ou carrefour". Vol. *Asie du Sud-Est, Océanie*. Géographie Universelle. Paris: Belin-RECLUS, pp. 164-175.

Taillard, C. (1998). "De l'enclavement à l'espace de connexion: l'insertion du Laos dans la péninsule Indochinoise". Special issue "Laos entre identité et intégration régionale". *Mutations Asiatiques*, no. 11, pp. 36-40.

UNDP (1996). *Human Development Report 1996: Economic Growth and Human Development*. New York: UNDP, 625 pp.

UNDP (1998). *Economic Circles in Thailand and Indochina: Enabling Policy Environment for Local and Community-based Initiatives to Promote Regional Economic Integration*. Bangkok: UNDP, 40 pp.

Uxo Lao/Handicap International (1997). *Living with Uxo: National Survey on the Socio-Economic Impact of Uxo in Lao PDR*. Vientiane: Ministry of Labour and Social Welfare, 148 pp.

Vienne M.S. de, Népote J., comp. (1995). "Laos 1975-1995: Restructuration et développement". *Cahiers Péninsule*, no. 3, Études orientales Olizane, 225 pp.

Vu Tu Lap, Taillard, C. (1993). *An Atlas of Vietnam*. Paris-Montpellier: La Documentation Française-RECLUS, coll. "Dynamiques du territoire", 422 pp., 308 maps, trilingual edition in French, Vietnamese and English.

Walker, A. (1999). *The Legend of the Golden Boat: Regulation, Trade and Traders in the Borderlands of Laos, Thailand, China and Burma*. Richmond: Curzon, 232 pp.

World Bank (1995). *LAO PDR Social Development Assessment and Strategy*. Washington, 118 pp.